FIRESIDE

Modern Chess Brilliancies

101 GAMES SELECTED AND ANNOTATED BY

INTERNATIONAL GRANDMASTER

Larry Evans

A FIRESIDE BOOK
PUBLISHED BY SIMON AND SCHUSTER

To Ingrid

ISBN 0-671-20578-1 casebound
ISBN 0-671-22420-4 paperback
Library of Congress Catalog Card Number 70-116505

Designed by Irving Perkins
Manufactured in the United States of America

1   2   3   4   5   6   7   8   9   10

Contents

INTRODUCTION   *Opening*   13

1   TAL–LARSEN
     6th MATCH GAME 1965   *Alekhine's Defense*   25

2   GURGENIDZE–TAL
     U.S.S.R. CHAMPIONSHIP 1961   *Benoni Defense*   27

3   GLIGORICH–MATULOVICH
     MAJORCA 1967   "   28

4   EVANS–BERGER
     AMSTERDAM 1964   *Caro-Kann Defense*   30

5   BAKULIN–BRONSTEIN
     U.S.S.R. CHAMPIONSHIP 1964   "   32

6   TAL–FUSTER
     PORTOROZ 1958   "   33

7   TRAPPL–PEREZ
     OBERHAUSEN 1961   "   35

8   TAL–PORTISCH
     2nd MATCH GAME 1965   "   36

9   TAL–SMYSLOV
     CANDIDATES' TOURNAMENT
     1959   "   38

10   BOTVINNIK–PORTISCH
     MONACO 1968   *English Opening*   40

11   SMYSLOV–LIBERSON
     RIGA 1968   "   42

12   FISCHER–CELLE
     CALIFORNIA 1964   *Evans Gambit*   44

13   IVKOV–PORTISCH
     BLED 1961   *French Defense*   45

14   TAL–DONNER
     BEVERWIJK 1968   "   48

15 FISCHER–TAL
      LEIPZIG 1960   *French Defense*   50
16 GHEORGHIU–UHLMANN
      SOFIA 1967   ,,   52
17 FISCHER–MIAGMARSUREN
      SOUSSE 1967   ,,   53
18 FISCHER–U. GELLER
      NATANYA 1968   ,,   55
19 ROSSOLIMO–REISSMAN
      PUERTO RICO 1967   *Giuoco Piano*   57
20 PACHMAN–UHLMANN
      HAVANA 1966   *Gruenfeld Defense*   58
21 GELLER–SMYSLOV
      1st MATCH GAME 1965   ,,   60
22 RESHEVSKY–SEIDMAN
      U.S. CHAMPIONSHIP 1968   ,,   62
23 R. BYRNE–FISCHER
      U.S. CHAMPIONSHIP 1964   ,,   64
24 SPASSKY–BRONSTEIN
      U.S.S.R. CHAMPIONSHIP 1960   *King's Gambit*   66
25 BRONSTEIN–TAL
      RIGA 1968   ,,   68
26 LETELIER–FISCHER
      LEIPZIG 1960   *King's Indian Defense*   73
27 GLIGORICH–FISCHER
      BLED 1961   ,,   74
28 POMAR–SZABO
      BEVERWIJK 1967   ,,   76
29 KAVALEK–MATULOVICH
      BUCHAREST 1966   ,,   78
30 VLADIMIROV–DODA
      LENINGRAD 1967   ,,   80
31 BOBOTSOV–TAL
      VARNA 1958   ,,   82
32 SAIDY–BEDNARSKY
      TEL AVIV 1964   ,,   84
33 NIKOLICH–FISCHER
      VINKOVCI 1968   ,,   86
34 KOZOMARA–R. BYRNE
      SARAJEVO 1967   ,,   88
35 POLUGAIEVSKY–PETROSIAN
      U.S.S.R. CHAMPIONSHIP 1960   *Nimzo-Indian Defense*   90

36 ADDISON–SIGURJONSSON
REYKJAVIK 1968   *Nimzo-Indian Defense*   91

37 POMAR–JOHANSSON
HAVANA 1966   ,,   93

38 DONNER–PORTISCH
BEVERWIJK 1968   ,,   94

39 EVANS–BISGUIER
U.S. CHAMPIONSHIP 1959   *Petrov Defense*   96

40 KONOVALOV–MORDKOVICH
U.S.S.R. 1958   *Philidor Defense*   99

41 TSCHESHKOVSKY–LUTIKOV
U.S.S.R. CHAMPIONSHIP 1969   ,,   101

42 PADEVSKY–MATANOVICH
HAVANA 1966   *Pirc-Robatsch Defense*   104

43 SOROKIN–DUBORIK
POSTAL GAME 1968   ,,   106

44 FISCHER–BENKO
U.S. CHAMPIONSHIP 1964   ,,   108

45 ZUCKERMAN–BENKO
U.S. CHAMPIONSHIP 1968   ,,   110

46 SMEJKAL–SMYSLOV
HASTINGS 1968–69   ,,   112

47 FOGUELMAN–BRONSTEIN
AMSTERDAM 1964   *Queen's Gambit Accepted*   114

48 RESHEVSKY–FISCHER
5th MATCH GAME 1961   *Queen's Gambit Declined*   116

49 KERES–GELLER
8th MATCH GAME 1965   ,,   118

50 AVERBACH–ESTRIN
MOSCOW CHAMPIONSHIP 1964   ,,   120

51 SZABO–SIGURJONSSON
REYKJAVIK 1968   ,,   121

52 LARSEN–MATANOVICH
ZAGREB 1965   ,,   123

53 D. BYRNE–BISGUIER
U.S. CHAMPIONSHIP 1967   ,,   125

54 TAL–HECHT
VARNA 1962   *Queen's Indian Defense*   127

55 BENKO–HOROWITZ
U.S. CHAMPIONSHIP 1968   *Reti Opening*   129

56 FISCHER–STEIN
SOUSSE 1967   *Ruy Lopez*   131

57 TAL–GLIGORICH
1st MATCH GAME 1968   *Ruy Lopez*   134

58 IVKOV–DONNER
HAVANA 1965   ,,   136

59 TAL–KERES
MOSCOW 1967   ,,   137

60 GUFELD–KAVALEK
MARIANSKE LAZNE 1962   ,,   139

61 TAL–NIEVERGELT
ZURICH 1959   *Sicilian Defense*   141

62 TAL–MOHRLOK
VARNA 1962   ,,   143

63 TAL–LARSEN
10th MATCH GAME 1965   ,,   146

64 VELIMIROVICH–NIKOLICH
BELGRADE 1964   ,,   149

65 VELIMIROVICH–SOFREVSKY
YUGOSLAV CHAMPIONSHIP
1966   ,,   151

66 MEDINA–POMAR
MALAGA 1969   ,,   152

67 TAL–BOLBOCHAN
HAVANA 1966   ,,   154

68 HENNINGS–MOEHRING
EAST GERMAN CHAMPIONSHIP
1967   ,,   156

69 FISCHER–GELLER
SKOPJE 1967   ,,   158

70 FISCHER–DELY
SKOPJE 1967   ,,   159

71 FISCHER–BENKO
CANDIDATES' TOURNAMENT
1959   ,,   160

72 O'KELLY–PENROSE
VARNA 1962   ,,   162

73 LUTIKOV–KLAVINS
U.S.S.R. 1962   ,,   165

74 KOEHLER–EVANS
U.S. NATIONAL OPEN 1968   ,,   166

75 TAL–OLAFSSON
BLED 1961   ,,   169

76 STEIN–PORTISCH
STOCKHOLM 1962   ,,   171

11

77 BOGDANOVICH–SUETIN
YUGOSLAVIA v. U.S.S.R. 1967   *Sicilian Defense*   172

78 SPASSKY–SUETIN
MOSCOW 1967   „   173

79 NEZHMETDINOV–TAL
U.S.S.R. CHAMPIONSHIP 1961   „   176

80 EVANS–BLACKSTONE
SANTA MONICA 1965   „   178

81 TAL–PETROSIAN
CANDIDATES' TOURNAMENT
1959   „   180

82 TAL–POLUGAIEVSKY
U.S.S.R. CHAMPIONSHIP 1959   „   181

83 PARMA–SZABO
SOLINGEN 1968   „   183

84 TAL–GLIGORICH
MOSCOW 1963   „   185

85 KHOLMOV–BRONSTEIN
U.S.S.R. CHAMPIONSHIP 1965   „   187

86 GLIGORICH–BOBOTSOV
HASTINGS 1959–60   „   189

87 GASPARIANTZ–EIDLIN
U.S.S.R. 1961   „   190

88 R. BYRNE–EVANS
U.S. CHAMPIONSHIP 1966   „   193

89 FISCHER–NAJDORF
VARNA 1962   „   194

90 FISCHER–BOLBOCHAN
STOCKHOLM 1962   „   196

91 FISCHER–LARSEN
PORTOROZ 1958   „   198

92 EVANS–ZUCKERMAN
U.S. CHAMPIONSHIP 1967   „   200

93 LITTLEWOOD–BOTVINNIK
HASTINGS 1961–62   „   202

94 LARSEN–PETROSIAN
CALIFORNIA 1966   „   204

95 SPASSKY–CIRICII
CZECHOSLOVAKIA 1962   „   206

96 GURGENIDZE–LEIN
U.S.S.R. CHAMPIONSHIP 1967   „   210

97 SUETIN–TAIMANOV
LENINGRAD 1967   „   211

98 SPASSKY–GELLER
     6th MATCH GAME 1968   *Sicilian Defense*   213
99 BILEK–GHEORGHIU
     BUCHAREST 1968   „   216
100 ESTRIN–BERLINER
     POSTAL GAME 1968   *Two Knights Defense*   217
101 KARAKLAICH–TRAIKOVICH
     YUGOSLAVIA 1968   „   221

     ALPHABETICAL LIST OF CONTESTANTS   224

Introduction

A win by an unsound combination, however showy,
fills me with artistic horror.—STEINITZ

MODERN CHESS had its inception in the great international tournament at London 1851, where already Staunton was complaining that championship matches were dragging endlessly and threatening public interest in professional competition:

> When a player, *upon system*, consumes hours over moves when minutes might suffice and depends, not upon out-maneuvering, but out-sitting his antagonist, patience ceases to be a virtue. . . .

Consequently Staunton proposed a sandglass to delimit each separate move. Crude mechanical clocks were introduced officially at Paris 1867, and players were fined for overstepping the time limit. The twentieth century opened with the now familiar double-faced push-button clock, heralding an equally significant development: allotting each side two hours for the first forty moves (or some such equivalent) and punishing noncompliance with an outright forfeit of the game instead of merely a fine. The clock had an obvious effect on not only the popularity but also the quality of chess; modern tournaments would be inconceivable without it.

The brilliancy prize is an institution which has survived intact. Traditionally after each major event an august body of critics selects those games with the greatest aesthetic appeal, as manifested by original, striking, intentional and successful combinations. At Carlsbad 1907 Cohn was awarded a brilliancy prize against Tchigorin "for a beautiful combination starting from an extra-ordinary deep Pawn sacrifice." Yet Cohn conceded later (presumably with the award tucked safely in his pocket) that he had *not intended* to sacrifice the Pawn —he had lost it, and the loss had forced him to play energetically to compensate for his material inferiority. Needless to say, the victims received no share of the swag, even when the board was "showered with golden pieces" (Lewitzky–Marshall, Breslau 1912). Their lot is negative immortality.

The convulsive combination that destroys the enemy on the spot is easily understood by duffer and grandmaster alike. In his classic work *The Art of Sacrifice*, Spielmann wrote: "The beauty of a chess game is assessed, and not without good reason, according to the sacrifices it contains." This pretty much expresses the feeling of the ages. But one problem has persistently plagued the judges: must a combination, to merit the crown, be correct in all variations and be able to withstand the most rigorous post-mortem analysis? Historically the answer has been yes, although many a red-faced jury has seen its selection posthumously exploded. The recipient of the award is concerned only that his brainchild worked over the board. What is often overlooked, however, is the performance of the loser, without whose unwilling cooperation no masterpiece is possible. This consideration raised its specter at Majorca 1968, where one of the judges reported:

> After a long and heated discussion . . . nobody could remember a drawn game ever having won a brilliancy prize. The question was: which of the players was responsible for the "brilliancy," and, if it was sound, why did he not win the game? On the other hand, if the "brilliancy" was sound but served only to save a lost game, should that player receive an award despite his having reached a lost position? An uproarious discussion (rather, melee) followed.*

When the smoke cleared it was decided the two players would share the prize jointly with still another game. (In my opinion, neither game deserved it, but that is beside the point; somebody had to get the award simply because it was available.)

Since a brilliancy is essentially an accident, it is not feasible to start any given game with the conscious intention of creating one. The opponent, the tension, the ticking of the clock—above all, the opportunity—must be present. Because combinations cannot always be calculated with precision and often are subject to surprising hazards, a master must have implicit faith in his own judgment. With typical candor, Najdorf confessed: "When I play chess, I hardly ever calculate the play in detail. I rely very much on an intuitive sense which tells me what are the right moves to look for."

Many cliff-hangers are fraught with uncertainty until the very last move, and it is impossible to be sure of one's ground at all times. Game 69 is a good example of a calculated risk that boomeranged. Players who strive to keep the draw in hand (which is the modern tendency) are not held in such high esteem

* The editor, *Chess Life*, April 1969, p. 144.

as the gamblers whose games are filled with thunderbolts, errors, flashes of insight, tension and luck. As Reti observed, "The pleasures to be derived from a chess combination lie in the feeling that a human mind is behind the game, dominating the inanimate pieces . . . and giving them the breath of life."

Indeed, how are bold and risky ventures to be assessed? That they work against inferior defense is no reason to reward them; and that they fail does not necessarily mean they are incorrect. It seems to me that an unclear sacrifice, apart from its beauty, should be evaluated by two criteria: (a) it should contain no *obvious* flaw; (b) it should serve the end for which it is intended even if it produces only a draw. Of course, the sacrifice must not be a wild trap based solely on the hope that the defender will overlook the refutation and go astray; there should always be an acceptable line available in case the right defense is found. It is unlikely that any master will employ such a wild weapon if he sees the hole in it, unless he is prompted by sheer desperation. Such an exigency is aptly termed a "swindle," and chess literature is replete with these saving resources. The following example is typical; several magazines dubbed it "the swindle of the century."

EVANS–RESHEVSKY
UNITED STATES CHAMPIONSHIP 1964

Black to move

Black is a Knight ahead and can win as he pleases. The simplest is *48* . . . Q–B3; *49* R–Q8 (of course the Knight cannot be captured because of *50* QxPch) N–N3, etc. I was toying with the idea of resigning but was curious to see if Reshevsky would snap at the bait.

48 . . . .   QxP??
49 Q–N8ch!   KxQ

Still unsuspecting, Reshevsky had no inkling of my plot. The Queen was captured as a formality, a last "spite check," and my opponent started to rise from his seat as he captured it. He actually thought I was reaching across the board to shake his hand, the customary accompanying gesture of resignation.

50 R×Pch!   Draw!!

The point is that Black must either capture the Rook (resulting in stalemate) or submit to perpetual check after *50* . . . K–B1; 51 R–B7ch K–K1; *52* R–K7ch, etc. This kind of fiasco could cause any player to lose his composure. Reshevsky merely paled and laughed wryly, then directed an audible reproach to himself ("Stupid!"); but otherwise there was no departure from his usual aplomb.

While it qualifies for nothing but a booby prize, I am proud of this Houdini-type escape. It has all the earmarks of surprise, originality, ingenuity and desperation. Despite its beautiful finish, the entire game does not belong in an anthology, because too much of its preceding play was erratic. Yet White's concluding coup adheres to the classical definition of a "combination"—a forced series of moves involving sacrifice.

> A combination is a blend of ideas—pins, forks, discovered checks, double attacks—which endow the pieces with magical powers.—CHERNEV

> Combinations have always been the most intriguing aspect of chess. The master looks for them, the public applauds them, the critics praise them. It is because combinations are possible that chess is more than a lifeless mathematical exercise. They are the poetry of the game; they are to chess what melody is to music. They represent the triumph of mind over matter. —FINE

Anderssen and Morphy, whose combinations have almost without exception withstood a century of criticism, loom as the towering masters of a swash-buckling era filled with naïve delight in the sacrifice as an end in itself. Even young Steinitz reveled in the fiery excitement of combinations, admitting that he "did not play with the object of winning directly, but to sacrifice a piece." Later in his career Steinitz discovered what we now know, that positional play is the best possible preparation for releasing accumulated energy in the explosion of a combination. But in those days the romantics were so enraptured with aesthetics that they almost felt cheated when good defense frustrated a brilliancy. The sacrifice was a ritual act by which the mighty paladins revealed their superiority; it was understandable, and even expected, that their benighted opponents would take umbrage—"What, you dare to sacrifice against me? I will show you that your puny offer can't be correct. I will devour everything and you shall lose miserably!" In *The Chess Sacrifice*, Vukovich remarks that "mature technique has long since blown away such ideas; now the content of the position is weighed objectively and not arrogantly."

When Anderssen was reproached by his admirers for not exhibiting his customary flair in his match against Morphy (1858), he replied:

> No, Morphy won't let me. He always plays the very best move . . . He who plays Morphy must abandon all hope of catching him in a trap, no matter how cunningly laid, but must assume that it is so clear to Morphy that there can be no question of a false step.

This magnanimous tribute failed to credit Morphy's revolutionary new approach, because Anderssen himself did not fully appreciate why he had lost! It is noteworthy that he displays a certain uneasiness in dismissing his own attacks as mere "traps." Morphy's attacks always flowed from the position organically, while Anderssen's were more often inspirations of the moment. Morphy knew not only how to attack but also when; and that is why he won.

A sample of the kind of game which must have delighted our forebears is found in Greco's manuscript (1625), a compilation of scintillating finishes to which the best defenses rarely were taken into consideration. It is easy to fathom the primitive appeal of these fairy tales: one side goes all out for mate, while the other gathers as much booty as possible—morality plays illustrating the age-old conflict between riches and honor.

	WHITE	BLACK
1	P–K4	P–K4
2	P–KB4	P–KB4
3	P×BP	Q–R5ch
4	P–N3	Q–K2
5	Q–R5ch	K–Q1
6	P×P	Q×Pch
7	B–K2	N–KB3
8	Q–B3	P–Q4
9	P–KN4	P–KR4
10	P–KR3	P×P
11	P×P	R×R
12	Q×R	Q–N6ch
13	K–Q1	N×P
14	Q×Pch	B–Q2
15	N–KB3	N–B7ch
16	K–K1	N–Q6ch
17	K–Q1	Q–K8ch
18	N×Q	N–B7mate

Position after 18 . . . N–B7; a piquant smothered mate. Look at White's Queen-side pieces: they are already set up for the next game; his King is glutted with wealth, yet he must die.

The principles of chess were still being discovered in the nineteenth century. In 1866 Steinitz, in his own words, "committed the crime" of wresting the unofficial title from Anderssen, who promptly conceded that his conqueror was even better than Morphy. Yet so bitter was the enmity toward Steinitz's style of play that even after he had held the world championship for twenty years, a self-appointed committee of three amateurs declared that "Morphy could have given Steinitz pawn and move." A *New York Times* critic referred to him condescendingly as a "persevering student." And another critic noted that Steinitz's two match victories over Zukertort were attributable to the sad fact that "Zukertort was not yet Zukertort in 1872, and was no longer Zukertort in 1886." Because his defensive play was so devastatingly accurate, Steinitz was maligned for "taking the beauty out of chess." To his enemies he attributed anti-Semitism. As I observed in *New Ideas in Chess*:

> Steinitz was the first to realize the necessity of evaluating a position—then *acting* on that evaluation. This objectivity forbade him from entering a speculative combination and then trusting to luck. It occurred to him that the master should not seek winning combinations unless he can first prove to himself that he holds an advantage. Thus, when his opponent went contrary to the objective demands of the position, Steinitz felt morally impelled to punish this crime. Steinitz himself made no attempt to win in the early stages of the game, as Morphy had done, because he was convinced that this was possible only after his opponent had made an error and not before. So he sought out of the openings minute advantages which gradually added up to one big winning combination. In an age where playing to win from the very start was considered the only honorable course, such a doctrine was assured a scornful reception.

Steinitz held the title until 1894. During this reign he was so anxious to vanquish those who scorned his system that his style became provocative. The purpose of his eccentric moves was to provoke his adversaries into playing for a win and thus overreaching themselves when the position really did not justify such an attempt. He fought on the chessboard and in the chess columns, tirelessly applying his "editorial birch rod." In a fascinating study, *The Psychology of the Chess Player*, Fine wrote:

> The gratification derived from being king of the chess world gradually led to a kind of Messiah complex in him. He almost literally felt called upon to rescue the lost chess players from the wilderness . . . Once he was the champion, he was the father, and he had to beat off the attacks by the sons. Accordingly his style underwent a radical transformation, and he became an invincible defensive player. But just as he had pushed the attack to extremes, he pushed the defense in the same way. He would get into the most fantastically lopsided positions, from which only his genius helped him to escape.

I linger on Steinitz because his influence still permeates modern chess. His teachings were elaborated and carried forward by Dr. Tarrasch and by Emanuel Lasker ("I who vanquished Steinitz must see to it that his great achievement, his theories, should find justice, and I must avenge the wrongs he suffered"). The credo of the classical school was expressed by Lasker, who kept a grip on the title until 1921.

> The delight in gambits is a sign of chess youth . . . In very much the same way as the young man, on reaching his manhood years, lays aside the Indian stories and tales of adventure, and turns to the psychological novel we with maturing experience leave off gambit playing and become interested in the less vivacious but withal more forceful maneuvers of the position player.

While Tarrasch was squabbling with the hypermoderns over such academic questions as control versus occupation of the center, Lasker was exploring new psychological dimensions:

> By some ardent enthusiasts Chess has been elevated into a science or an art. It is neither; but its principal characteristic seems to be—what human nature mostly delights in—a fight.

It was obvious to Lasker that when evenly matched opponents play correctly, the games seldom have any fighting content and frequently end in draws:

> Balanced positions with best play on either side must lead again and again to balanced positions.

To this mathematician it was both a theorem and an ethical demand that with best play the perfect game must end in a draw; the problem was how to introduce a dynamic imbalance. There is no chance to win without a fight, and there can be no fight without upsetting the balance—even if this involves dubious moves that rattle one's opponent. "It is no easy matter," despaired a contemporary, "to reply correctly to Lasker's bad moves."

Lasker felt that chess is a struggle of total involvement in which the dominant personality, the rounded individual and not necessarily the better player, is bound to triumph. He was a great fighter who was thoroughly at home in both open and closed positions, freely strewing tactical complications into a game that was really strategical in essence. It is noteworthy that he accepted an invitation to teach chess in the U.S.S.R. during the mid-thirties, thereby leaving his imprint on the postwar dynamic Russian school.

By the time Alekhine and Capablanca dominated the scene, the age of innocence was over. Sophisticated technique was the order of the day. At Carlsbad 1929 Rubinstein extracted a win from such a "hopelessly drawn"

Rook-and-Pawn ending that the editors of the tournament book united in the assertion that had it happened three hundred years ago he would have been burned at the stake for being in league with evil spirits!

Obviously a rise in the quality of defense necessitated a corresponding adjustment in the standard of attack. In modern chess most of the beauty resides in the annotations; brilliancies exist chiefly as grace notes, unheard melodies, because the enemy anticipates and thwarts them with appropriate rejoinders. Despite Lasker's injunction to shun "the ragtime and vaudeville of chess," the public grew increasingly restive with inchworm gambits and grubby Pawn-snatching. The hypermoderns were reproached with being dull and colorless once their novelty wore off. The average player is not equipped with the patience or ability to appreciate this subtle brand of chess, the slow jockeying for position in which all the action seems to take place beneath the surface. Nothing happens, no slam-bang attacks, no flimflam—yet somehow the technicians emerge triumphant. Naturally, chess seems duller when masters are closely matched. Naturally, the brilliancies of yore are impossible when an opponent refuses to stumble into the silly pitfalls which render them possible. But the aesthetic grasp of many chess fans often does not extend beyond the flashy smothered mate or the tawdry stroke. To the uninitiated, some of the most hard-fought struggles seem devoid of all bravura. This is comparable to the jazz buff's announcing that Bach bores him.

Alekhine and Tal are the two geniuses of attack in this century. Their games are characterized by sheer will and pulsating nervous energy—a legacy of masterpieces imbued with artistry, originality, imagination and brilliance. Both were obsessed with chess. Both explored lines of fantasy which their contemporaries rejected. Tal did not hesitate to express his attitude toward the game:

> I like to grasp the initiative and not give my opponent peace of mind. I will not hide the fact that I love to hear the spectators react after a sacrifice of a piece or Pawn. I don't think that there is anything bad in such a feeling; no artist or musician is indifferent to the reactions of the public.

Victor Korchnoi amassed a crushing plus score against his compatriot, even though he never rose to the same heights as Tal. Famous for counterattacking with ferocious energy, Korchnoi revealed a different temperament:

> I like to coax my opponents into attacking, to let them taste the joy of the initiative, so that they may get carried away, become careless, and sacrifice material.

One can detect here a clear echo of Steinitz. Tal's brilliancies (*any* successful brilliancy, for that matter) can be summoned into existence only after the opponent has erred. Perhaps Korchnoi's superlative *sangfroid* enabled him to detect subtle flaws without succumbing to nervousness. He stated in a recent interview:

> I am not a fan of Tal's. Several months ago I said that Tal is a stereotyped, mechanical player, and people attacked me. Tal has always been a player with wonderful energy, he played with great effort. But his opponents could not always match him in their efforts. I was one of the rare players, who could. Do you remember the Candidates' Tournament of 1959 and the way he beat Smyslov? [See Game 9.] It was his golden era. I think he knows better chess today, he understands it better. But his health is not good, and he cannot endure those terrible nervous struggles.

There can be no doubt that Tal's luck in sacrifice is to be classed as the luck of the strong. He generally loosed his salvo in a rough setting when his opponent, pressed for time, would flounder in a sea of variations. What operated in Tal's favor was a factor which might be called sacrificial shock. Dr. Tarrasch observed long ago that an unexpected sacrifice gives rise to an element of shock, which precludes calm and clear thought. This unsettling effect explains many blunders committed by the defender when he finds himself in unfamiliar terrain. Korchnoi, apparently, was spurred to his keenest efforts by such a sacrifice; it invigorated him. Today's sacrificial luck can be ascribed mostly to time pressure, which was never the case in the previous century. (For a discussion of the clock, see Game 25, note at move 40.)

When Tal was reproached for launching an unsound sacrifice which "luckily" succeeded (see Game 61), he retorted:

> I did not see at what point I was dead lost; and concerning the other accusations of the wise critics, I console myself with pleasure that the chess fan, the spectator, and the reader are happy only when the grandmaster risks, rather than just "pushes wood."

Fischer, on the other hand, will have little truck with such psychological ploys. He grimly insists on soundness and is almost apologetic when he deviates (see Game 90, note at move 25)—"Ironically, I wouldn't have been awarded the brilliancy prize had I chosen the best line here. They don't give medals for endgame technique!"

Most players don't care how they win so long as they win. Nevertheless, there *are* two distinct styles: the tactician seeks a knockout; the strategist is content to win on points. Top honors nowadays generally go to the latter, the stolid grinders like Smyslov, Petrosian, and Spassky. Their manner engenders no seething or turbulence; it is slow-paced and usually evolves from positions which seem drab, stodgy and drawish. Their efforts are stylish rather than sensational, abounding with smooth power. One often feels that they win by boring their opponents to death. Chernev comments:

> Petrosian's play is like no other great master past or present . . . you get the impression that he regards a King-side attack as a primitive attempt to force a win . . . Very often he seems to be . . . maneuvering his pieces back to the first rank, or even into a corner of the board.

Commenting admiringly on one of Petrosian's defensive coups (see Game 6, note at move 10), Fischer writes:

> This super-refinement reduces all of White's attacking prospects. Petrosian has a knack of snuffing out such dreams twenty moves before they even enter his opponent's head.

Most grandmasters are gifted with Petrosian's prophylactic instinct, and they have no intention of contenting themselves with negative immortality. The last decade consequently has yielded a slender harvest of golden brilliancies. The tyranny of the point system has fostered an attitude of safety first and a spate of grandmaster draws. The routine, the plodding, the necessity to squeeze out points in order to finish in the money or earn a higher title—all these factors argue against taking risks. Keres, for one, fears that this situation may lead to the death of creative chess:

> . . . the point is the King. As the participants are of uneven strength, every leading Grandmaster will plan his "simple mathematics," where to get the necessary points. And, of course, it is not reasonable to take a risk against any of the rivals when points can be obtained more easily from the weaker opponents. Only if the mathematics does not go according to plan may it become necessary to "bite" some of the rivals. . . . But in these tournaments, only a few players are really interested in coming first. One needs his ten points, another nine, a third seven, etc., in order to get their corresponding titles. Here again, mathematics dominates. But what about the tournament, the games, the fight for leadership, the dying art of chess?

The chess pro on the tournament circuit earns his crust of bread, to be sure, but his burning ambition is to create a handful of masterpieces. It is a tribute that he still is able to forge fresh material despite adverse conditions and the reams of analysis to which all phases of the game, particularly the opening, have been subjected. There is even talk of two world championships—one for machines, the other for humans. In *The Royal Game*, Stefan Zweig sums up the agony and ecstasy of the chessmaster:

> It stands to reason that so unusual a game, one touched with genius, must create out of itself fitting matadors. This I always knew, but what was

difficult and almost impossible to conceive of was the life of a mentally alert person whose world contracts to a narrow, black-and-white, one-way street; who seeks ultimate triumphs in the to-and-fro forward-and-backward movement of thirty-two pieces; a being who, by a new opening in which the Knight is preferred to the pawn, apprehends greatness and the immortality that goes with casual mention in a chess handbook—of a man of spirit who, escaping madness, can unremittingly devote all of his mental energy during ten, twenty, thirty, forty years to the ludicrous effort to corner a wooden king on a wooden board!

It should be made clear at the outset that the present collection consists solely of personal favorites. Many official brilliancies have been excluded and so have traps, on the grounds that undoubtedly they will wend their way into appropriate anthologies. My major task was weeding out brilliancies which require too much cooperation from the loser; when one side falters too often, the over-all quality of the game is spoiled. I have tried to skim the cream of tournament chess, the best games of the world's best, and the reader can be assured that each effort has outstanding merit. They are arranged by opening, the period is mainly the sixties, with nothing prior to 1958. If there is an important omission or a gross oversight it is due simply to the fact that one person scarcely can keep abreast of the vast and accumulating body of chess literature.

It should be noted that of these 101 games, White wins 74, Black wins 21, and 6 are drawn—a glaring confirmation of the advantage of the first move. Brilliancies by Black are relatively rare, because it is difficult for the second player to snatch the initiative unless White has obliged with several ugly errors, thus spoiling the game for this anthologist. As for draws, both masters must contribute their best to create an immortal game and it makes no difference to me if the result is decisive or not.

To the best of my ability the annotations are crisp and objective without laying claim to being exhaustive. Whenever feasible, I have let the actual combatants speak for themselves. These games are approached impartially without regard for the outcome, although in each instance it is necessary to suggest a vital improvement for the victim since, after all, it was his initial error which spawned the brilliancy. Often it is no easy matter to identify that culprit known as "the losing move." The critic, in tranquillity, can contribute a valuable perspective, provided that he is willing to work as hard on the game as the contestants did. All too frequently, however, he remains merely a friendly guide to the complexities of master play who first cites the *MCO** column for the game under review, then remains silent until White is a Rook ahead and, finally, points out how Black could have held out longer.

* The chessplayer's bible, *Modern Chess Openings*, by Evans & Korn (1965).

Botvinnik, Keres and Fischer are the fewamong irreproachable annotators who are self-critical at all times and aim to instruct rather than merely exhibit their prowess. It has been argued that only those who actually played the game in question should annotate it, because they are the only ones who really know what that game is all about. But even the generally trustworthy comments of the emotion-laden participants should be taken with a grain of salt. The mighty Alekhine, on more than one occasion, was not above "editing" some of his game scores so that they conformed with what he deemed to be a more appropriate finish. All too often, alas, notes are copied indiscriminately from "authoritative" sources, thereby relaying the original errors. Spielmann pointed out a long time ago:

> Many chessplayers . . . are loath to admit subsequently that at a critical point they were guided by instinct, and some have been known to demonstrate how uncommonly far ahead and with what accuracy they had made their calculations. It strikes me as poverty-stricken rather than heroic.

To the serious student, demolishing faulty annotations is not only a sport but also an excellent way to improve. Another book could be devoted to this subject alone.

An astute reader may question the inclusion of several thwarted brilliancies such as Games 42, 57, 72, 93, 95. Strictly speaking, these belong in a volume dedicated to great defenses. In my opinion, each major tournament should present an award for the best defense as well as for a brilliancy. At any rate, chess remains one of the last bulwarks of the individual in this machine age. There is still scope for imagination and fantasy before the computer overtakes it. It is my hope that you will enjoy these 101 exciting struggles as much as I did. These great games of the sixties offer a modest oasis in a troubled world.

August 1969   LARRY EVANS

1
6th MATCH GAME 1965
Alekhine's Defense

WHITE: TAL BLACK: LARSEN

Tal has an uncanny knack for infusing life into prosaic settings. His brinkmanship pays off when Black loses his way in a welter of fantastic variations.

1 P–K4	N–KB3
2 P–K5	N–Q4
3 P–Q4	P–Q3
4 N–KB3	....

Many modern masters distrust the Four Pawns Attack, with *4 P–QB4 N–N3; 5 P–B4,* after which White has his center to defend.

4	PxP
5 NxP	P–K3

Earlier, in their fourth match game, Larsen scored a psychological success with *5 ... N–Q2!?* "daring" Tal to sacrifice *6 NxP* (he should have). Instead, White chose the tame *6 B–QB4* and actually got the worst of it.

One of Larsen's later innovations is *5 ... P–KN3!*

6 Q–B3	Q–B3
7 Q–N3	P–KR3
8 N–QB3	N–N5
9 B–N5ch	P–B3
10 B–R4	N–Q2
11 O–O	NxN
12 PxN	Q–N3
13 Q–B3	Q–B4

Larsen reckons that the doubled Pawns cannot be exploited in the ending, and he also knows how Tal hates to exchange Queens. Naturally not *13 ... NxBP?; 14 BxPch!*

14 Q–K2	B–K2
15 P–QR3	N–Q4
16 N–N5!?	....

Nine out of ten masters would settle for the safer *16 B–Q2.* What characterizes Tal's style is a disdain for the obvious. Even if there are a thousand good reasons for rejecting a given move, the alert tactician is ready to consider it—and he often gains an advantage in this totally unexpected manner.

Position after 16 N–N5

16	PxN

The "bluff" must be accepted, since *16 ... O–O?; 17 N–Q4 Q–R2; 18 P–QB4* followed by *B–B2* would allow White a commanding position.

25

17 Q×Pch	K–Q1
18 P–QB4	Q×P?

A world of fantasy arises after *18* . . . N–B5; *19* R–Q1ch K–B2; *20* R–Q7ch B×R; *21* Q×Bch K–N1; *22* Q×B Q×P; *23* B–K3 N–N3; *24* Q×BP Q–B3; *25* B–K8! Q–K2; *26* Q×N R×B; *27* B–B5 Q–Q2; *28* B–Q6ch K–B1; *29* P–B5, and Tal remarks that the Bishop on Q6 is more powerful than the hemmed-in Rook.

The right defense is *18* . . . N–N3!; *19* Q–R5 K–B2; *20* P–B5 K–N1; *21* P×N P×P; *22* Q–N5 R–R4 with at least equal chances.

19 P×N	B–Q3
20 P–KN3	Q×QP
21 Q–K2	K–K2
22 R–Q1	Q–QR4
23 Q–N4	Q–KB4
24 Q–QB4	. . . .

Not *24* Q×P? B–K4. White is a Pawn behind, but he has ample compensation in view of Black's exposed King.

Position after 24 Q–QB4

24	Q–B4

This defense doesn't work, but the question is whether Black has anything significantly better. If *24* . . . B–B4; *25* B–K3! B×B; *26* Q–B7ch K–B3; *27* P×B wins.

The most reasonable try at consolidation looks like *24* . . . R–Q1; but after *25* B–K3, Black still can't develop his Queen side. *25* . . . B–Q2 is refuted by *26* R×B! And *25* . . . P–QN3; *26* Q–B6 B–R3; *27* R×B puts an end to resistance.

25 Q–Q3	Q–Q4
26 Q–QB3	B–K4

Not *26* . . . Q–K4?; *27* B–B4. Now Black is hoping for a repetition of moves with *27* Q–N4ch B–Q3; etc.

27 Q–K1	Q–B4
28 B–Q2	K–B3
29 QR–B1	Q–N3
30 B–K3	Q–R3

There is no respite. *30* . . . Q×P loses to *31* P–B4 B–N1; *32* B–Q4ch.

31 Q–N4	. . . .

Now the threat is *32* B–N5.

31	P–QN4
32 B×NP	Q–N2
33 P–B4	B–N1
34 B–B6	Resigns

His Rooks stayed at home all game.

2

34th U.S.S.R. CHAMPIONSHIP 1961
Benoni Defense

WHITE: GURGENIDZE   BLACK: TAL

Black's victory did much to popu-
larize the Hromadka System by
revealing its double-edged potential.
After a careless move by White, Tal
uncorks a sparkling attack.

1	P–Q4	N–KB3
2	P–QB4	P–B4
3	P–Q5	....

3 N–KB3 is occasionally played to
steer the game into positional channels more to White's taste. After
3 ... PxP; *4* NxP P–K3, Black
has no worries. Also without bite is
3 PxP P–K3; *4* N–KB3 BxP transposing into a reverse Queen's Gambit
Accepted.

3	....	P–K3
4	N–QB3	PxP
5	PxP	P–Q3
6	N–B3	P–KN3
7	P–K4	B–N2
8	B–K2	O–O
9	O–O	R–K1
10	N–Q2	....

More flexible is *10* Q–B2 N–R3;
11 B–KB4 N–QN5; *12* Q–N1 Q–
K2; *13* R–K1!

10	....	N–R3
11	R–K1	....

If *11* P–B4 (or *11* P–B3 N–Q2;
12 N–B4 N–K4=) N–B2; *12* B–
B3 N–Q2; *13* P–QR4 R–N1; *14*
N–B4 N–N3= (Steinmeyer–Evans,
U.S. Championship 1964).

11	....	N–B2
12	P–QR4	....

12 B–B1 is more consistent. The
text should be played only after
Black threatens ... P–QN4.

12	....	P–N3
13	Q–B2	N–N5
14	P–R3?	....

Meets with drastic punishment. Correct is *14* N–B4.

14	....	NxBP!
15	KxN	Q–R5ch
16	K–B1	B–Q5
17	N–Q1	....

Position after 17 N–Q1

17	....	QxRP!
18	B–B3	....

Of course not *18* PxQ? BxRP mate.
The text allows the King access to
K2. But a series of quiet moves now
decides the issue.

18	....	Q–R7
19	N–K3	....

A better try is *19* N–B4 followed by B–K3.

19	P–B4
20 N/2–B4	P×P
21 B×P	B–R3

Piling on the pressure. White is a piece up but his men are uncoordinated and his King is exposed.

22 B–B3	R–K4
23 R–R3	R/1–K1
24 B–Q2	N×P

This collapses the house of cards.

25 B×Nch	R×B
26 K–K2	....

The Rook is immune because of Q–R8 mate.

26	B×N
27 R×B	B×Nch
Resigns	

After *28* Q×B Q×Pch; *29* K–Q1 Q×B mate.

3

MAJORCA 1967
Benoni Defense

WHITE: GLIGORICH   BLACK: MATULOVICH

Black seems to be overcoming his opening difficulties when a sudden positional sacrifice immobilizes him. Keep your eye on White's center Pawns!

1 P–Q4	N–KB3
2 P–QB4	P–B4

To compel White to make an early decision in the center.

3 P–Q5	P–KN3

Usually *3* ... P–K3 is played first. Now the opening could also be classified as a King's Indian Defense.

4 N–QB3	B–N2
5 P–K4	P–Q3
6 N–B3	....

For *6* P–B4 see Games 28–30.

6	O–O

7 B–K2	P–K3
8 O–O	P×P
9 BP×P	B–N5

Black prepares to part with the two Bishops as the price for relieving his cramp. There are two main alternatives:

A. *9* ... N–R3; *10* N–Q2 N–B2; *11* P–B3 (unsound is *11* P–B4 R–K1; *12* B–B3 R–N1; *13* N–B4 P–QN4; *14* N–R5 B–Q2; *15* P–K5 P×P; *16* P×P R×P; *17* B–B4 R–B4!; *18* P–N3 P–N5—Zinser–Evans, Venice 1967) N–B2; *12* P–QR4 P–N3; *13* N–B4 B–QR3; *14* R–N1 (or *14* N–R3 or *14* B–N5), with double-edged play (Gligorich–Lobigas, Manila 1968).

B. *9* ... R–K1; *10* N–Q2 P–N3!?; *11* P–B3 B–QR3; *12* B×B N×B;

13 N–B4 Q–Q2; *14* P–QR4 (R. Byrne–Evans, U.S. Championship 1964), and now *14* . . . N–QN5; *15* B–B4 B–B1 leaves Black with a passive game, since his Knight has been deprived of K1 to defend the QP.

10 P–KR3   . . . .

Also playable is *10* B–KB4 P–QR3; *11* P–QR4 Q–K2; *12* Q–B2!? QN–Q2; *13* KR–K1 P–B5!= (Pachman–Kaplan, Puerto Rico 1968).

10	BxN
11 BxB	QN–Q2
12 B–B4	N–K1

Again we see why it is sometimes important for Black to abstain from . . . R–K1 too early in this variation.

13 Q–Q2   P–QR3

Position after 13 . . . P–QR3

14 B–N5!   . . . .

"A remarkable idea. Almost all masters play *14* P–QR4 automatically in this type of position to delay the Black advance on the Queen side. But if this advance comes later, it then has greater force, because White has weakened his position" (Larsen).

14 . . . .   B–B3

15 B–R6	B–N2
16 B–N5	B–B3

As the theoretical underdog Black would naturally be content with a draw. He cannot move his Queen in view of *17* B–K7. And White keeps an edge on *16* . . . P–B3; *17* B–R4 P–QN4; *18* B–N4.

17 BxB	N/1xB
18 KR–K1	R–K1

A loss of time. Black should play *18* . . . P–QN4! while the getting is good. It is not wise to commit this Rook before the best post for it has been established.

19 B–Q1!	P–QN4
20 B–B2	P–B5

The difference now is that White's pieces are all on the right squares to undertake action in the center by P–B4.

21 P–B4	P–N5
22 N–R4	P–N6
23 PxP	PxP
24 B–Q3	Q–B2
25 K–R2	N–B4
26 NxN	QxN
27 QR–B1	. . . .

White cannot capture the RP, because his KP hangs at the end. Black now seems to have succeeded in obtaining an adequate grip on the dark squares. His main lookout is preventing P–K5.

27 . . . .   Q–R2

27 . . . Q–Q5 is met by *28* R–B4.

28 R–B4   . . . .

28 R–B6 is met by . . . Q–Q5. Not *28* Q–B3 N–Q2; *29* QxP N–B4;

30 Q–B2 N×B; *31* Q×N Q–B7 regaining the Pawn.

| 28 | .... | N–Q2 |
| 29 | KR–QB1 | .... |

Now White's threat is *30* Q–B3. Again *29* R–B6 meets with the pesky ... Q–Q5.

| 29 | .... | N–B4 |

Although this provokes a stunning refutation, it is difficult to suggest anything better.

Position after 29 ... N–B4

| 30 | R×N! | .... |

The natural *30* B–N1 P–B3! might give Black time to consolidate.

| 30 | .... | P×R |
| 31 | P–Q6 | Q–N3? |

Black should get his counterplay

started with *31* ... P–QR4–5; he might still be able to make a fight of it.

| 32 | B–B4 | R–R2 |
| 33 | P–K5 | P–QR4 |

Too little too late.

34	Q–Q5	P–R5
35	P–Q7	R–KB1
36	R–Q1	R/2–R1

Now Black's further loss of time is apparent. The next blow smashes his blockade to smithereens.

| 37 | P–K6! | P×P |

The beauty part is *37* ... Q×P; *38* Q×R!

| 38 | Q–K5 | K–B2 |
| 39 | R–Q6 | Q–B2 |

Readers who cannot stand the sight of blood had better cover their eyes.

| 40 | B×Pch | K–K2 |
| 41 | P–Q8(Q)ch | .... |

Of course *41* B–B4ch K–Q1; *42* Q–N5ch also mates.

| 41 | .... | KR×Q |
| 42 | B–B4ch | Resigns |

4
AMSTERDAM INTERZONAL 1964
Caro-Kann Defense

WHITE: EVANS   BLACK: BERGER

White's speculative Knight sacrifice does not yield any immediate dividends. It soon becomes apparent, however, that Black's uncastled King will find no haven, though he strives mightily to do so.

1	P–K4	P–QB3
2	P–Q4	P–Q4
3	N–QB3	P×P
4	N×P	B–B4
5	N–N3	B–N3
6	N–B3	N–Q2
7	P–KR4	....

This weakening of the Pawn structure is compensated by the subsequent control of space. The alternative 7 B–Q3 P–K3; 8 O–O KN–B3; 9 R–K1 B–K2; 10 P–B4 O–O; 11 P–N3 Q–R4; 12 B×B RP×B; 13 Q–K2 gives White a slight pull (Evans–Benko, U.S. Championship 1962).

7	....	P–KR3
8	P–R5	B–R2
9	B–Q3	B×B
10	Q×B	Q–B2
11	B–Q2	KN–B3
12	O–O–O	P–K3
13	K–N1	....

13 P–B4 B–Q3; 14 N–K4 B–B5! allows simplifications.

13 ....   P–B4

Before undertaking action in the center Black should castle long, either here or on the next move. If 13 ... B–Q3; 14 N–K4 B–B5; 15 B–K1 followed by P–KN3 maintains the tension.

14	P–B4	P×P?
15	N×P	P–R3

Black had intended 15 ... N–K4; but after 16 Q–K2 N×BP; 17 N×P! N×Bch; 18 R×N P×N; 19 Q×Pch Q–K2 (or 19 ... B–K2; 20 N–B5 K–B1; 21 R–QB1 wins); 20 Q–B4

(threatening R–K2) Black's King cannot escape the central crossfire.

Black must submit to 15 ... O–O–O; 16 N–N5 Q–N1; 17 N–K4! N×N; 18 Q×N, but his defensive task is extremely difficult—e.g., 18 ... P–R3 (or 18 ... N–B3; 19 Q–K3 P–R3; 20 N–R7ch K–B2; 21 B–R5ch P–N3; 22 R×R wins); 19 B–B4 P–K4; 20 R×N! R×R; 21 B×KP Q–R1; 22 N–B7 (or Q–B5) R×N; 23 Q–B5ch K–N1 (if 22 ... R–Q2; 23 R–Q1 wins); 24 Q×P mops up.

Position after 15 ... P–R3

16	N×P!	P×N
17	Q–N6ch	K–Q1
18	KR–K1	....

After this quiet developing move Gibraltar crumbles.

18 ....   K–B1

Giving up a second Pawn to gain a sanctuary for the King. On 18 ... P–K4 (or 18 ... Q×P; 19 B–B3); 19 B–B3 K–B1; 20 P–B4! is powerful.

19	R×P	P–N3
20	Q–B5!	....

Another quiet move, intending B–B4.

20	....	K–N2
21	B–B4	Q–B4

Loses, but so does *21* ... Q–B1; *22* N–K4 K–R2 (if *22* ... NxN; *23* QxNch K–R2; *24* R–QB6!);

25 NxN NxN; *26* RxN! PxR; *27* R–Q7ch etc.

22 RxN/6!   Resigns

If *22* ... NxR; *23* R–Q7ch K–B3; *24* R–B7, mate.

5

U.S.S.R. CHAMPIONSHIP 1964
Caro-Kann Defense

WHITE: BAKULIN   BLACK: BRONSTEIN

Black's patient strategic buildup is rewarded when he gets the opportunity to splurge a Rook and a Bishop. The finish is artistic and original.

1	P–K4	P–QB3
2	P–Q4	P–Q4
3	N–QB3	PxP
4	NxP	N–B3
5	NxNch	NPxN

The alternative *5* ... KPxN gives Black a lifeless position wherein all he can look forward to is a draw. The text is double-edged, anticipating eventual use of the open KN file in return for the ugly Pawn structure.

6	B–K3	B–B4
7	Q–Q2	P–K3
8	N–K2	N–Q2
9	N–N3	B–N3
10	B–K2	....

White's Knight is not particularly well-placed. More consistent is *10* P–KR4 P–KR4; *11* B–Q3 followed by Queen-side castling.

10	....	Q–B2
11	O–O	....

A courageous but risky decision. White anticipates Black's castling long and hopes to use his Queen-side Pawns as battering rams. His own King, however, will be equally vulnerable. Safer is *11* O–O–O.

11	....	P–KR4
12	KR–Q1	P–R5
13	N–B1	P–R6
14	P–KN3	O–O–O
15	P–QB4	....

More clean-cut is *15* P–QN4 P–K4; *16* P–QB4. Now Black can establish a blockade.

15	....	P–QB4
16	P–Q5	P–K4
17	QR–B1	P–B4
18	P–QN4	B–Q3

Stronger than *18* ... PxP; *19* P–B5. While White seems to have reached his maximum, Black still has the dynamic break ... P–B5.

Position after 18 ... B–Q3

19 P–B3? ....

The cause of White's future trouble. More active is *19* P–B4, though already he has lost his precious initiative.

19	....	P–B5
20	B–B2	QR–K1
21	K–R1	KR–N1
22	R–K1	P–K5

Now it's clear that Black has all the play. The threat of ... P–K6 compels White's reply, after which his game is strategically lost.

23	BxP	NxB
24	PxN	QxP
25	B–Q1	B–B2!
26	PxBP	....

Hoping to answer *26* ... B–N3 with *27* N–N3.

26	....	P–K6!
27	Q–K2	....

The Pawn is poisoned: *27* RxP (or *27* NxP BxP; *28* R–B3 R–K4 and the pin is unbearable) RxR; *28* QxR QxQ; *29* NxQ BxP; *30* R–B3 R–K1 wins.

27	....	B–Q6!
28	QxB	R–N8ch!

Position after 28 ... R–N8ch

29	KxR	P–K7ch
30	N–K3	....

On *30* K–R1 Q–B7; *31* Q–B5ch K–N1; *32* QxRP R–N1 wins.

30	....	RxN
31	Q–B5ch	R–K3ch
32	K–R1	Q–B7
	Resigns	

6

PORTOROZ 1958
Caro-Kann Defense

WHITE: TAL   BLACK: FUSTER

This is one of the games with which Tal burst upon the world chess scene. Spectacularly sacrificing a Bishop for only two Pawns, he succeeds in pinning Black's King in the center while mounting an attack.

1 P–K4	P–QB3
2 P–Q4	P–Q4
3 N–QB3	PxP
4 NxP	N–Q2
5 N–KB3	KN–B3
6 NxNch	....

To avoid simplifications Spassky later revived *6* N–N3, but the retreat only loses a tempo and places the Knight on a dubious post.

6	NxN
7 B–QB4	B–B4

A mistake is *7* . . . B–N5?; *8* BxPch KxB; *9* N–K5ch etc.

8 Q–K2	P–K3
9 B–KN5	B–K2
10 O–O–O	P–KR3

The refinement *10* . . . B–KN5!; *11* P–KR3 BxN; *12* QxB N–Q4!; *13* BxB QxB snuffs out White's budding initiative (Fischer–Petrosian, Bled 1961).

11 B–R4	N–K5

More sensible is *11* . . . N–Q4. The text gives White an opportunity to complicate, although he holds the edge in any case.

12 P–KN4!	....

Surprising and effective. Of course, White had to reckon with *12* . . . BxB; *13* PxB (on *13* NxB B–R2 is sufficient) NxP; *14* PxP O–O; *15* PxPch, with ample compensation for the loss of the exchange.

12	B–R2
13 B–KN3	NxB
14 BPxN!	Q–B2
15 N–K5	B–Q3
16 P–KR4	P–B3?

Unfortunately *16* . . . O–O–O fails against *17* NxKBP! QxN; *18* BxPch. And on *16* . . . O–O; *17* P–N5 pursues the attack.

But Black should seek some relief with *16* . . . BxN; *17* PxB R–Q1; *18* RxRch KxR. The reduction in material would give drawing chances.

17 BxP!	....

Naturally! Black was hoping for *17* N–B3 O–O–O.

17	PxN
18 PxP	B–K2

Not *18* . . . BxKP; *19* KR–K1 B–Q3; *20* B–Q7ch!

19 KR–B1	R–KB1
20 RxRch	BxR
21 Q–B3	Q–K2

Position after 21 . . . *Q–K2*

Apparently Black has secured a measure of safety, intending to free himself with . . . R–Q1.

22 Q–N3!	R–N1

To fend off the threat of R–Q7. *22* . . . R–Q1 is refuted by *23* B–B7ch! QxB; *24* RxRch K–K2; *25* R–Q7ch. It's all over now, anyway.

23	B–Q7ch	Q×B
24	R×Q	K×R
25	Q–B7ch	B–K2
26	P–K6ch	K–Q1

26 ... K–Q3 meets with *27* Q–B4ch followed by Q×R.

27	Q×P	Resigns

The Bishop has no refuge: *27* ... B–K5; *28* Q–R8ch K–B2; *29* Q–K5ch, et cetera.

7

OBERHAUSEN 1961
Caro-Kann Defense

WHITE: TRAPPL   BLACK: PEREZ

Many of the teams at this event contained young players who were given their first international trials. The nineteen-year-old Czech, Trappl, walked off with the brilliancy prize.

1	P–K4	P–QB3
2	P–Q4	P–Q4
3	N–QB3	P×P
4	N×P	N–Q2
5	B–QB4	....

After *5* Q–K2!? Black must avoid *5* ... KN–B3?; *6* N–Q6 mate, with which Keres once won a tournament game and Alekhine defeated four players in consultation.

5	....	P–K3

Somewhat inconsistent, since the theme of this defense is to leave the QB diagonal unclogged. Stronger is *5* ... KN–B3; *6* N–N5˙ N–Q4! (again fighting to defer ... P–K3 until after the QB has been developed); *7* KN–B3 P–KR3; *8* N–K4 QN–N3; *9* B–N3 (better is *9* B–Q3), B–B4; *10* N–N3 B–R2; *11* O–O P–K3= (Fischer–Portisch, Stockholm 1962).

6	Q–K2	KN–B3
7	N–N5	N–N3
8	B–N3	P–KR3

Naturally not 8 ... Q×P?; *9* KN–B3 followed by N–K5.

9	N/5–B3	P–B4
10	P×P	B×P?

This obvious recapture allows Black's pieces to become entangled on the Queen side; and he can neither defend his own King properly nor mount a quick enough counterattack. More systematic is *10* ... QN–Q2 (Petrosian), to recapture with the knight and control K5 as an outpost.

11	B–Q2	O–O
12	N–K5	QN–Q4
13	KN–B3	P–QN3
14	O–O–O	Q–B2
15	P–N4!	P–QR4
16	P–N5	P×P
17	B×NP	P–R5

Both attacks are fast, but White comes first.

18	B×N/Q5	N×B
19	KR–N1	P–R6

19 ... P–B3 fails against *20* B–R6.

20 R×N!   ....

Eliminating the main defender of Black's King and clearing KB6 for the Bishop. There is also another deeper and very pretty point.

| 20 | .... | P×Pch |
| 21 | K–N1 | Q–R2 |

If *21* ... P×R; *22* B–B6 P–N3; *23* Q–Q3 R–K1 (meeting *24* R×Pch); *24* N×NP wins.

| 22 | Q–B4 | P×R |
| 23 | B–B6! | .... |

Jettisoning the Queen for just one tempo.

| 23 | .... | P×Q |

Also insufficient is *23* ... P–N3; *24* Q×QP B–K3; *25* R×Pch! P×R

Position after 22 ... *P×R*

(forced); *26* Q×Bch R–B2 (forced); *27* N–N5 Q×Pch; *28* Q×Q R×Q; *29* N/N5×R with a winning endgame.

| 24 | R×Pch | K–R1 |
| 25 | R–N5ch | Resigns |

Black gets mated—*25* ... K–R2; *26* R–R5ch K–N1; *27* R–R8 mate.

8

2nd MATCH GAME 1965
Caro-Kann Defense

WHITE: TAL   BLACK: PORTISCH

An engrossing psychological study. Tal's combination is good for no more than a draw, but Portisch misjudges the position and plays for a win, thereby succumbing to a bit of wizardry.

1	P–K4	P–QB3
2	N–QB3	P–Q4
3	N–B3	P×P
4	N×P	B–N5

White's avoidance of P–Q4 is not accidental and is designed to exclude the normal development *4* ... B–B4 which could now be met with *5* N–N3

B–N3; *6* P–KR4 P–KR3; *7* N–K5 B–R2; *8* Q–R5 P–KN3; *9* B–B4! P–K3; *10* Q–K2 (threatening N×KBP), with a beautiful game.

5	P–KR3	B×N
6	Q×B	N–Q2
7	P–Q4	KN–B3
8	B–Q3	N×N
9	Q×N	P–K3

More forcing is *9* ... N–B3, which would compel White to place his Queen on an awkward square (K3, B4 or R4) to defend his QP, or to offer a gambit with *10* Q–K2!?

10	O–O	B–K2
11	P–QB3	N–B3
12	Q–R4	N–Q4

12 . . . O–O looks perfectly safe.

13	Q–N4	B–B3
14	R–K1	Q–N3
15	P–QB4!?	. . . .

Perhaps too forcing. Simpler is 15 P–R3.

15	. . . .	N–N5

After 15 . . . N–K2; 16 B–K3 (16 P–Q5 BP×P; 17 P×P N×P; 18 Q–R4ch K–B1; 19 B–K4 B–Q5!; 20 R–K2 R–Q1 denies White anything for his Pawn) Q×NP; 17 QR–N1 Q–B6; 18 Q–K2 White has play for the Pawn.

16	R×Pch	. . . .

A logical consequence; otherwise the QP falls without compensation.

16	. . . .	P×R
17	Q×Pch	. . . .

A tense moment.

Position after 17 Q×Pch

17	. . . .	K–B1?

A difficult decision, not undertaken lightly. But Black should have allowed a draw with 17 . . . K–Q1; 18 Q–Q6ch K–K1; 19 Q–K6ch (there is nothing better) etc. However, Portisch decides to play to win.

Tal's genius consists of confronting his opponents with tempting ways to go wrong. He gives a beautiful winning line after 17 . . . B–K2; 18 B–N6ch! P×B (if 18 . . . K–Q1; 19 B–B5 Q–B2; 20 B–B4 Q–B1; 21 Q–K4); 19 B–N5 Q–B2; 20 R–K1 Q–Q2; 21 Q×Pch followed by R×B.

18	B–B4	R–Q1
19	P–B5	. . . .

Ever accurate. Not 19 R–K1? P–B4!

19	. . . .	N×B

And not 19 . . . Q–R4?; 20 R–K1 N×B; 21 B–Q6ch R×B; 22 Q–K8 mate.

20	P×Q	N×B
21	Q–N4	N–Q4

Fischer suggests 21 . . . P–N4 as a better chance. But not 21 . . . R×P?; 22 Q–B8ch R–Q1; 23 Q×Rch! B×Q; 24 P×P.

22	P×P	K–K2

Portisch gives as correct 22 . . . P–KN3. Were it not for White's tiny Pawn on QR7, he would be lost materially. Even so, it is hard to see how he can capitalize on it. Black's King seems headed for refuge via Q3 and B2.

23	P–N4!	R–R1

If 23 . . . N×P; 24 R–N1 R×P;

Position after 22 . . . K–K2

25 Q–K2ch K–Q3; *26* P–R3 and R×P next.

24 R–K1ch   K–Q3?

Correct is *24* . . . K–Q1; *25* R–K6 (*25* P–N5 R×P; *26* Q–K6 K–B2;

27 R–QB1 R–Q1; *28* P×P P–QN3 also holds) K–B2; *26* P–N5 KR–QB1 (Fischer).

25 P–N5!   R×P

A blunder, but he's lost anyway. If *25* . . . K–B2 (or *25* . . . KR–Q1; *26* P–N6! N×P; *27* R–N1); *26* R–N1 KR–Q1; *27* P–N6ch N×P; *28* Q–N3ch R–Q3; *29* R×N R×P; *30* R–N4, and White should win (Fischer).

26 R–K6ch   K–B2
27 R×B!   Resigns

On *27* . . . P×R; *28* Q–N7ch is decisive.

9
CANDIDATES' TOURNAMENT 1959
Caro-Kann Defense

WHITE: TAL   BLACK: SMYSLOV

The "magician from Riga" conjures rabbits from his hat to create a game for the ages. Each time Black is on the verge of consolidating, Tal unleashes another surprise.

1 P–K4   P–QB3
2 P–Q3   P–Q4

It is better to foil White's passive setup by *2* . . . P–K4 or *2* . . . P–KN3.

3 N–Q2   P–K4
4 KN–B3   N–Q2
5 P–Q4   P×KP

White's last is open to the theoretical objection that it allows a premature

clarification in the center. Black could ease the pressure with *5* . . . P×QP!; *6* N×P P×P; *7* N×P N–B4.

6 QN×P   P×P

Tal opines that the active *6* . . . P–KB4; *7* N–N3 P–K5; *8* N–N5 is too dangerous for Black.

7 Q×P   . . . .

7 Q–K2 B–N5ch; *8* P–B3 P×P; *9* P×P B–K2; *10* N–Q6ch K–B1 does not offer enough compensation for the Pawn.

7 . . . .   KN–B3
8 B–KN5   B–K2
9 O–O–O   O–O

10	N–Q6	Q–R4
11	B–QB4	P–N4

The stage is set for sharp tactics with the Kings aligned on opposing wings. The text is Black's most active chance. He is hoping for *12* B–N3? P–B4, followed by . . . P–B5.

Inferior is *11* . . . BxN; *12* QxB N–K5; *13* Q–B4 NxB; *14* NxN N–B3; *15* KR–K1. Also risky is *11* . . . N–N3; *12* BxPch RxB; *13* NxR KxN; *14* KR–K1 QN–Q4; *15* Q–K5!

12	B–Q2!	Q–R3?

Probably the losing move. It must be remembered, however, that Smyslov might have been playing for a win here with Black—and it takes two to create a brilliancy. The simplest is *12* . . . Q–R5; *13* NxB QRxN;

Position after 12 . . . Q–R3

14 B–N3 QxQ with only a slight disadvantage in the endgame. *12* . . , Q–N3 (or *12* . . . Q–B2); *13* N–B5 B–B4; *14* Q–R4! leads to variations similar to that in the note to Black's next move.

13	N–B5!	. . . .

Black was relying on the retreat of the attacked Bishop, which would give him time for . . . P–B4.

13	. . . .	B–Q1

Again everything seems to be in order. Bad would have been *13* . . . B–B4; *14* Q–R4 PxB; *15* B–B3! QxP; *16* RxN! BxR; *17* N–R6ch K–R1; *18* QxN!

14	Q–R4!	PxB

Black would not survive long by *14* . . . N–K4; *15* N–R6ch! PxN; *16* BxRP N–N3; *17* RxB!

15	Q–N5	N–R4

If *15* . . . P–N3 (*15* . . . N–K1?; *16* QxB wins); *16* N–R6ch K–N2; *17* B–B3 QxP; *18* KR–K1! and Black cannot meet the threat of N–N4.

16	N–R6ch	K–R1
17	QxN	QxP

After *17* . . . PxN; *18* QxP White has too many threats—*e.g.*, *17* . . . R–KN1 (or *17* . . . P–QB4; *18* B–B3ch P–B3; *19* N–N5 wins); *18* B–B3ch P–B3; *19* KR–K1 P–B4; *20* N–N5 RxN; *21* QxR, and the threat of R–K8ch is devastating.

18	B–B3	N–B3
19	QxP	. . . .

Position after 19 QxP

A remarkable concept. Black cannot avoid material loss. Of course, the Queen cannot be taken, because of R×Bch.

19	....	Q–R8ch
20	K–Q2	R×Q
21	N×Rch	K–N1
22	R×Q	K×N

23	N–K5ch	K–K3
24	N×P/6	N–K5ch
25	K–K3	B–N3ch
26	B–Q4	Resigns

When the great Smyslov loses in twenty-six moves, that is chess history.

10

MONACO 1968
English Opening

WHITE: BOTVINNIK   BLACK: PORTISCH

Botvinnik is noted for his strategic depth; his best games rarely feature brilliancies. Here, however, when given the opportunity, he demonstrates that he is always alert to all the dormant tactical implications.

1	P–QB4	P–K4
2	N–QB3	N–KB3
3	P–KN3	P–Q4
4	P×P	N×P
5	B–N2	B–K3

Another try is 5 ... N–K2; 6 N–B3 QN–B3; 7 P–Q3 N–B4; 8 O–O B–K2; 9 P–QR3 B–K3; 10 P–QN4 P–QR3; 11 B–N2 P–B3; 12 P–K3 O–O: 13 Q–B2 Q–Q2 (Pachman–Cobo, Havana 1964).

6	N–B3	N–QB3
7	O–O	N–N3

The main drawback is that Black is essaying a well-known variation of the Sicilian a move down; the entire approach is suspect.

8	P–Q3	B–K2
9	P–QR3	P–QR4

This restraining maneuver was supposed to be an improvement, but it turns out to be just another weakness. Black might strive for more activity with 9 ... P–B4; 10 P–QN4 B–B3.

10	B–K3	O–O
11	N–QR4	N×N

If 11 ... N–Q4; 12 B–B5 P–QN4?; 13 B×B Q×B; 14 R–B1, etc.

12	Q×N	B–Q4
13	KR–B1	R–K1

Portisch himself queries this lackluster developing move but fails to give a satisfactory alternative. After 13 ... P–B4; 14 Q–N5, B–B3 (15 Q×NP? N–Q5) Black's game looks playable but shaky.

14	R–B2	B–B1
15	QR–B1	N–N1?

White's control of the QB file is extremely annoying, and Black hopes to neutralize it with ... P–QB3 on the next move. The text, however, is an error of judgment. Necessary is *15 . . . P–K5; 16 PxP BxP; 17 R–Q2 Q–B3; 18 R–B4!* despite the fact that White keeps the initiative.

Ajedrez considers *15 . . . P–R3; 16 N–Q2 BxB; 17 KxB N–Q5; 18 BxN PxB; 19 RxP RxP; 20 N–K4 RxP; 21 R–Q7*—with a distinct White advantage.

16 RxP! ....

Falling for the "trap," Botvinnik initiates a deep and well-calculated combination.

16 ....   B–B3
17 R/1xB   PxR

All according to plan. Black has gained an exchange and White's Rook is in trouble.

18 RxKBP! ....

Position after 18 RxKBP

The Rook is immune—*18 . . . KxR?; 19 Q–B4ch K–N3; 20 N–N5 Q–B3; 21 B–K4ch K–R4; 22 B–B3ch K–N3; 23 B–R5ch! KxB; 24 Q–R4ch K–N3; 25 QxP* mate.

Had Black seen what was in store he would have tried *18 . . . R–K2.*

18	**P–R3**
19 R–N7	**Q–B1**
20 Q–B4ch	**K–R1**

Black can avert the holocaust with *20 . . . Q–K3; 21 NxP QxQ; 22 NxQ P–R5;* but, with strong diagonals for his Bishops and two Pawns for the exchange, White should win the ending.

21 N–R4!	**QxR**
22 N–N6ch	**K–R2**
23 B–K4	**B–Q3**
24 NxPch	**P–N3**

Forced. If *24 . . . K–R1?; 25 N–B7ch* wins the house.

25 BxPch	**K–N2**
26 BxPch!	**Resigns**

Final position after 26 BxPch

Neat to the end. If *26 . . . KxB; 27 Q–R4ch K–N2; 28 Q–R7ch K–B3; 29 N–N4ch K–K3; 30 QxQ* wins. No better is *26 . . . K–B3; 27 Q–B4ch K–K3; 28 B–B7ch K–K2; 29 Q–N5ch.* Finally if *26 . . . K–R1; 27 N–B7ch K–N1; 28 NxBch* etc. This was voted the best game of 1968 by the *Chess Informant* jury of eight grandmasters.

11
RIGA 1968
English Opening

WHITE: Smyslov   BLACK: Liberson

"My best game in ten years," said former World Champion Smyslov. White's Queen sacrifice is very deep and has many fine points, an unexpected bonus for his positional superiority.

1	P–QB4	P–K4
2	N–QB3	N–QB3
3	P–KN3	P–KN3
4	B–N2	B–N2
5	R–N1	P–Q3
6	P–QN4	P–QR3

Better is 6 ... P–B4 immediately, so as not to create a Queen-side target. Evans–Spassky, Lugano Olympics 1968, continued: 7 P–Q3 N–B3; 8 P–N5 N–K2; 9 P–K4 O–O; 10 KN–K2 P–QR3=.

7	P–K3	P–B4
8	KN–K2	N–B3
9	P–Q3	O–O
10	O–O	B–Q2
11	P–QR4	R–N1
12	P–N5	P×P
13	RP×P	N–K2
14	B–QR3	....

"To prevent the advance of Black's QBP. If now 13 ... P–B4; 14 P×Pe.p., and Black's pawn weaknesses will be readily exploited" (Smyslov).

42

14	....	B–K3
15	Q–N3	P–N3
16	P–Q4	P–K5
17	P–Q5	B–B2
18	N–Q4	Q–Q2
19	B–N2	....

"According to the great teachers of the past—Anderssen, Lasker, Alekhine—before one attacks, every piece must be on its best square. Since the QB has served its purpose on QR3, it is moved to its best attacking post" (Smyslov).

19	....	P–N4

If 19 ... R–R1; 20 R–R1 followed by 21 R–R6, and if Black then exchanges Rooks, White will have a dangerous passed Pawn. White's next is to prevent ... P–B5.

20	N/3–K2	K–R1
21	R–R1	N–N3
22	P–B4	P×Pe.p.
23	R×P	N–K2
24	N–B6	QR–K1
25	N/2–Q4	N/3×P!?

Black's KBP is difficult to defend; the text is his best practical chance to end his slow strangulation.

26	P×N	B×P

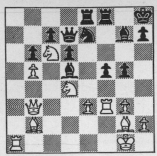

Position after 26 . . . BxP

27 NxP!   ....

Black had expected *26 Q–B2 BxR; 27 BxB N–N3*, with good counterplay.

27 ....   **RxN**

The Queen cannot be accepted—*27 . . . BxQ; 28 BxBch K–N1; 29 N/6xNch RxN; 30 BxR KxB; 31 R–R8ch K–B2* (not *31 . . . R–K1; 32 NxPch); 32 N–Q4ch*, followed by *33 NxB* wins.

Also bad is *27 . . . NxN/4; 28 QxB BxB; 29 QR–KB1*, with great advantage.

28 BxBch   **K–N1**

If *28 . . . KxB; 29 Q–B3ch K–N1; 30 RxR QxR; 31 R–KB1 Q–K3; 32 R–B6!* and Black cannot avoid material loss.

29 RxR!   **BxQ**
30 RxP   **N–N3**

Best. Not *30 . . . P–R3; 31 NxNch RxN; 32 R–R8ch R–K1; 33 BxPch K–R2; 34 R–N7ch*, etc.

31 B–R6   **Q–K3**

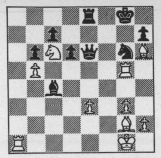

Position after 31 . . . Q–K3

Time to take stock. White has only a Rook and Bishop for the Queen, but Black's Queen will be subjected to unrelenting harassment.

32 P–R4!   **QxPch**
33 K–R2   **Q–QB6**

The threat was *34 RxNch.*

34 R–KB1   **B–B5**
35 R–B2   ....

But not *35 R–QB1? QxR; 36 RxNch PxR; 37 BxQ BxP*, with Black on top.

35 ....   **Q–K8**
36 R/5–KB5   **BxP**

"The best practical chance" (Smyslov).

37 B–Q2   **Q–N8**

The Queen is almost more trouble than it's worth: it has to be constantly protected and is inefficient both for defense and attack.

38 B–Q5ch   **K–R1**

If *38 . . . K–N2; 39 R–B7ch K–R1; 40 B–B3ch N–K4; 41 NxN PxN; 42 RxP*, with a won ending.

39 B–B3ch   **N–K4**
40 NxN   **PxN**
41 RxP   **Resigns**

12
CALIFORNIA 1964
Evans Gambit

WHITE: FISCHER   BLACK: CELLE

This is one of ten clock games played simultaneously at Davis College. Continuing with restraint and circumspection, Fischer builds up an irresistible attack culminating in a sacrificial orgy.

1	P–K4	P–K4
2	N–KB3	N–QB3
3	B–B4	B–B4
4	P–QN4!?	....

The Evans Gambit still makes for enterprising chess despite the fact that it was exhaustively analyzed last century.

| 4 | .... | B×P |
| 5 | P–B3 | B–K2 |

5 ... B–R4; 6 P–Q4 P–Q3; 7 O–O B–N3 is the famous Lasker Defense which put this gambit out of commission. The text is also good.

| 6 | P–Q4 | P–Q3? |

Correct is 6 ... N–QR4!; 7 N×P N×B; 8 N×N P–Q4.

| 7 | P×P | N×P |

On 7 ... P×P (7 ... N–R4?; 8 B×Pch K×B; 9 Q–Q5ch regains the piece with an extra Pawn); 8 Q–N3 N–R4; 9 B×Pch K–B1; 10 Q–R4 wins a Pawn.

| 8 | N×N | P×N |
| 9 | Q–R5! | .... |

44

White gets nothing after 9 Q–N3 B–K3!

9	....	P–KN3
10	Q×KP	N–B3
11	B–R3	R–B1
12	O–O	N–N5

12 ... N–Q2 followed by ... N–N3 is better, but the text is hard to refute.

13	Q–N3	B×B
14	N×B	Q–K2
15	B–N5ch!	....

The only way to retain the initiative. If 15 N–B2 Q–K4. And 15 N–N5 is disarmed by N–K4.

| 15 | .... | P–B3 |

Not 15 ... B–Q2?; 16 Q×P! (16 Q×N? P–QB3).

| 16 | N–B4! | .... |

Position after 16 N–B4

| 16 | .... | Q–K3! |

Fischer gives *16* ... PxB; *17* N–Q6ch K–Q1; *18* KR–Q1 B–Q2; *19* NxNPch K–B1; *20* N–Q6ch K–Q1; *21* R–Q4! N–K4; *22* QR–Q1 K–B2; *23* P–B4 N–N5; *24* P–KR3 N–B3; *25* P–B5 K–N3; *26* Q–K3 K–B2 (if *26* ... K–R3; *27* P–QR4); *27* R–B4ch! PxR; *28* Q–B5ch B–B3; *29* N–N5ch wins.

17 QR–Q1! ....

White's attack is blunted after *17* Q–B7 Q–Q2!; *18* N–Q6ch K–K2; *19* NxBch QRxN; *20* QxQch KxQ; etc.

17	....	PxB
18	Q–B7!	B–Q2
19	N–Q6ch	K–K2
20	N–B5ch!	....

"The attack needs fresh fuel. Material is not what counts now, but open lines. Black is forced to capture against his will. *20* ... K–K1 is out because of *21* N–N7ch. And *20* ... K–B3; *21* R–Q6 PxN; *22* QxB! wins outright" (Fischer).

| *20* | .... | PxN |
| *21* | PxP | QR–B1 |

The best try. *21* ... QxBP; *22* Q–Q6ch K–Q1 (or *22* ... K–K1;

23 KR–K1ch B–K3; *24* Q–Q7 mate); *23* QxRch K–B2; *24* QxR wins.

Position after 21 ... QR–B1

22	RxBch!	QxR
23	P–B6ch!	NxP
24	R–K1ch	....

"Note the amusing piece configuration. All Black's pieces are stepping on each other's toes" (Fischer).

24	....	N–K5
25	RxNch	K–B3
26	QxQ	KR–Q1
27	Q–N4	Resigns

Fischer chided himself for missing *27* Q–K7ch with mate in four. Fortunately his nonmaster opponent offered a good enough fight to make this game worthy.

13

BLED 1961
French Defense

WHITE: IVKOV BLACK: PORTISCH

The Queens disappear after a sharp theoretical opening. White's attack continues to rage, however, and a holocaust descends.

1	P–K4	P–K3
2	P–Q4	P–Q4
3	N–QB3	B–N5
4	P–K5	P–QB4

5 P–QR3   BxNch
6 PxB   Q–B2

One of Botvinnik's opening contributions, initiating a sharper fight than the older *6 . . . N–K2; 7 Q–N4 N–B4; 8 B–Q3 P–KR4.*

7 Q–N4   ....

7 N–B3 is tamer but perhaps more dependable in the long run. The question is whether this excursion with the Queen is or is not premature.

7 ....   P–B4

Nowadays Black prefers to reserve this square for his pieces. *7 . . . N–K2; 8 QxNP R–N1; 9 QxRP PxP; 10 K–Q1 QN–B3; 11 N–B3 PxP; 12 N–N5 NxP; 13 P–B4 RxN; 14 PxR N/4–N3; 15 B–K2* (better is *15 P–KR4 P–K4; 16 P–R5 N–B1; 17 B–N5ch) P–K4; 16 R–B1 B–K3; 17 B–N5ch K–Q1!* with advantage (Matulovich–Tatai, Venice 1969).

Inferior is *7 . . . P–B3; 8 N–B3 N–B3; 9 Q–N3 Q–B2; 10 PxQBP KN–K2; 11 B–Q3 PxP; 12 NxP* (Smyslov–Botvinnik, 20th Match Game 1957).

8 Q–N3   N–K2

8 . . . PxP; 9 PxP N–K2; 10 N–K2 O–O; 11 P–QB3 solves White's problems. The famous Reshevsky-Botvinnik encounter, Moscow 1948, continued: *8 . . . PxP; 9 PxP N–K2; 10 B–Q2 O–O; 11 B–Q3 P–QN3; 12 N–K2 B–R3; 13 N–B4 Q–Q2; 14 BxB* (if *14 B–N4 R–B2; 15 N–R5 K–R1* is correct) *NxB; 15 Q–Q3 N–N1; 16 P–KR4* with a White pull.

9 QxP   R–N1
10 QxP   PxP

Position after 10 . . . PxP

11 K–Q1   ....

Tal's idea, in order to develop the Knight at KB3, where it is more aggressively placed than after *11 N–K2.* Opinions are divided as to White's best. R. Byrne–Botvinnik, Monte Carlo 1968, went: *11 N–K2 QN–B3; 12 P–KB4 B–Q2; 13 Q–R3 PxP; 14 QxP O–O–O; 15 P–N3* (stronger is *15 B–N2 B–K1; 16 O–O–O B–R4; 17 R–Q2) B–K1!; 16 B–KN2 B–R4; 17 B–Q2 Q–N3; 18 R–KB1 K–N1=.*

11 ....   B–Q2

"Black's theme is clear. He scorches his King-side earth in return for powerful pressure on the other wing and in the center" (Byrne). Gligorich-Petrosian, Candidates' Tournament, 1959, continued: *11 . . . QN–B3* (not *11 . . . QxBP; 12 R–N1 P–Q6; 13 BxP QxKP; 14 Q–R5ch); 12 N–B3 NxP; 13 B–N5! N/4–N3 (13 . . . NxN?; 14 B–N5ch);* and now Euwe suggests *14 B–B6!* followed by P–KR4–5.

12 Q–R5ch   K–Q1

Varying from Tal–Botvinnik, 1st Match Game 1960: *12 . . . N–N3;*

13 N–K2 P–Q6; *14* PxP B–R5ch (better is *14* . . . QN–B3); *15* K–K1 QxP; *16* B–N5! N–B3; *17* P–Q4 Q–B2; *18* P–R4! P–K4; *19* R–R3 with advantage.

13 N–K2	B–R5

Lands Black in brackish waters, since the Bishop is needed where it has been standing, to defend the KP. Correct is *13* . . . PxP; *14* P–B4 Q–B4; *15* Q–B3 P–Q5! and, if anything, the complications favor Black. At its best the Winawer French is actually a dynamic countergambit.

14 N–B4	QxKP

14 . . . QxBP; *15* R–R2 B–Q2; *16* Q–B7 Q–B3; *17* P–KR4 is powerful.

15 Q–B7	B–Q2

Has the gain of a Pawn justified this loss of time?

16 B–Q3	Q–Q3
17 R–K1!?	. . . .

Disdaining a safe advantage with the prosaic *17* PxP and deciding upon a genuine risk.

17	P–K4?

Portisch overestimates his influence in the center and underestimates White's coming sacrificial attack. His chance lay in *17* . . . QN–B3; *18* NxPch BxN; *19* RxB QxKRP, after which double-edged play may develop—*e.g.*, *20* BxP NxB; *21* QxRch K–Q2; *22* QxR KxR; etc.

18 P–QR4!	. . . .

Having opted for the oversharp *17* R–K1, White must now tread the sacrificial road. The threat is B–R3.

18	B–K1

Relatively best. If *18* . . . QN–B3 (or *18* . . . PxN?; *19* B–R3); *19* B–R3 Q–R3; *20* NxP! NxN; *21* QxRch K–B2; *22* QxN wins.

19 Q–K6!	. . . .

"That White also retains a winning attack after the exchange of Queens gives his conception particular subtlety" (Vukovich).

19	QxQ
20 NxQch	K–Q2

Had he foreseen the sequel, Black might have gone to B1 directly. *21* PxP RxP (not *21* . . . P–K5; *22* B–B1) offers some slim hopes.

21 N–B5ch	K–B1
22 RxP	QN–B3
23 R–K2	RxP
24 BxPch	K–Q1

Not *24* . . . NxB?; *25* RxBch. No help either is *24* . . . K–B2?; *25* B–B4ch K–N3; *26* R–N1ch KxN; *27* R–N5ch and mates shortly.

25 NxPch	K–B2
26 B–B4ch!	. . . .

Position after 26 B–B4ch

26	N–K4

Disagreeably forced. On *26* ...
K×N; *27* R–N1ch K–R3; *28* B–Q3ch
K–R4; *29* B–B7ch mates.

27 R×N	N×B
28 R–K7ch!	K–B3

29 R–B7ch	K–N3
30 R–N1ch	K–R3
31 R–B6ch!	**Resigns**

On *31* ... B×R; *32* N–B5ch K–R4;
33 B–B7 is mate.

14

BEVERWIJK 1968
French Defense

WHITE: TAL   BLACK: DONNER

Ordinarily, because of the barricaded
Pawn structure, it is difficult to
launch an attack in this variation.
Tal succeeds in confining Black's
King to the center, then proceeds to
open lines with wild abandon.

1 P–K4	P–K3
2 P–Q4	P–Q4
3 N–QB3	B–N5
4 P–K5	P–QB4
5 P–QR3	B×Nch
6 P×B	Q–B2

White has reinforced his center at the
cost of a doubled QBP, and Black
hastens to exert pressure along the
semiopen file. Black has a recent
idea in mind, indicated by his next
two moves—exchanging the QB, his
"problem child."

7 N–B3	P–QN3
8 P–QR4	B–R3
9 B×B	....

9 B–N5ch B×B; *10* P×B P–QR4;
11 O–O N–K2 (Stein–R. Byrne,
Sousse 1967) will hold for Black if
properly defended.

9	N×B
10 Q–K2	N–N1

Bad is *10* ... P×P; *11* Q–N5ch!

K–Q1 (if *11* ... K–B1; *12* B–R3ch);
12 Q×N Q×BPch; *13* K–K2 Q×R;
14 B–N5ch—winning the Queen.

11 P–R5!?	....

White tries to open up the game
before his opponent can catch up in
development. *11* O–O is the tamer
alternative.

11	P×RP

11 ... P×QP; *12* O–O! is unclear,
but White's attacking prospects
remain bright.

12 B–R3	N–Q2?!

It is essential to prepare for castling
by *12* ... N–K2; then on *13* P×P
(if *13* B×P N–Q2), QN–B3 maintains
a blockade.

13 P×P	N–K2
14 P–B6!	....

A clearance sacrifice, quite thematic,
which opens the Bishop's diagonal
and hems the Black King in the
center.

14	Q×BP
15 O–O	Q×P

The purpose is not so much to gain
another Pawn as to prevent N–Q4.

16 **KR–Q1** **N–QB3**

Tal feels that *16 . . .* Q–B5; *17* Q–Q2 N–QB3 may be somewhat better; in that event White can continue his attack with *18* B–R3 followed by *19* R–R3.

17 **B–Q6** **Q–B5**
18 **Q–K3** **Q–K5**
19 **Q–N3** **N–N3**

Preventing Q–N7. With two extra Pawns Black's position looks cozy. White's initiative seems to have come to a standstill and Black's King is ready to go to Q2 with a measure of safety.

Position after 19 . . . N–N3

20 **P–B4!** **. . . .**

Offering yet another Pawn in order to effect a breach.

20 **. . . .** **QxBP**

Or *20 . . .* PxP (*20 . . .* NxBP?; *21* Q–N7); *21* Q–N5 R–QB1 (the threat was R–Q4); *22* RxP followed by *23* RxP with an irresistible attack.

21 **Q–R3** **Q–R3**
22 **QR–B1** **R–QB1**

Black could organize a better defense with *22 . . .* N–B5 immediately.

23 **N–Q2!** **. . . .**

Not only discouraging . . . N–B5, but threatening *24* N–N3–B5 as well.

23 **. . . .** **P–B3**

It is hard to concede that Black's solid position is already lost. On *23 . . .* N–Q5; *24* RxRch (or would Tal have played his post-mortem suggestion of *24* K–R1!?) QxR; *25* QxP Q–B7 gives strong counterplay.

24 **PxP** **PxP**
25 **Q–KB3** **K–Q2?**

Tal says *25 . . .* N–Q2 is relatively better. But *25 . . .* P–B4 is also difficult to refute.

26 **QxBP!** **. . . .**

Position after 26 QxBP

26 **. . . .** **KR–K1**

26 . . . KxB loses to *27* N–K4ch K–B2; *28* N–B5 Q–K7; *29* Q–N7ch.

27 **N–K4** **. . . .**

Clearer than *27* Q–B7ch N–K2 (*27 . . .* KxB?; *28* N–K4 mate); *28* R–K1 K–Q1; *29* QxKP Q–N2.

27 **. . . .** **N–K2**

Also hopeless is *27* ... Q–K7; *28* R–K1.

28	N–B5ch	R×N
29	B×R	N–B5

Black is lost no matter what he does.

30	B×N	Resigns

The point is *30* ... R×B; *31* R×Pch! etc. Again one is left with the impression that Black could have considerably improved his defense somewhere along the way; but that does not detract from Tal's courageous performance.

15
LEIPZIG OLYMPICS 1960
French Defense

WHITE: FISCHER   BLACK: TAL

Any meeting between these two antagonists arouses interest, and this one could have gone either way. After a seesaw struggle, it settles in perpetual check—a valid, if frustrating, result.

1	P–K4	P–K3
2	P–Q4	P–Q4
3	N–QB3	B–N5
4	P–K5	P–QB4
5	P–QR3	B–R4!?

This reply has never been a popular alternative to *5* ... B×Nch; but it has never been refuted either.

6	P–QN4	P×QP

Also playable is *6* ... P×NP; *7* N–N5 N–QB3 (*7* ... P×Pch; *8* P–B3 gives White a strong attack); *8* KN–B3 P–QR3; *9* N–Q6ch K–B1; *10* B–Q3 P–N6ch; *11* K–B1 B–B2 (Boleslavsky–Katalimov, U.S.S.R. Championship Preliminaries 1960).

7	Q–N4	....

Sharper than *7* N–N5 (not *7* Q×P B–B2; *8* N–B3 N–QB3; *9* Q–N4? N×KP; *10* Q×NP N×Nch; *11* P×N Q–B3; *13* B–KR6 Q–K4ch [Keres]) B–B2; *8* P–KB4 N–K2; *9* N–KB3 B–Q2!= (Smyslov–Botvinnik, 3rd Match Game 1954).

7	....	N–K2
8	P×B	....

An interesting gamelet was Zuckerman–Barsukov, Washington D.C. 1962: *8* N–N5 B–B2; *9* Q×NP R–N1; *10* Q×P B×P (better is *10* ... P–R3; *11* N×Bch Q×N; *12* N–K2 B–Q2!); *11* N–KB3 R–R1; *12* Q–Q3 B–B3; *13* B–B4 N–R3; *14* N–Q6ch K–B1; *15* N–K5! with a winning position.

8	....	P×N
9	Q×NP	R–N1
10	Q×P	QN–B3

10 ... N–Q2; *11* N–B3 N–B1; *12* Q–Q3 Q×P; *13* P–KR4! is given by theory as good for White

(Smyslov–Botvinnik, 9th Match Game 1954).

Position after 10 . . . QN–B3

11 N–B3   Q–B2

Probably the best line is *11 . . .* QxP; *12* R–QN1 Q–B2; *13* B–KB4 B–Q2; *14* B–N3 O–O–O (Damjanovich–Udovchich, Yugoslav Championship Preliminaries 1963).

12 B–QN5!   B–Q2

White's KRP heads for a touchdown after *12 . . .* RxP; *13* K–B1! R–KN1; *14* R–KN1! RxRch; *15* KxR.

13 O–O   O–O–O

If *13 . . .* NxKP; *14* NxN QxN; *15* BxBch KxB; *16* Q–Q3! (Fischer) keeps White on top; for if *16 . . .* Q–K5?; *17* QxQ PxQ; *18* P–B3! wins a Pawn.

14 B–N5?   . . . .

Underestimating Black's reply. Fischer claims a win with *14* BxN! BxB (or *14 . . .* NxB; *15* R–K1 followed by B–N5 and P–KR4); *15* QxP P–Q5; *16* QxPch B–Q2 (if *16 . . .* K–N1; *17* N–N5); *17* QxN RxPch; *18* KxR B–R6ch; *19* KxB QxQ; *20* B–N5 with a decisive

material advantage as soon as White consolidates.

14 . . . .   NxKP!
15 NxN   . . . .

Black survives after *15* BxBch RxB; *16* NxN QxN; *17* BxN R–R1!; *18* QR–K1 RxQ; *19* RxQ RxB; etc.

15 . . . .   BxB

Playing for a win. After *15 . . .* QxN; *16* BxN R–R1; *17* KR–K1! (*17* QR–K1? loses to Q–N1) QxRch; *18* RxQ RxQ; *19* BxR KxB; *20* BxB KxB; *21* R–K3! bails White out (Fischer).

16 NxP   . . . .

Leads to an exciting draw. White could have maintained some tension with *16* BxN QxB; *17* KR–K1.

16 . . . .   BxR
17 NxR   RxB
18 NxKP   RxPch

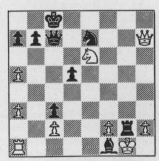

Position after 18 . . . RxPch

19 K–R1!   . . . .

Not the hasty *19* KxB? RxP; *20* Q–B7 R–R8ch and Black wins.

19 . . . .   Q–K4

White saves everything after *19 ....*
Q–QB5; *20* QxN R–N1; *21* N–B4!
(*21* ... QxN?; *22* Q–K6ch K–B2;
23 QxR Q–B6ch; *24* K–N1).

20 RxB   QxN

A discreet decision. *20* ... R–N3

21 QxN RxN; *22* Q–B8ch R–K1;
23 Q–B3 is in White's favor.

21 KxR   Q–N5ch
                 Draw

In view of his material deficit Black
must take the perpetual check after
22 K–R1 Q–B6ch; etc.

16
SOFIA 1967
French Defense

WHITE: GHEORGHIU   BLACK: UHLMANN

A quiet opening gives rise to some
splendid tactics. White's positional
sacrifice of the exchange is fully
justified, and the final twist is simply
delicious.

1 P–K4	P–K3
2 P–Q3	P–Q4
3 N–Q2	N–KB3
4 KN–B3	B–K2
5 P–KN3	P–B4
6 B–N2	N–B3
7 O–O	O–O
8 R–K1	....

Experience has shown that White
should avoid *8* P–B3, which presents
a Queen-side target. This is a well-
known position, wherein each side
will attack on the opposite wing;
chances are equal.

8	P–QN4
9 P–K5	N–Q2
10 N–B1	P–QR4
11 P–KR4	P–N5
12 B–B4	P–R5
13 P–R3	....

An attempt to improve on the
customary *13* N/1–R2 P–R6; *14*
P–N3 N–R2! where Black's counterplay against the weakened dark
squares may prove adequate.

13	PxP
14 PxP	B–R3
15 N–K3	N–Q5

Two alternatives which merit consideration are *15* ... N–N3 and
15 ... P–B3.

16 P–B4!	N–N6?!

Stronger is *16* ... PxP; and if
17 NxN PxN; *18* BxR PxN; *19*
B–B3˙PxPch gives Black very active
play. On *16* ... PxP; *17* NxP
N–N6 is tenable.

17 PxP!?	NxR
18 QxN	PxP
19 NxP	BxP?

19 ... N–N3 is much safer. Now
Black cannot recover.

20 P–K6	N–B3

Weak is *20 . . .* P×P; *21* N–B7 R×B;
22 N×P!

21 N×Bch	Q×N
22 N–K5	B–N3
23 N–B6!	. . . .

Much better than *23* B×R R×B, after
which White haṣ no clear-cut win.

23	Q–N2

The only square. Not *23 . . .* Q–
K1? *24* P–K7.

24 B–Q6	. . . .

Very forceful. Now the threat is
N–K7ch.

24	B–K5

Allows a pretty finish. After *24 . . .*
K–R1; *25* B×R R×B; *26* P–K7 R–K1;
27 Q–K5, it's just a matter of time
before White's KP wins material.

Position after 24 . . . B–K5

25 R×B!	Q×N
26 B×R	R×B (and Resigns)

26 . . . N×R would have allowed
27 Q×P mate.

It has now become apparent that
White emerges a piece ahead after
27 Q×N! Q×R (or *27 . . .* P×Q;
28 R–N4ch K–R1; *29* B×Q); *28*
Q×BPch! R×Q; *29* P×Rch K×P
30 B×Q, etc.

17

SOUSSE INTERZONAL 1967
French Defense

WHITE: FISCHER   BLACK: MIAGMARSUREN

Black is so intent on breaking
through on the Queen side that he
forgets about his King. Fischer's
concluding Queen sacrifice is captiv-
ating and perfectly timed.

1 P–K4	P–K3
2 P–Q3	P–Q4
3 N–Q2	N–KB3
4 P–KN3	P–B4

5 B–N2	N–B3
6 KN–B3	B–K2
7 O–O	O O

White's quiet buildup delays the
sharp hand-to-hand battle until the
middle game, and then operations
take place behind closed lines.
Black and White will attack on
opposite wings. The question is:
Who comes first?

8	P–K5	N–Q2
9	R–K1	P–QN4
10	N–B1	P–N5
11	P–KR4	P–QR4
12	B–B4	P–R5
13	P–R3	....

"Believe it or not, I actually spent more time on this innocuous push (fifteen minutes) than on any other move in the game! I didn't want to allow Black to get in ... P–R6, thereby creating 'holes' (weak squares) on QB3 and QR6. On the other hand, by stopping to meet his positional threat I am forced to postpone my own schemes for at least one move. Chess is a matter of delicate judgment, knowing when to punch and how to duck" (Fischer).

| 13 | .... | PxP |
| 14 | PxP | N–R4 |

This decentralization may be inadvisable. Black might try 14 ... N–Q5 or 14 ... B–R3, as in the previous game.

| 15 | N–K3 | B–R3 |
| 16 | B–R3 | .... |

Permanently discouraging the freeing maneuver, ... P–B3.

| 16 | .... | P–Q5 |
| 17 | N–B1 | .... |

Fischer is a law unto himself. He abstains from the natural 17 N–N4 because this Knight is headed for K4 instead. On the other hand, Black has secured Q4 for his Knight.

| 17 | .... | N–N3 |
| 18 | N–N5 | .... |

Position after 18 N–N5

18 ....   N–Q4?

Black is too intent on occupying his new outpost. Instead 18 ... P–R3!; 19 N–K4 P–B5 gives reasonable counterplay. It is remarkable that such an obvious move leads to trouble.

19 B–Q2!   BxN

19 ... P–B5 was still a better try. But not 19 ... P–R3?; 20 NxKP! PxN; 21 BxPch K–R1; 22 QBxN QxB; 23 BxN, gaining two buttons.

| 20 | BxB | Q–Q2 |
| 21 | Q–R5 | .... |

"Make way for the heavy artillery" (Fischer).

21 ....   KR–B1

Black might try taking the precaution of 21 ... K–R1.

22 N–Q2   N–B6?

Ruinous. Black should proceed 22 ... P–B5 with counterplay.

23 B–B6!   ....

With all Black's pieces clustered on the other wing, his King is ripe for mayhem.

Position after 23 B–B6

23 ....   Q–K1

Forced. Not 23 ... PxB; 24 PxP
K–R1; 25 N–B3 N–Q4 (or 25 ...
R–KN1; 26 N–K5); 26 N–N5 NxP;
27 Q–R6 Q–K2; 28 B–B5! and wins.

24 N–K4	P–N3
25 Q–N5	NxN
26 RxN	P–B5
27 P–R5	....

White avoids the cheap trap of
27 RxP? PxP; 28 PxP N–N6.

| 27 .... | PxP |
| 28 R–R4! | R–R2 |

To defend the second rank. Not
28 ... PxP; 29 PxP P–B8(Q)ch;
30 RxQ RxRch; 31 K–R2 BPxP;
32 RxP! wins.

29 B–N2!   ....

A subtle move, miraculously timed.
Its sly purpose soon becomes apparent.

29 ....   PxP

Overlooking the main point. The
only defense is 29 ... Q–B1; but
White still wins with 30 B–K4! PxP;
31 PxP BPxP; 32 BxNP! PxB; 33
R–R8ch K–B2; 34 R–R7ch! (more
convincing than 34 RxQch RxR)
K–K1; 35 RxR B–Q6; 36 RxN, and
an extra Rook should do the trick.

30 Q–R6   Q–B1

30 ... P–B8(Q)ch; 31 RxQ RxRch;
32 K–R2 leads to the same finish.

31 QxRPch!   Resigns

Black gets mated after 31 ... KxQ;
32 PxPch KxP; 33 B–K4.

18

NATANYA 1968
French Defense

WHITE: FISCHER   BLACK: U. GELLER

Fischer is renowned for defeating
weaker opponents with flair. Here is
another example of his forceful style
against token resistance.

1	P–K4	P–K3
2	P–Q3	P–Q4
3	N–Q2	P–QB4

4	P–KN3	N–KB3
5	B–N2	B–K2
6	KN–B3	O–O
7	O–O	N–B3
8	R–K1	Q–B2
9	P–K5	N–Q2
10	Q–K2	P–QN4
11	P–KR4	P–QR4

This formation has become almost a ritual, and it has not been determined whether Black can break through on the Queen side in time to frustrate White's imminent attack.

12 N–B1   N–Q5!?

An interesting idea which enables Black to utilize the semiopen QB file at the cost of doubled Pawns. More customary is *12* . . . P–N5.

13 N×N   P×N
14 B–B4   R–R3
15 N–R2!   . . . .

Abstaining from the tempting *15* B×P!? B–N5; *16* KR–N1! (not *16* KR–QB1? P×B; *17* P–K6 R×P; *18* Q×R Q×B; *19* Q×N Q×Rch; etc.) P×B; *17* P–K6 B–Q3; *18* P×N B×P, with equal chances.

15 . . . .   R–B3
16 QR–B1   B–R3?

The Bishop has a dismal future here. Correct is *16* . . . Q–N3, which would prevent White's combination.

17 B×P!   P×B

Perhaps Black should settle for *17* . . . R–B4; *18* B–K4 KR–B1; *19* N–B3 R×P; *20* R×R Q×R; *21* N×P Q×Q; *22* R×Q N–B4, with counterplay for the Pawn.

18 P–K6   Q–Q1

18 . . . B–Q3; *19* B×B R×B; *20* P×N Q×P; *21* N–B3 mops up.

19 P×N   R–K3
20 Q–N4   P–B4

0 . . . Q×P? would allow *21* B–K5.

21 Q–R5   Q×P
22 N–B3   P–N3
23 Q–R6   B–B3
24 R×R   Q×R

Position after 24 . . . Q×R

Black seems to have emerged tolerably well from the staggering blows. Now he is hoping for *25* R–K1? Q×Rch!; *26* N×R B–N2; *27* Q–N5 B–B3; when White must take the draw by repetition.

25 B–K5!   . . . .

A neat twist. White will capture the King file next move after eliminating the defensive Bishop.

25 . . . .   B×B
26 R–K1   P–B5

The only hope. If *26* . . . B–N2; *27* Q×Bch K×Q; *28* R×Q wins the loose Pawns.

27 R×B   Q–Q2
28 P–R5!   P×NP
29 RP×P!   P×Pch

White's control of the dark squares is already decisive. Black's Bishop is no more than an overgrown Pawn. *29* . . . R×N loses to *30* R–K8ch! Q×R; *31* Q×Pch K–B1; *32* P–N7ch etc.

30	K×P	P×P
31	Q×Pch	Q–N2

Again Black is hoping for a break after *32 Q×B? Q×R.*

| 32 | R–N5! | .... |

Now *32 ... Q×Q; 33 R×Qch* picks up the stranded Bishop.

| 32 | .... | **R–B2** |
| | | **(and Resigns)** |

He sees that simply *33 Q–R6* wins his Queen.

19

PUERTO RICO OPEN 1967
Giuoco Piano

WHITE: ROSSOLIMO   BLACK: REISSMAN

The elegant finale is reminiscent of Marshall's famous win over Lewitzky (Breslau 1912) where the spectators were so delighted that they reportedly showered the board with gold pieces.

1	P–K4	P–K4
2	N–KB3	N–QB3
3	B–B4	B–B4
4	P–B3	N–B3
5	P–Q4	P×P
6	P×P	B–N5ch
7	B–Q2	....

7 N–B3 N×KP; 8 O–O B×N; 9 P–Q5 N–K4; 10 P×B N×B; 11 Q–Q4 O–O permits Black to emerge unscarred.

7	....	B×Bch
8	QN×B	P–Q4
9	P×P	KN×P
10	Q–N3	N/3–K2

Not quite sound is *10 ... O–O!?; 11 B×N N–R4; 12 B×Pch R×B; 13 Q–B3 R–K2ch; 14 N–K5* etc.

11	O–O	P–QB3
12	KR–K1	O–O
13	P–QR4	P–QN3

An ill-advised attempt to improve on the main line with *13 ... Q–N3.*

14	N–K5	B–N2
15	P–R5	R–B1
16	N–K4	Q–B2

Black must try *16 ... R–B2* to allow the Bishop a retreat to B1.

17	P–R6	B–R1
18	Q–KR3	N–B5
19	Q–N4	N/2–Q4
20	R–R3!	....

A fine idea. This Rook, which is now inactive, will swing over to the King side.

| 20 | .... | N–K3 |

Black's predicament is already critical. *20 ... P–B3* fails to *21 B×Nch N×B; 22 Q–K6ch K–R1; 23 N–N6ch P×N; 24 R–R3* mate.

The best chance is *20 ... P–QB4.*

21	B×N	P×B
22	N–B6ch	K–R1
23	Q–N6!	....

Position after 23 Q–N6

A sizzler. Black has no defense any more.

23 . . . .   Q–B7

If *23* . . . BP×Q; *24* N×Pch P×N; *25* R–R3 mate. Black can last a few moves by giving up his Queen for two Knights—*23* . . . P×N; *24* Q×BPch N–N2; *25* R–KN3 R–KN1; *26* N×Pch Q×N. The text evokes a beautiful point.

24 R–R3!   Resigns

Again if *24* . . . Q×Q (on *24* . . . N–N4; *25* Q×N resumes the threat of Q–N6); *25* N×Qch P×N; *26* R×P mate.

20
HAVANA OLYMPICS 1966
Gruenfeld Defense

WHITE: PACHMAN   BLACK: UHLMANN

Uhlmann is a specialist in this defense, and Pachman is one of the world's leading opening theoreticians. Their clash gives off uncommon sparks, notably after White bravely sacrifices the exchange.

1 P–Q4   N–KB3
2 P–QB4   P–KN3
3 N–QB3   P–Q4
4 P×P   . . . .

The sharpest way to proceed against this sturdy defense. The alternatives are not known to give White any advantage.

4 . . . .   N×P
5 P–K4   N×N
6 P×N   B–N2

At one time this was branded an error. Reuben Fine said that Black had to play *6* . . . P–QB4 first, so as to prevent the reply *7* B–R3. This reflected the advanced state of theory in 1940.

7 B–QB4   . . . .

Against Korchnoi, at Buenos Aires 1960, I implemented the aforementioned "wisdom" and ended up fighting for a draw after *7* B–R3 (never again!) N–Q2!; *8* N–B3 P–QB4; *9* Q–N3 O–O; *10* B–Q3 Q–B2; *11* O–O R–N1; etc.

Also toothless is Fine's other recommendation *7* P–KB4 P–QB4; *8* B–K3 Q–R4; *9* K–B2 O–O; *10* Q–N3 P×P;

11 PxP N–Q2; and if now *12* P–KR3? N–B4!

7	....	O–O
8	N–K2	N–B3

More usual is *8* . . . P–B4. The idea of the text is to defer this blow at the center until Black has completed his development with . . . P–N3; . . . B–N2; . . . N–R4; etc., so that he will then be able to maintain his Pawn on QB4 instead of being compelled to exchange it for White's QP.

9	O–O	P–N3
10	B–K3	B–N2
11	R–B1	P–K3
12	B–Q3	Q–Q2
13	Q–Q2	N–R4
14	P–QB4	P–KB4

The disadvantage of Black's setup now becomes apparent: he has great difficulty getting in the thematic . . . P–QB4—so he assails the center from another direction.

Position after 14 . . . P–KB4

15	P–B3	N–B3
16	B–N1	N–R4
17	KR–Q1	Q–R5

Black is bankrupt of ideas and decides to play for a draw. A reasonable alternative is *17* . . . B–QR3.

18	N–B3	....

He could try *18* N–B4 immediately, since the same position is reached on move 20 anyway.

18	....	Q–Q2

Kmoch recommends *18* . . . QxBP; *19* N–Q5 (if *19* N–K2 Q–R5; *20* RxP N–B5; *21* B–QB2 QxP; *22* N–B3 Q–R3 holds) PxN; *20* RxQ NxR; *21* Q–K2 NxB; *22* QxN QPxP; *23* PxP PxP; *24* BxP BxB; *25* QxB QR–K1, with little chance for White to make headway despite his small material edge.

19	N–K2	Q–R5
20	N–B4	....

Spurning the proffered repetition. Usually Pachman is more agreeable.

20	....	NxP?!

It is always interesting to observe a player's reaction when his offer of a draw is refused. After *20* . . . KR–K1 the game could go either way. The text gives White a chance to speculate—at least it looked like a speculation at the time.

Position after 20 . . . NxP

21	RxN!	QxR
22	R–QB1	Q–R5

23 NxKP   R–B2

To return material with 23 ... PxP was to be considered.

24 NxB   KxN

24 ... RxN loses more slowly after 25 PxP PxP; 26 BxP BxP; 27 B–K6ch K–R1; 28 B–N5! R–KB1; 29 R–B1!

25 PxP   PxP
26 B–B4   P–KR3
27 B–K5ch   K–N3
28 Q–B4   B–B1
29 P–N4   P–KR4
30 PxBPch   BxP
31 Q–N3ch   Resigns

If 31 ... K–R2; 32 BxBch RxB; 33 Q–N7 mate.

21
1st MATCH GAME 1965
Gruenfeld Defense

WHITE: GELLER   BLACK: SMYSLOV

The way Smyslov is dispatched may have demoralized him at the outset; he lost the match 5½–2½. Geller makes it all look so easy, winding up with a neat Queen sacrifice.

1 P–Q4   N–KB3
2 P–QB4   P–KN3
3 N–QB3   P–Q4
4 PxP   NxP
5 P–K4   NxN
6 PxN   B–N2
7 B–QB4   P–QB4
8 N–K2   O–O
9 O–O   N–B3

The main alternative is 9 ... PxP; 10 PxP N–B3; 11 B–K3 B–N5; 12 P–B3 N–R4; 13 B–Q3 (13 BxPch wins a Pawn, but is frowned upon because Black gets strong counterplay) B–K3; 14 P–Q5!? BxR; 15 QxB P–B3; this sacrifice of the exchange was introduced by Bronstein, and it has never been completely solved.

10 B–K3   Q–B2

Indirectly menacing the KB and freeing Q1 for the Rook to attack White's QP.

Another popular variation is 10 ... N–R4; 11 B–Q3 P–N3; 12 R–B1! (weaker is 12 PxP PxP; 13 BxP Q–B2) B–N2; 13 P–Q5 P–B5; 14 B–B2 Q–Q2; 15 N–Q4 with the freer game (Portisch–Uhlmann, Zagreb 1965).

11 R–B1   R–Q1
12 P–B4   ....

Spassky–Fischer, Piatigorsky Cup 1966, continued: 12 Q–K1 P–K3; 13 P–B4 N–R4; 14 B–Q3 P–B4; 15 R–Q1 P–N3; 16 Q–B2 PxQP; 17 BxP BxB; 18 PxB B–N2; 19 N–N3 and now with Q–N2! (instead of ... Q–B2; 20 P–Q5!) Black could have obtained the better chances.

12 ....   P–K3

After *12* . . . N–R4; *13* B–Q3 P–B4;
14 KPxP BxP; *15* BxB PxB; *16* N–
N3 Black's King side is exposed
(Ivkov–Jiménez, Havana 1965).

The crucial theoretical line is *12*
. . . B–N5; *13* P–B5 PxBP; *14*
BxPch! K–R1! (unclear is *14*
. . . KxB; *15* Q–N3ch P–K3; *16* N–
B4 Q–Q2; *17* KPxP N–R4!—
Spassky–Shiskin, U.S.S.R. Cham-
pionship Preliminaries 1959); *15*
PxBP PxP; *16* PxP BxN; *17* QxB
BxP and shortly drawn (Shiskin-
Bondarevsky, U.S.S.R. Champion-
ship Preliminaries 1960).

Position after 12 . . . *P–K3*

13 K–R1   P–N3

In retrospect Black's troubles may be
traced to this lackluster response.
Safer is *13* . . . N–R4; *14* B–Q3
P–B4. White now seizes the opportunity to prevent this defense.

14 P–B5!   N–R4?

Inconsistent. Black has two other
options which must be examined
with great care: (A) *14* . . . KPxP;
15 B–N5 R–B1; *16* N–N3 PxP; *17*
NxP with good attacking chances;
(B) *14* . . . N–K4!; *15* B–KB4 Q–
K2; *16* B–QN3 B–QR3 with promising counterplay.

15	B–Q3	KPxP
16	KPxP	B–N2
17	Q–Q2	R–K1
18	N–N3	Q–B3
19	R–B2	QR–Q1

Black's game does not look bad, but
he lost several tempi while regrouping his forces; White has achieved
steady development without wasting
any moves. Simagin gives *19* . . .
RxB!?; *20* QxR PxQP; *21* PxQP
BxP; *22* Q–Q2 QxRch; *23* QxQ
BxR; *24* Q–R6 B–Q5 (if *24* . . .
B–B4; *25* N–R5! PxN; *26* P–B6);
25 PxP RPxP; *26* BxP PxB; *27*
QxPch K–R1; *28* Q–R5ch K–N1;
29 Q–N4ch K–R2; *30* QxB and wins.

20	B–KR6	B–KR1
21	Q–B4	R–Q2
22	N–K4	P–B5

On *22* . . . Q–B2 (*22* . . . RxN?;
23 BxR QxB; *24* Q–N8ch); *23*
R–K1! BxN; *24* RxB RxR; *25* QxR
maintains the grip. But the text re-
leases the tension in the center, upon
which Black's counterplay is based.

23	B–B2	R/2–K2
24	QR–KB1!	RxN

Position after 24 . . . *RxN*

25 PxP!   . . . .

This *zwischenzug* is deadly. It cannot be met by *25 ... RxQ* because of *26 PxRP* mate! But after *25 BxR? RxB*, Black could muster up saving resources.

| 25 .... | P–B3 |
| 26 Q–N5! | .... |

Again the Queen cannot be captured, this time because R–B8 mates.

| 26 .... | Q–Q2 |
| 27 K–N1 | .... |

Equally good is *27 PxPch KxP; 28 Q–R5*. The text also wins.

| 27 .... | B–N2 |
| 28 RxP! | R–N5 |

Or *28 ... BxR; 29 QxB PxP; 30 QxPch K–R1; 31 B–N5 R/5–K3; 32 B–B6ch RxB; 33 RxR* wins— apparently the point of White's moving his King back to N1 (preventing mate on the 1st rank).

29 PxPch	K–R1
30 BxBch	QxB
31 QxR	Resigns

On *31 ... QxQ; 32 R–B8ch* forces mate.

22

UNITED STATES CHAMPIONSHIP 1968
Gruenfeld Defense

WHITE: RESHEVSKY   BLACK: SEIDMAN

Facing stout resistance, White transports a minimal advantage into the endgame. He sacrifices a Knight for two Pawns in a startling setting, demonstrating once more the full fury of the two Bishops.

1 P–Q4	N–KB3
2 P–QB4	P–KN3
3 N–QB3	P–Q4
4 N–B3	B–N2
5 B–B4	O–O
6 R–B1	....

This system was popularized by the gifted Hungarian grandmaster Lajos Portisch. It is quiet and positional, yielding White a shaded advantage at best. Petrosian also betrays a fondness for it.

| 6 .... | P–B4 |

More vigorous than *6 ... P–B3.*

7 PxBP	B–K3
8 P–K3	Q–R4
9 N–Q4	N–B3
10 NxB	....

If *10 N–N3 Q–Q1; 11 N–Q4!?* (better is *11 PxP) NxN; 12 PxN PxP; 13 B–K5 P–N3; 14 N–N5 N–K1; 15 BxB KxB=* (Panno–Benko, Hollywood 1963).

10	PxN
11 Q–R4	QxP
12 Q–N5	QxQ
13 PxQ	N–N1

More forceful is *13 ... N–QR4* as in Portisch–Evans, Havana 1964.

Portisch told me later that he had been unable to find an essential improvement for White after *14* B–K2 QR–B1; *15* O–O N–B5; *16* P–QN3 N–Q7; *17* KR–Q1 N/7–K5; *18* N–R4 P–N4; *19* B–B7 N–K1; *20* B–R5 R×R; *21* B×R R×P; *22* B–KN4 R×P; *23* B×Pch K–B1; *24* B×P N/1–Q3, with rough equality.

14	B–Q3	QN–Q2
15	K–K2	P–K4
16	B–N3	P–K5
17	B–N1	QR–B1
18	N–R4	N–N5
19	KR–Q1	P–K3
20	R×R	R×R
21	P–B3	....

Unproductive is *21* P–KR3 (*21* B×P? R–B5 wins a piece) N–R3, followed by either ... N–B4 or ... B–K4 with a comfortable position.

21	....	P×Pch
22	P×P	N/5–K4
23	P–K4	P×P
24	B×P	P–N3
25	R–Q6	....

The tempting *25* P–B4 N–KB3; *26* B–N7 R–B7ch; *27* R–Q2 R×Rch; *28* K×R N/4–Q2 produces only even chances.

| 25 | .... | N–B1 |

Reshevsky gives *25* ... K–B2; *26* P–B4 R–B5 (if *26* ... QN–B3; *27* B–N7 R–B7ch; *28* K–Q1 wins); *27* N–B3 N–KB3; *28* B–QB2 N/4–Q2; *29* B–N3 R–N5; *30* P–B5! NP×P; *31* B×Pch K–K2; *32* B×P R×Pch; *33* K–B3 N–B4; *34* R–B6 "with a strategically won position." Black can still offer some resistance with *34* ... N–R4; *35* R–B7ch K–K1.

| 26 | P–N3 | P–N4? |

Tighter is *26* ... N–B2; *27* R–B6 R–Q1.

Position after 26 ... P–N4

Judging from a casual inspection, Black's worries are over. White's reply now is so startling that Seidman can almost be forgiven for having overlooked it.

| 27 | N×P! | .... |

A bolt from the blue. While the game was in progress it was not clear that this sacrifice was entirely sound. Later analysis, however, revealed it to be so.

27	....	P×N
28	R×NP	P–R4
29	R–R6	....

Reshevsky suggests *29* P–QR4 as stronger.

29	....	P–R5
30	B–KB2	N/4–N3
31	R–R8?	....

Again, stronger was *31* R–B6, cutting off Black's Rook.

| 31 | .... | R×R? |

A much better try is *31* ... N–B5ch; *32* K–Q2 R×R; *33* B×R N–R6; *34* B–R7 B–K4; *35* K–K2 B×P;

36 K–B1, and White's Pawns would have prevailed, but not without a struggle (Reshevsky).

32	BxR	B–K4
33	B–N1	N–B5ch
34	K–B1	N–Q2
35	P–R4	B–B2
36	B–B6	N–N1
37	B–K4	N–Q4
38	BxN!	PxB
39	P–N4!	....

The winning move. Insufficient is *39* P–N6 B–Q3; *40* P–R5 K–B2; *41* P–N7 K–K3;. *42* B–R7 K–Q2; *43* P–N4 K–B3; etc. It is imperative to advance the RP, and in order to effect this advance White's QNP has to be at N5 (Reshevsky).

Position after 39 P–N4

39	....	K–B2
40	P–R5	N–Q2
41	P–N6	B–Q1
42	P–N7	N–N1
43	B–R7	B–B2
44	P–N5	N–Q2
45	P–R6	BxP
46	P–N8(Q)	Resigns

23

UNITED STATES CHAMPIONSHIP 1964
Gruenfeld Defense

WHITE: R. BYRNE   BLACK: FISCHER

"After White's 11th move I should adjudicate his position as slightly superior, and at worst completely safe. To turn this into a mating position in 11 more moves is more witchcraft than chess" (K. F. Kirby, editor of the *South African Chess Quarterly*).

1	P–Q4	N–KB3
2	P–QB4	P–KN3
3	P–KN3	P–B3
4	B–N2	....

Byrne–Fischer, U.S. Championship 1963 continued: *4* P–Q5 P–QN4!; *5* PxBP NPxP; *6* PxPch QNxP; *7* B–N2 R–QN1; *8* N–KB3 B–KN2; *9* O–O O–O=.

4	....	P–Q4
5	PxP	PxP
6	N–QB3	B–N2
7	P–K3	....

Or *7* N–B3 O–O; *8* N–K5 B–B4; *9* O–O N–K5; *10* Q–N3 N–QB3; *11* QxQP NxQN; *12* PxN QxQ;

13 BxQ NxN; *14* PxN BxP, with a draw shortly (Benko–Fischer, U.S. Championship 1963).

7	....	O–O
8	KN–K2	N–B3
9	O–O	P–N3
10	P–N3	B–QR3
11	B–QR3	R–K1
12	Q–Q2	P–K4!

Apparently risky, because it weakens the QP, but the only way to introduce a dynamic imbalance. After the "natural" *12* ... P–K3 a draw would be the most likely result of the symmetrical formation.

13	PxP	NxP
14	KR–Q1?	....

Strangely enough, this automatic developing move leads to difficulties. Fischer gives *14* QR–Q1 Q–B1!; *15* B–N2 (not *15* NxP NxN; *16* BxN R–Q1; *17* P–B4 RxB!; *18* QxR B–N2!) Q–KB4, and Black keeps a slight initiative.

14	....	N–Q6!
15	Q–B2	....

There is hardly any other defense to ... N–K5. If *15* N–B4 N–K5!; *16* NxN/4 PxN; *17* QR–N1 QR–B1; *18* NxN B–B6!; *19* Q–K2 BxN; *20* Q–N4 P–B4; *21* Q–R3 BxR!; *22* RxQ KRxR; *23* B–KB1 R–Q8; *24* K–N2 B–Q6!; *25* BxB PxB wins (Fischer).

15	....	NxP!
16	KxN	N–N5ch
17	K–N1	NxKP
18	Q–Q2	....

Position after 18 Q–Q2

White is expecting *18* ... NxR; *19* RxN with advantage.

18	....	NxB!

"This dazzling move came as the shocker. It is obvious now that Black is going all out for a mating attack, but what is almost uncanny is that, with all his pieces so well developed, White should be so utterly helpless against it" (R. Byrne).

19	KxN	P–Q5!
20	NxP	B–N2ch
21	K–B1	Q–Q2!
	Resigns	

"The culminating combination is of such depth that, at the very moment at which I resigned, both grandmasters who were commenting on the play for the spectators in a separate room believed that I had a won game" (Byrne).

It is a pity that White did not continue with *22* Q–KB2 Q–R6ch; *23* K–N1 R–K8ch!; *24* RxR BxN, and mate follows at his KN2.

Also hopeless is *22* N/4–N5 Q–R6ch; *23* K–N1 B–R3 followed by ... B–K6.

Final position after 21 ... Q–Q2

"The Byrne game was quite fabulous, and I cannot call to mind anything to parallel it. . . . Quite honestly, I do not see the man who can stop Bobby at this time," Mr. Kirby said.

Fischer termed White's resignation a "bitter disappointment." He was expressing the natural desire to have his beautiful combination lodged in the text rather than in the notes; that way the final position would require no explanations.

24
27th U.S.S.R. CHAMPIONSHIP 1960
King's Gambit

WHITE: SPASSKY   BLACK: BRONSTEIN

White's offer of a Rook is simply stunning and so is the follow-up, a throwback to last century. Fischer was ecstatic—possibly this influenced him in naming Spassky one of the ten greatest players of all time, long before the latter won the title.

1	P–K4	P–K4
2	P–KB4	....

This opening alone is cause for surprise in modern tournaments. Ironically, Bronstein himself was the one who revived it in the late forties.

2	....	P×P
3	N–KB3	P–Q4

The famous encounter Spassky–Fischer, Mar Del Plata 1960, continued: *3* ... P–KN4; *4* P–KR4 P–N5; *5* N–K5 N–KB3; *6* P–Q4

P–Q3; *7* N–Q3 N×P; *8* B×P B–N2 and Black, with an extra Pawn, has every reason to be content—although in this contest he eventually blundered and lost.

Spassky–Kholmov, U.S.S.R. Championship playoff 1963, went: *3* ... B–K2; *4* N–B3 N–KB3 (*4* ... B–R5ch; *5* K–K2 has features of an old Steinitz gambit); *5* P–K5 N–N5; *6* P–Q4 N–K6; *7* B×N P×B; *8* B–B4 P–Q3; *9* O–O O–O; *10* Q–Q3 regaining the Pawn with freer development.

4	P×P	B–Q3

4 ... N–KB3; *5* B–N5ch P–B3; *6* P×P N×P was Hartston–Spassky, Hastings 1965–66.

5	N–B3	N–K2

With the possibility of retaining the gambit Pawn by ... N–N3. If 5 ... N–KB3 White best proceeds with 6 B–N5ch B–Q2; 7 Q–K2ch Q–K2; 8 QxQch KxQ; 9 B–B4 with an edge. This modern way of treating the King's Gambit would have caused an uproar last century.

6	P–Q4	O–O
7	B–Q3	N–Q2
8	O–O	P–KR3

Spassky recommends 8 ... N–KB3; 9 N–K5 N/2xP; 10 NxN NxN; 11 Q–R5 P–KN3; 12 Q–R6 Q–B3, "with not bad play for Black." Also possible is 8 ... N–N3; 9 N–K4 N–B3; 10 NxB QxN; 11 P–B4 B–N5.

9	N–K4!	NxP
10	P–B4	N–K6
11	BxN	PxB
12	P–B5	B–K2

If 12 ... B–B5; 13 P–KN3 B–N4 (or 13 ... P–B4; 14 N–B3 B–N4; 15 P–KR4 B–K2; 16 N–Q5 with a strong attack); 14 N/3xB PxN; 15 Q–R5 with a winning attack.

| 13 | B–B2 | R–K1 |

The position is difficult to assess after 13 ... N–B3; 14 Q–Q3 NxN; 15 QxN P KN3; 16 QxP K–N2.

| 14 | Q–Q3 | P–K7 |
| 15 | N–Q6!? | .... |

A Rubinstein or a Capablanca probably would have played 15 R–B2; and the game would run a normal course after 15 ... N–B1.

Position after 15 N–Q6

Spassky gambled everything on one trap. He admits that he was carried away a little with the concept, but Bronstein had left himself with only twenty minutes for the next 26 moves.

| 15 | .... | N–B1 |

Correct is 15 ... PxR(Q)ch; 16 RxQ BxN; 17 Q–R7ch K–B1; 18 PxB PxP; 19 Q–R8ch K–K2; 20 R–K1ch N–K4; 21 QxNP R–KN1; 22 QxRP Q–N3; 23 K–R1 B–K3; 24 PxN P–Q4; 25 Q–B6ch K–Q2, after which the King reaches safety with a probable draw in sight.

| 16 | NxBP! | PxR(Q)ch |
| 17 | RxQ | B–B4? |

Not 17 ... KxN?; 18 N–K5ch K–N1; 19 Q–R7ch NxQ; 20 B–N3ch and mates. The only defense is 17 ... Q–Q4; 18 B–N3 QxB (if 18 ... QxQN; 19 BxQch KxB; 20 Q–B4ch K–N3; 21 Q–N8! B–B3; 22 N–R4ch BxN; 23 Q–B7ch K–R2; 24 QxR with the Black pieces badly congested); 19 QxQ (if 19 PxQ KxN is safe) B–K3; 20 NxPch PxN; 21 Q–K3. White keeps the initiative, but the outcome of the game is still in doubt.

18	QxB	Q–Q2
19	Q–B4	B–B3
20	N/3–K5	Q–K2
21	B–N3	BxN

If *21* ... N–K3; *22* Q–N4.

22	NxBch	K–R2
23	Q–K4ch	Resigns

On *23* ... K–R1; *24* RxNch followed by N–N6ch is decisive.

25
RIGA 1968
King's Gambit

WHITE: Bronstein   BLACK: Tal

Excitement in the tournament hall—Bronstein is playing the King's Gambit! But he must be mad to risk it against Tal, the greatest living combinative genius in the world!

1	P–K4	P–K4
2	P–KB4	....

The success of Fischer and Spassky with this swashbuckling gambit speaks in favor of reviving little-known opening variations, particularly against opponents who can be thrown off balance by such sharp tactics. Wildness may be wisdom.

2	....	P–Q4

The gambit seems to have a magical effect on the second player, who employs the sound Falkbeer Counter Gambit instead of aiming for outright refutation with *2* ... PxP! Fischer–Wade, Vinkovci 1968, continued: *2* ... N–KB3; *3* PxP NxP; *4* N–KB3 N–N4; *5* P–Q4 NxNch; *6* QxN Q–R5ch; *7* Q–B2 QxQch; *8* KxQ. Black lost an ending which

he should have held, bearing out the judgment I pronounced in *Modern Chess Openings* (10th ed.): "Today it is played with a view to obtaining a positional advantage, even if it means an early exchange of Queens, and the question of whether this is an opening of the future or of the past still remains."

3	PxQP	P–K5
4	P–Q3	N–KB3
5	PxP	....

This is one of the oldest and best continuations. The reader will find both 5 Q–K2 and 5 N–Q2 rather thoroughly analyzed in the opening manuals.

5	....	NxKP
6	N–KB3	B–QB4

Several books still quote a musty Tartakower analysis giving *6* ... B–N5ch?; *7* P–B3 B–QB4; overlooking *8* Q–R4ch! which wins a piece!

7	Q–K2	B–B4

Best. The text move was introduced by Dr. Tarrasch against Spielmann at Mährisch–Ostrau 1923. The idea is that after *8 P–KN4? O–O; 9 PxB R–K1* gives Black a strong attack for the sacrificed piece.

The alternatives *7 ... P–B4; 8 B–K3*, or *7 ... QxP; 8 KN–Q2!*, or *7 ... B–B7ch; 8 K–Q1 QxPch; 9 KN–Q2!* all confer an advantage on White.

8	N–B3	Q–K2
9	B–K3	....

Position after 9 B–K3

| 9 | .... | NxN? |

Keres writes:

"The books do not approve, and since Tal, as we see, has no improvement in mind, we may repeat the question mark which theory gives this move. Here we see the advantages for the player who chooses opening variations which are not popular at the moment. In our time, almost every master makes a thorough study of opening schemes that are popular and often used in modern tournaments. These variations are often prolonged deep into the middle game, with almost every possibility already analyzed at home. This way players have little to create over the board, they just repeat home analysis. "Now if such a theory-oriented player encounters new situations in over-the-board games, he often does not find the right line, because he is not accustomed to making decisions in unfamiliar positions. He is often willing to accept a quiet line, a 'not-to-lose' technique, in order to have time to study the situation at home for the next game. Thus we see that the importance of opening preparation in home analysis is often overestimated and the ability of the chess master to solve these problems at the chessboard is not adequately cultivated.

"I certainly do not want to place Tal in this company of players who cannot find the right way in comparatively unknown positions. But the fact is that even a Tal can be misled. . . . It would be a pity if, in modern tournaments, the game of chess actually began with the middle game!"

Best for Black now is considered to be *9 ... BxB; 10 QxB NxN; 11 QxQch KxQ; 12 PxN BxP (or 12 ... B–K5)*.

10	BxB	NxQ
11	BxQ	NxP
12	B–R3	....

Also good is *12 B–KN5 (or 12 P–Q6) NxQP; 13 O–O–O*.

| 12 | .... | N–Q2? |

Also out of the question is *12 ... BxP?; 13 R–B1 N–Q6ch; 14 BxN BxB; 15 RxP* etc.

Already the major work, Tartakower's *Die Hypermoderne Schachpartie* (1924), points out *12 ...*

NxQP; *13* O–O–O with White better, but after the recommended *13* . . . B–K3 Black can return his extra Pawn and complete his development in the process.

13 O–O–O   B–K5

Keres, on this, writes:
"Here Tal suddenly got upset and thought about his reply for almost an hour. Only now he has noticed that the intended *13* . . . O–O–O would be a grave mistake that loses a piece after *14* R–Q4 followed by *15* P–KN4—a surprising point! But if Black cannot castle, his previous move makes no sense and he encounters great difficulties.

"There is no adequate defense against the many threats, such as *14* R–Q4, *14* R–K1ch, *14* N–Q4, etc. The text is an attempt to get away with a somewhat acceptable game."

14 N–N5   . . . .

"White had many strong continuations here, such as *14* R–Q4 P–KB4; *15* N–N5; and *14* . . . BxN; *15* PxB; and *14* R–K1 P–KB4; *15* N–N5 etc. The text is not bad either, but it somehow complicates matters" (Keres).

14 . . . .   BxQP
15 P–KN3!?   . . . .

"The most surprising move, typically Bronstein! Few players would have considered a move like this here, especially as White has a lot of other promising continuations. Very strong would have been simply *14* R–K1ch! and only after *15* . . . K–Q1 or

Position after 14 . . . BxQP

15 . . . B–K3 may White continue with *15* P–KN3! etc.

"When I asked Bronstein after the game why he did not play simply *15* R–K1ch first, he looked at me as if I could not understand anything about the position and then said: 'I could not miss the opportunity to play a move like *15* P–KN3 against Tal, which I may never repeat in my whole life!'

"That's Bronstein. Now I am glad he played *15* P–KN3, which leads to very interesting complications" (Keres).

15 . . . .   BxR
16 PxN   P–QB4!

Now Tal begins to find some fine defensive moves. After *16* . . . O–O–O; *17* B–R3 B–B3; *18* NxBP White would regain his material with a bind.

17 B–B4   . . . .

Black gets counterplay on *17* R–K1ch K–B1; *18* B–B4 B–B3; *19* NxBP P–QN4!

17 . . . .   B–B3
18 NxBP   . . . .

If *18* BxPch K–K2!; *19* R–K1ch K–Q3.

18 ....   P–QN4!

"This saves the Exchange, as *19* NxR PxB would leave White with a trapped Knight on KR8. Now we can see that the beautiful move *15* P–KN3 did not make White's task any easier" (Keres).

19 N–Q6ch   K–K2
20 NxP   ....

"White still has a nice game. With his two Bishops, a good Pawn for the Exchange and Black's exposed King, his chances are a little superior, but by no means should his possibilities be overestimated.

"But everybody knows how difficult it is to adapt to new circumstances when the situation takes a sudden change. Having obtained some chances to save a lost game, Tal cannot find the right way to defend himself and again gets a lost position" (Keres).

20 ....   KR–KB1?

"He should have simplified the situation here by *20* ... BxN!; *29* BxB KR–Q1. Although White would remain with two Bishops and a Pawn for Rook and Knight, Black's position would be by no means hopeless; and with careful defense he would have good chances to save the game" (Keres).

21 N–Q4!   ....

"Tal must have overlooked this strong reply. He cannot protect the Bishop, as *21* ... R–B3 is met by *22* NxBch RxN; *23* B–Q5; and *21* ... QR–B1 is met by *22* NxBch

Position after 21 N–Q4

RxN; *23* B–N5 or even *22* R–K1ch. A nice mate would have followed *21* ... B–N2; *22* R–K1ch K–Q3; *23* N–N5ch and *24* R–K6 mate" (Keres).

21 ....   B–N7
22 N–K6   R–B4

On *22* ... R–B3; *23* NxBP is enough for a winning advantage.

23 R–N1   ....

"Both players have already used a lot of time for the complicated first part of the game and are now forced to play almost move on move. This explains the inaccuracies of the second part. Very strong here was *23* P–N4! as the Pawn could not be captured and White would have won a Pawn with continuing pressure" (Keres).

23 ....   B–K5
24 N–B7   ....

"It is good tactics in time trouble to make moves the opponent does not expect, but here *24* RxPch K–Q3; *25* RxNch KxR; *26* NxPch RxN; *27* BxR gave a rather simple win. Of course, the text is not bad either" (Keres).

24	....	R–Q1
25	R×Pch	K–B3

"Better was *25 . . . K–Q3; 26 N–N5ch K–B3; 27 N×Pch K–N3; 28 B–K3 R×P!* with complications. But White can play, of course, *26 N–K6 R–K1; 27 N–Q4 R×P; 28 N–N5ch* etc., winning the QRP under advantageous circumstances. After the text, White could still have taken a Pawn without risk by *26 R×P,* but—the time" (Keres).

26	R–B7ch	K–N3
27	R–K7	N–B3
28	N–K6	R–QB1

"On *28 . . . R–K1* the maneuver *29 R–N7ch K–R3; 30 R–N1* threatening *31 N–N7* or *31 B×P* or *31 N×P* is very annoying. Now White takes the time to activate his Queen Bishop" (Keres).

29	P–N3	R–R4
30	N–N5	B–Q4

"Black is lost, of course. It makes no sense to criticize both sides for their play in time trouble, here anything can happen!" (Keres).

31	B–Q3ch	K–R3
32	B–N2	P–B5
33	B–B5	P–B6
34	B×R	P×Bch
35	K×P	R×P
36	R×P	R–B7

"That must have been something for the spectators! Black simply does not have the time to resign" (Keres).

37	R–R4	K–N3
38	R–Q4	P–R4
39	P–R4	P–R5
40	P–R5	B–N7

"Who comes first? It seems to me that modern masters and grand-masters do not use their time in the best way. What good is it to have a fine first part of the game, when often the second part is spoiled by 'lightning chess,' by time trouble? I think it would be better to have a less deeply played first part, in order to have the time to play the second part in at least an acceptable manner" (Keres).

I wonder whether a solution to the problem of compelling players to distribute their time more equitably would be to have two time controls (after each 20 moves) instead of only one control at the end of the customary move 40. There can be no doubt that this innovation would revolutionize master chess, which many authorities fear is in danger of being played out. If such a reform were instituted, would it merely encourage players to memorize the openings even more deeply? Would time-pressure play an even greater role, thereby enhancing the human element (which I believe is desirable)? Hopefully, the experiment would produce a brisker pace in opening play, accentuating the now neglected middle game and ending.

41	P–R6	N–R4
42	B–N7	N×P

"They do not even notice that it is already the 42nd move" (Keres).

43	R×N	Resigns

"A game with the points to win new friends for our game of chess" (Keres).

LEIPZIG OLYMPICS 1960

King's Indian Defense

WHITE: LETELIER   BLACK: FISCHER

White overextends his center in his hunt for material and neglects to safeguard his rear. His hapless monarch, unable to castle, is soon forced to abdicate.

1 P–Q4	N–KB3
2 P–QB4	P–KN3
3 N–QB3	B–N2
4 P–K4	O–O
5 P–K5	....

White should resist this invitation and continue his development serenely with *5* N–B3 or *5* P–B3.

5	N–K1
6 P–B4	P–Q3
7 B–K3	....

7 N–B3 PxP; *8* QPxP leads to a better foothold on the center.

7	P–QB4
8 PxBP	N–QB3
9 BPxP	....

Overly aggressive. Safer is *9* N–B3 B–N5; *10* B–K2.

9	PxP
10 N–K4	....

A further violation of principle by moving a developed man twice. More realistic is *10* N–B3.

10	B–B4

Naturally Black pursues rapid development at any price.

11 N–N3?	....

The only chance lay in the consistent *11* NxP NxN; *12* QxN QxQ; *13* PxQ BxP; *14* R–Q1 N–N5!; *15* K–B2 NxP; *16* N–K2 P–QR4 (Fischer). White could still offer resistance in this endgame.

11	B–K3
12 N–B3	....

Now White would gladly disgorge his Pawn in order to consolidate.

12	Q–B2

Also good is *12* ... PxP; *13* QxQ RxQ; *14* B–B5 PxP. But Black justifiably seeks more out of the middle game.

13 Q–N1	....

One contortion leads to another. On *13* Q–B2 (or *13* B–K2 PxP; *14* B–B5 Q–R4ch; *15* P–N4 NxP; *16* BxR KxB!; *17* O–O PxP; *18* N–K4 B–B4) PxP; *14* P–B5 PxP; *15* NxBP N–N5; *16* Q–N3 BxN; *17* QxN N–B3; *18* Q–B5 Q–N1— (threatening ... N–N5) (Fischer).

13	PxP
14 P–KB5	P–K5!

Black opens lines for a quick kill.

15 PxB	....

No better is *15* QxP PxP; *16* NxP? Q–R4ch winning a piece.

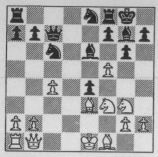

Position after 14 . . . P–K5

| 15 | . . . . | P×N |
| 16 | P×P | P–B4 |

The Pawn on K6 can be ignored in favor of the attack.

17	P–B4	N–B3
18	B–K2	KR–K1
19	K–B2	R×P

Black has regained the Pawn with an overwhelming position. The finish is elegant.

| 20 | R–K1 | QR–K1 |

21	B–B3	R×B!
22	R×R	R×R
23	K×R	Q×Pch!
	Resigns	

Final position after 23 . . . Q×Pch

A likely continuation is *24* K–B2 (or *24* K×Q B–R3 mate!) N–N5ch; *25* K–N2 N–K6ch; *26* K–B2 N–Q5; *27* Q–R1 N–N5ch; *28* K–B1 N×B; etc.

The moral: Abstain from complications before having completed your development.

27

BLED 1961
King's Indian Defense

WHITE: GLIGORICH   BLACK: FISCHER

This draw has the charm of perfection. The timing and ingenuity displayed by both players produce a harmonious flow of movement, remarkable in its aesthetic appeal.

| 1 | P–Q4 | N–KB3 |

2	P–QB4	P–KN3
3	N–QB3	B–N2
4	P–K4	P–Q3
5	N–B3	O O
6	B–K2	P–K4
7	O–O	N–B3
8	P–Q5	. . . .

Larsen–Fischer, Monaco 1967, continued: *8* B–K3 R–K1!; *9* P×P P×P; *10* Q×Q N×Q (right is *10* . . . R×Q!; *11* B–N5 R–B1!); *11* N–QN5 N–K3; *12* N–N5 R–K2; *13* KR–K1 P–N3=.

8	N–K2
9 N–K1	N–Q2
10 N–Q3	. . . .

The older *10* P–B3 P–KB4; *11* B–K3 P–B5; *12* B–B2 P–KN4 gives Black a strong attack.

10	P–KB4
11 P×P	. . . .

The best line against Larsen's *11* B–Q2 is P–B4!; *12* P–B3 P–B5!

11	N×BP

More viable is *12* . . . P×P; *13* P–B4 N–KN3. After the text Black's grip on his Q5 compensates for White's control of K4.

12 P–B3	N–B3

An alternative is *12* . . . N–Q5.

13 N–B2	N–Q5
14 N/2–K4	N–R4
15 B–N5	Q–Q2
16 P–KN3	P–KR3

Inferior is *16* . . . P–B4?; *17* N–N5! N×N; *18* P×N with a bind (Tal–Gligorich, Bled 1961).

17 B–K3	P–B4!

Launching an intricate Pawn sacrifice. After *17* . . . N×Bch; *18* Q×N P–KN4; *19* P–B5 White would have a comfortable space advantage.

18 B×N	KP×B
19 N–QN5	P–R3

Not *19* . . . B–K4?; *20* P–B4, etc.

20 N/5×P/6	. . . .

Position after 20 N/5×P/6

Apparently Black has lost a Pawn without any return.

20	P–Q6!

And now he gives up a second Pawn, to open the diagonal for his KB. A fine concept.

21 Q×P	. . . .

21 B×P B–Q5ch; *22* K–R1 N×Pch; *23* N×N Q×N; *24* Q–B2 B–R6 affords Black adequate counterplay.

21	B–Q5ch
22 K–N2	. . . .

After *22* K–R1 N×Pch; *23* N×N Q×N, White retains his extra Pawn, but his weak squares would provide Black with even chances. Another possibility is *22* R–B2!? to try for an advantage.

22	N×P!

Black had to visualize this resource and determine its absolute soundness, when he embarked on his combination on move 17.

Position after 22 ... NxP

23 NxB   ....

Unclear is *23* NxN (not *23* PxN??
Q–R6 mate) QxN; *24* QR–N1—
where White's extra Pawn is offset by
his weakened King side.

Gligorich takes a cleaner course,
virtually assuring a draw.

23 ....   NxR
24 N–N6   Q–QB2

Blow for blow. Black now threatens
mate in two.

25	RxN	QxN
26	P–N4!	....

Now it is White, behind in material,
who finds the saving clause.

26 ....   QxP

Too precarious is *26* ... PxP; *27*
P–B5! BxP; *28* NxB QxN; *29*
QxPch and wins.

27 R–QN1   Q–R4
28 NxP   ....

Black comes out on top after *28*
RxP R–B2.

28	....	QxN
29	QxPch	B–N2
30	RxP	Q–Q5
31	B–Q3	R–B5
32	Q–K6ch	K–R1
33	Q–N6	Draw

Neither side dares disturb the surface
tension.

28
BEVERWIJK 1967
King's Indian Defense

WHITE: POMAR   BLACK: SZABO

This important theoretical contest
overturned the evaluation that the
variation is in White's favor. Black is
not given the opportunity to score a
flashy point, but that hardly detracts
from the muted charm of his performance.

1	P–Q4	N–KB3
2	P–QB4	P–KN3
3	N–QB3	B–N2
4	P–K4	P–Q3
5	B–K2	O–O
6	P–B4	....

The pendulum has swung. Once considered the scourge of the King's Indian, the Four Pawns Attack has now been shorn of its terror.

6	....	P–B4
7	P–Q5	P–K3
8	N–B3	PxP
9	BPxP	....

The insipid 9 KPxP is drawish.

9	....	R–K1

Keres–Spassky, 10th Match Game 1965, went: 9 . . . P–QN4; 10 P–K5 PxP; 11 PxP N–N5; 12 B–KB4! N–Q2; 13 P–K6 with dangerous threats.

10	N–Q2	....

For the spicy 10 P–K5!?, see Game 30.

10	....	P–QR3

10 . . . P–B5; 11 B–B3 (better is 11 P–QR4) QN–Q2; 12 O–O P–QN4 is Pomar–Fischer, Havana Olympics 1966.

11	P–QR4	N–N5
12	BxN	Q–R5ch
13	P–N3	QxB
14	QxQ	....

Interesting is 14 O–O B–Q5ch!; 15 K–R1 Q–R6!; 16 N–B3 B–N5; 17 Q–Q3 N–Q2!; 18 B–Q2 BxNch!; 19 QxB P–B4; 20 PxP PxP; 21 KR–K1 N–B3; and White's QP is a source of infection (Kerr–Evans, Washington 1969).

14	....	BxQ
15	K–B2	B–Q5ch

Better than 15 . . . P–B4; 16 P–R3 PxP; 17 N–B4! B–B6; 18 R–K1

B–B1; 19 N–N6 R–R2; 20 P–R5 N–B3!? (White gets a bind after 20 . . . B–N2; 21 QN–R4 R–Q1; 22 B–K3 N–Q2; 23 QR–N1); 21 PxN PxP; 22 N–B4 R–N2 with insufficient compensation for the piece (Zaitsev–Priyodovsky, U.S.S.R. 1965).

16	K–N2	N–Q2
17	P–R3	BxN
18	NPxB	B–K7
19	R–K1	B–Q6
20	R–K3	P–B5
21	B–R3	....

Position after 21 B–R3

A critical position, important for the judgment of the whole variation, and the subject of an article by Zaitsev in which he concluded that White's chances were favorable. The key move which he considered was 21 . . . P–B4; 22 P–K5 N–N3 (22 . . . PxP; 23 PxP RxP; 24 RxR NxR; 25 R–K1 N–B2; 26 B–K7! R–K1; 27 K–B2 is difficult for Black); 23 BxP NxQP; 24 RxB! PxR; 25 P–B4 and all the winning chances are with White after he fixes the Queen side with P–R5 and P–B5, then wins the QP.

21	....	N–N3!

It is questionable whether this is a prepared variation, even though it was well known that Pomar is fond of the White side. Such moves are usually found in the heat of battle.

| 22 | BxP | NxQP |
| 23 | R/3–K1? | .... |

White places too much reliance on his next move. The only interesting course is *23* RxB PxR; *24* P–B4 (*24* PxN? R–K7ch) N–B6; *25* K–B3 P–QN4!; *26* BPxP PxP; *27* P–R5 with a stiff fight.

23	....	NxBP
24	B–K5	RxB!
25	PxR	R–QB1
26	R–R3	....

There is no time for *26* K–B3 P–QN4; *27* R–R3 P–N5, etc.

26	....	N–K7
27	K–B2	P–B6
28	N–N3	....

Willy-nilly White should try his luck in the Rook-and-Pawn ending resulting from *28* RxN BxR; *29* KxB P–B7!; *30* N–N3 R–B6; *31* R–R2 (forced) RxN; *32* RxP, although *32* ... RxP (or ... R–N5) wins. The actual game is even worse for White.

| 28 | .... | P–B7 |
| 29 | N–B1 | .... |

29 RxN would transpose into the previous note.

29	....	NxN
30	RxN	BxP
31	K–K3	R–B5
32	P–R5	P–R4
33	K–Q2	R–B4

Picking up a third Pawn for the exchange, after which White might as well surrender.

34	R–K1	RxKP
35	K–B1	P–B4
36	R–N3	RxP
37	RxB	PxR
38	RxP	R–R6
39	P–N4	P–R5
40	R–N6	K–B2
41	KxP	RxP
42	P–N5	R–KN6
	Resigns	

A good illustration of the "creative evolution" which makes up the judgment of a variation. The middle game and ending flowed harmoniously from the opening. Theory now decrees that White should abstain from this unless he has an improvement—the burden of proof has alternated.

29

BUCHAREST 1966
King's Indian Defense
WHITE: KAVALEK   BLACK: MATULOVICH

Black's aggressive formation boomerangs when he runs into a surprising Rook sacrifice. What is remarkable is that his position appears perfectly safe one move earlier.

1	P–Q4	N–KB3
2	P–QB4	P–B4
3	P–Q5	P–Q3
4	N–QB3	P–KN3
5	P–K4	B–N2
6	P–B4	O–O
7	B–Q3	P–K3
8	PxP	....

The game has transposed into the Four Pawns Attack, and the text is an improvement on *8* N–B3 PxP; *9* BPxP Q–N3.

8 .... PxP

An alternative is *8* ... BxP; *9* P–B5 B–Q2; *10* N–B3 PxP; *11* PxP R–K1ch; *12* N–K2 B–B3; *13* O–O QN–Q2; *14* B–N5 P–KR3; *15* B–R4 Q–N3=.

9	KN–K2	N–B3
10	O–O	N–Q5
11	N–N3	N–K1

More consistent is *11* ... P–QR3, striving for a rapid expansion with ... P–QN4.

12 B–K3 Q–R5!?

Risky. Again *12* ... N–B2 followed by ... P–QR3 is thematic.

13	P–B5!?	KPxP
14	Q–Q2!	P–B5

Less clear is *14* ... PxP; *15* B–N5 Q–N5; *16* BxP. White's initiative compensates for his Pawn, but Black has numerous resources.

15	BxP	N–K3
16	B–K3	RxRch
17	RxR	B–Q2?

Correct is *17* ... N–B3 immediately, threatening ... N–N5.

18 N–Q5 N–B3

Overlooking White's combination, but the position is already difficult. If *18* ... B–QB3; *19* Q–KB2 is hard to meet.

Position after 18 ... N–B3

19	RxN!	BxR
20	N–B5!	PxN
21	P–KN3!	B–B6

Forced. On *21* ... Q–R6?; *22* NxBch K–B2; *23* B–B1! wins the Queen.

22 PxB Q–Q1

Black has averted immediate disaster, but his exposed King is now the target.

23 PxP N–N2

No better is *23* ...N–B1; *24* B–N5 Q–R4; *25* B–B6.

24	B–N5	Q–KB1
25	N–B6ch	K–R1
26	NxB	Q–B2
27	N–B6	N–R4
28	NxN	QxN
29	B–B6ch	K–N1
30	B–K4	P–KR3
31	QxP	R–K1
32	B–Q5ch	Resigns

LENINGRAD 1967
King's Indian Defense

WHITE: VLADIMIROV   BLACK: DODA

White's ultrasharp opening variation has all the tang of home cooking. Black quite properly nibbles at the dish, as befits a polite guest; his mistake is accepting a second helping.

1 P–Q4	N–KB3
2 P–QB4	P–B4
3 P–Q5	P–KN3

More forcing is *3* ... P–K3 (or *3* ... P–K4) which is characteristic of the Benoni Defense.

4 N–QB3	P–Q3
5 P–K4	B–N2
6 P–B4	O–O
7 N–B3	P–K3
8 B–K2	PxP
9 BPxP	....

An interesting gambit is *9* P–K5!? PxKP; *10* PxKP N–N5; *11* B–N5 Q–R4; *12* PxP NxKP; *13* O–O (Nei–Westerninen, Helsinki 1966). Black should be able to defend successfully.

9	R–K1

Earlier in my career I learned to avoid *9* ... P–QN4!?; *10* BxP NxKP; *11* NxN Q–R4ch; *12* K–B2 QxB; *13* NxQP, where Black had to fight hard for a draw (Wood–Evans, Hastings 1949–50).

10 P–K5!?	....

Suggested by Keres, this involves a risky Pawn sacrifice. It is questionable whether White can undertake such action before having castled; yet after *10* N–Q2 Black obtains a satisfactory position without special difficulty.

10	PxP

Black rises to the occasion. Also playable perhaps is *10* ... KN–Q2; *11* PxP P–QR3; *12* P–QR4 N–KB3; *13* O–O B–N5; *14* N–K5 BxB; *15* QxB QxP (Lehmann–Toran, Munich 1954).

11 PxP	....

11 NxP QN–Q2 merely hastens Black's development, but it does not seem to have been tested yet.

11	N–N5
12 B–KN5	....

An attempt to improve on *12* P–K6!? (or *12* B–KB4 NxKP; *13* NxN BxN; *14* O–O) PxP; *13* O–O PxP! with a sharp struggle and mutual chances.

12	Q–N3
13 O–O	NxKP

Averting the pitfall *13* ... P–B5ch?; *14* K–R1 N–B7ch; *15* RxN QxR; *16* N–K4 Q–N3; *17* N–Q6 R–B1; *18* B–K7 N–Q2; *19* NxQBP—regaining material with a clear advantage.

14 NxN	BxN
15 B–QB4	QxP!?

A bold choice. Kupka–Zaitsev, Prague versus Moscow 1968, continued: *15* ... B–B4 (not *15* ...

Q–N5; *16* Q–B3 B–B4; *17* P–N4!
QxB; *18* PxB P–B3; *19* PxP! PxP;
20 BxP R–B1; *21* Q–N2 Q–Q5ch;
22 K–R1 RxB; *23* RxR BxR; *24*
QxPch B–N2; *25* Q–K8ch K–R2;
29 R–KN1); *16* N–N5 (if *16* B–N5
B–Q2; *17* Q–B3 P–B4) N–Q2; *17*
P–QR4 P–B3!; *18* B–R6 B–Q5ch;
19 K–R1 P–R4; *20* RxB!? PxR;
21 B–Q3 B–K6; and Black is better.

16 P–Q6 ....

A logical extension of White's idea
to utilize the open KB file. Black's
problems are now more easily solved
in analysis than over the board.

16 .... B–B4

Kholmov gives *16* ... B–K3; *17*
BxB PxB (if *17* ... RxB; *18* Q–B3
P–B4; *19* Q–Q5 K–B2; *20* QR–N1!);
18 Q–B3 N–B3 (or *18* ... N–Q2;
19 Q–B7ch K–R1; *20* QxN QxN;
21 QR–Q1 R–KB1; *22* QxKP
RxRch; *23* RxR B–Q5ch; *24* K–R1
Q–Q6; *25* B–B6ch BxB; *26* QxBch
K–N1; *27* Q–B7ch K–R1; *28* P–Q7
with an easy win); *19* Q–B7ch K–R1;
20 B–B6ch BxB; *21* QxBch K–N1;
22 QR–N1 Q–Q7; *23* Q–B7ch K–R1;
24 RxP Q–R3; *25* Q–B6ch K–N1;
26 N–K4! with a winning attack.

Position after 16 ... B–B4

17 BxPch!? ....

First *17* RxB! seems more accurate,
the point being that *17* ... PxR;
18 BxPch! forces a transposition into
the game without allowing Black the
option pointed out in the next note.
And if *17* ... QxN; *18* BxPch
K–N2; *19* R–B3 Q–Q5ch! (not
19 ... QxQR; *20* QxQ BxQ; *21*
BxR followed by P–Q7 wins); *20*
QxQ BxQch; *21* K–B1 R–KB1; *22*
R–K1! N–B3! (not *22* ... RxB;
23 RxRch KxR; *24* R–K7ch K–N1;
25 R–K8ch K–B2; *26* P–Q7); *23*
B–Q5! with a dangerous initiative
for the Pawn.

17 .... KxB
18 RxBch! PxR?

No better is *18* ... K–N1; *19* Q–
Q5ch K–R1; *20* R–K1! B–Q5ch;
21 QxBch!

Kholmov opines that, after the text,
"White's attack becomes irresistible.
The quiet retreat *18* ... K–N2
places before White a hardly solvable
problem: his Rook is left hanging in
the air, as is the entire Queen side."
But complications still arise from
19 P–Q7 (not *19* R–B3 BxN; *20* R–
N1 QxR!; *21* QxQ R–K8ch) NxP!;
20 QxNch K–R1; *21* RxB QxRch;
22 Q–Q1 (not *22* K–B2? R–B1ch and
... QxN next) QxQch; *23* NxQ
RxR; *24* B–B6ch K–N1; *25* BxR
R–K1 and Black's Rook with two
Pawns probably must triumph over
the two minor pieces.

19 Q–R5ch K–B1

Kholmov gives *19* ... K–N2?; *20*
B–R6ch K–B3; *21* R–KB1 B–Q5ch
(or *21* ... Q–B7; *22* N–Q5ch! K–

K3; *23* Q×Rch K×N; *24* P–Q7! N×P; *25* Q×Nch K–B5; *26* R–B1ch); *22* K–R1 R–K4; *23* Q–N5ch K–B2; *24* Q–N7ch K–K1; *25* N–Q5! N–Q2; *26* Q–N8ch N–B1; *27* N–B6ch! mates.

20	R–KB1!	B–Q5ch
21	K–R1	R–K3
22	R×Pch	B–B3
23	B–R6ch	K–N1

Position after 23 . . . K–N1

Apparently Black's King is secure, and Black now seeks salvation in the mate threat on the first rank.

24 Q–N5ch! K–B2

If *24* . . . K–R1 (of course not *24* . . . B×Q; *25* R–B8 mate); *25* B–N7ch! K–N1 (*25* . . . B×B; *26* Q–Q8 mates); *26* B×Bch K–B1; *27* B–N7ch K–K1; *28* R–B8ch K–Q2; *29* Q–Q8ch K–B3; *30* Q–B7 mate.

25 R×Bch! . . . .

White cannot afford to stop checking without getting mated himself!

25	. . . .	R×R
26	Q–N7ch	K–K3
27	Q–K7ch	Resigns

He does not care to take his King for a stroll with *27* . . . K–B4; *28* Q–K4 mate.

31

VARNA 1958
King's Indian Defense

WHITE: BOBOTSOV BLACK: TAL

What a blow to tradition! Black sacrifices his Queen, revolutionizing the whole evaluation of this variation; it is amazing how his attack gains momentum with each move.

1	P–Q4	N–KB3
2	P–QB4	P–KN3
3	N–QB3	B–N2
4	P–K4	P–Q3
5	P–B3	O–O
6	KN–K2	P–B4
7	B–K3	QN–Q2
8	Q–Q2	P–QR3
9	O–O–O	Q–R4
10	K–N1	P–QN4!?

This sets the stage for Black's next by ignoring the threat of N–Q5. More prudent is *10* . . . R–K1; *11* N–B1 (Evans–Mednis, U.S. Championship 1964) R–N1—with a cramped but solid position.

11 N–Q5 . . . .

It is better to interpolate *11* P×BP! QP×P (also possible is *11* . . . P–

N5); *12* N–Q5 NxN; *13* QxQ NxB; *14* R–B1 (difficult is *14* RxN BxR; *15* N–B3 KR–B1) NxBP; *15* RxN PxR; *16* N–B3 R–N1 (*16* ... N–K4; *17* B–K2 B–K3; *18* R–Q1 QR–N1; *19* K–B1 KR–B1 is unclear—Saidy–Marovich, Malaga 1969); *17* BxP N–K4; *18* B–K2 B–K3—with tricky play, as in the original game with this variation (Zamikhovsky-Nezhmetdinov, U.S.S.R. 1956).

11 ....   NxN!

The logical consequence. Bad is *11* ... Q–Q1?; *12* PxBP.

12 QxQ   NxB

Position after 12 ... NxB

Here is the outcome of Black's speculation. He has two Knights for the Queen and hopes to use the latent power of his KB for an attack against White's QN2. White should be able to exploit his material advantage, but how? The theorists are still in disagreement about who stands better: probably the better player!

13 R–B1   ....

This variation was tested again in Beyen–Klompus, correspondence game, 1968, which continued: *13* R–Q3 NxBP; *14* Q–K1 R–N1; *15* P–KR4 PxP; *16* NxP N–B4; *17* R–Q1 N–R5!; *18* BxN (if *18* P–QN3 N–R6ch; *19* K–B1 B–K3!) PxB; *19* P–QN3 PxP; *20* PxP B–K3; *21* Q–R5 BxP; *22* R–Q2 KR–B1; *23* NxB N–B4; *24* R–QB2 RxNch; *25* K–R2 R–N4; *26* Q–R3 KR–N1; *27* P–B4 R–N5; *28* P–K5 R–R5; *29* QxR NxQ; *30* P–B6 PxP; White Resigns.

13 ....   NxBP
14 RxN?   ....

It is questionable whether White should so willingly return material and open the QN file in the bargain. The sturdiest defense is *14* Q–K1 PxP; *15* N–B4.

14 ....   PxR
15 N–B1   R–N1
16 BxP   N–N3
17 B–N3   ....

A little better is *17* B–K2. It is clear, however, that Black already has ample compensation for the Queen, which is a helpless spectator.

17 ....   BxP
18 Q–Q2   B–KN2
19 N–K2   P–B5
20 B–B2   P–B6!

Of course. Black opens lines. *21* NxP N–B5 would allow an immediate finish.

21 Q–Q3   PxP
22 N–Q4   B–Q2
23 R–Q1   KR–B1
24 B–N3   N–R5
25 BxN   BxB
26 N–N3   R–B6
27 QxRP   BxN
28 PxB   QR–QB1

Position after 28 ... QR–QB1

Anything wins now. Even *28 ...* R/6–B1, followed by *...* R–R1 and *...* R–R8ch.

| 29 | Q–R3 | .... |

White would love to play *29* K×P if it didn't lose the Queen by *29 ...* R/6–B3ch.

29	....	R–B8ch
30	R×R	R×Rch
	Resigns	

32

TEL AVIV OLYMPICS 1964
King's Indian Defense

WHITE: SAIDY   BLACK: BEDNARSKY

White's intricate combination was launched because he believed his position to be inferior. Saidy criticizes himself, yet his sacrifice turns out to be even sounder than its author's faith in it.

1	P–QB4	P–KN3
2	N–QB3	B–N2
3	P–Q4	N–KB3
4	P–K4	P–Q3
5	P–B3	P–B3
6	B–K3	P–QR3
7	Q–Q2	P–QN4

Black's anti-Saemisch system was introduced by Robert Byrne. Instead of passively waiting for White to mount an attack, Black launches an immediate Queen-side diversion.

| *8* | B–Q3 | .... |

On *8* O–O–O Q–R4! solves Black's opening problems.

8	....	QN–Q2
9	KN–K2	O–O
10	O–O	P×P

A good alternative is *10 ...* P–K4.

11	B×P	N–N3
12	B–N3	P–QR4
13	N–R4	B–QR3
14	KR–B1	KN–Q2
15	R–B2	....

"White's Saemisch Attack seems to have established a satisfactory sway in the center. The Black QBP is backward, but capturing it by *15* R×P would give Black strong play via *15 ...* B–N4; *16* N×N N×N; and *17 ...* P–R5. But now White's serenity is destroyed by the text move" (Saidy).

| *15* | .... | P–QB4!? |

"Keres queries this move. Nevertheless, in my considered opinion,

it is impeccable. At this point I
pondered for forty valuable minutes,
appalled by the disjointed position of
my own pieces and the fact that
Black had so swiftly freed his position. *16 PxP NxN; 17 BxN NxP*
gives Black a fine game. I must admit
now that, had I seen a quiet way to
retain an edge, no 'brilliancy' would
have been hatched (with such a long
gestation period)" (Saidy).

Position after 15 . . . P–QB4

16 NxP!   . . . .

Keres also rewards this with a pure
"!" adding, "The combination is
original and easily overlooked."
("Perhaps it should have been" was
Saidy's pessimistic evaluation.)

Without it, however, Black gets a
fine position after *16 PxP NxN;
17 BxN NxP.*

16	**PxN**
17 PxP	**P–R5**

Sturdier is *17 . . . N–B1; 18 R–Q1
BxN; 19 QxB Q–B2*—with a hard
fight in the offing.

18 BxPch	**RxB**
19 PxN	**BxN**

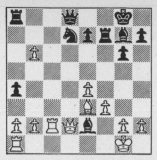

Position after 19 . . . BxN

Keres considers this "the best practical
chance," but Saidy was pessimistic
about the reply *19 . . . P–R6.* Keres
gives *20 R–Q1 PxP* (or *20 . . . BxN;
21 QxB PxP; 22 P–N7 R–N1; 23
Q–N5* with good play); *21 N–B3.* He
concludes that after winning the
QNP White would have three Pawns
for the piece and certainly no reason
to complain.

20 QxB   . . . .

"Played automatically—why waste
precious time on the obvious? But,
as I never suspected until reading
Keres' notes, *20 P–N7!* gives White
the advantage" (Saidy). A possible
continuation is *20 . . . R–N1; 21
R/1–QB1 B–QR3; 22 R–B8 R–B1;
23 RxQ KRxR; 24 R–B7 N–B1;
25 Q–R5 QBxP; 26 QxP BxNP;
27 B–R7!* wins material.

20	**NxP**
21 R–Q1	**Q–N1?**

The decisive error in a flawed contest.
Correct is *21 . . . N–Q2!; 22 R/2–
Q2 P–K3;* and if *23 Q–N5, Q–N1*
saves the piece. Instead of an uphill
battle, White now has an easy win.

22 Q–N5	**N–B1**

Black cannot save the Knight by 22 ... R–B3; *23* R–B6 R×R; *24* Q×R, etc.

23 R–Q8ch	**R–B1**
24 Q–Q5ch	**Resigns**

Because after *24* ... K–R1; *25* R×R B×R; *26* B–Q4ch, Black must surrender either his King or most of his material. The errors generated by tension make this fight all the more instructive. As Keres puts it: "I hope Dr. Saidy does not mind if I do not agree with his rather pessimistic opinion. Although not a model performance, I nevertheless like this game and the original combination very much . . . I think most chess fans do too."

33

VINKOVCI 1968
King's Indian Defense

WHITE: NIKOLICH   BLACK: FISCHER

Fischer's games are characterized by a relentless search for the sharpest continuation. In a placid setting he unexpectedly offers a piece, forging a mating net which does not become apparent for another half dozen moves.

1	P–QB4	P–KN3
2	N–QB3	B–N2
3	P–KN3	P–K4
4	B–N2	P–Q3
5	P–K3	N–KB3
6	KN–K2	O–O
7	O–O	P–B3
8	P–Q4	R–K1
9	R–N1	....

This system is passive and yields the initiative; it is not considered honorable to play for a draw with the White pieces, but a draw could be achieved by *9* P×P P×P; *10* Q×Q R×Q; *11* P–N3, etc.

9	....	P–K5
10	P–QN4	B–B4
11	P–KR3	....

White should avoid making new weaknesses and proceed immediately with *11* P–N5.

11	....	P–KR4
12	N–B4	QN–Q2
13	P–QR4	N–B1
14	P–B5	....

A strategical error, which permits Black to close the center. More dynamic is *14* P–N5 to open lines.

14	....	P–Q4
15	P–N5	N/1–R2
16	B–Q2	N–N4
17	R–N2	....

One of those "mysterious" Rook moves, because Black was threatening 17 ... N–B6ch; *18* B×N P×B; *19* R–N2 P–N4, trapping the Knight.

17	....	Q–Q2
18	K–R2	B–R3
19	P–R5	....

Consistent, if nothing else. Had White seen what was in store, he might have tried *19* R–R1, followed by a flight of his King to the Queen side. Fischer thought a long time here. *19* ... P–R5 does not pose an immediate threat, but it's not a bad move. Another possibility is *19* ... N–B6ch; *20* BxN PxB; *21* QxP BxN; *22* NPxB PxP, and Black regains his Pawn with a good game because *23* NxP? is refuted by ... B–Q6. But neither of these lines is sufficiently forcing to suit his taste.

| 19 | .... | B–N5! |

Position after 19 ... B–N5

| 20 | PxB | .... |

This elegant offer cannot be refused. Fischer gives *20* Q–N3 N–B6ch; *21* BxN BxB; *22* PxP PxP; *23* Q–N7 Q–B4; *24* QxBP BxN; *25* NPxB N–N5ch; *26* K–N3 P–R5ch; *27* KxP K–N2; *28* QxP R–R1; *29* K–N3

R–R6ch; *30* KxR N–K4ch and mates shortly.

| 20 | .... | RPxP! |

The ventilated KR file will prove White's undoing.

| 21 | R–R1 | .... |

The only chance. A weird defensive try is *21* B–R1 N–B6ch; *22* K–N2 BxN; *23* KPxB Q–B4; *24* R–KN1 Q–R4; *25* K–B1 Q–R7; *26* BxN KPxB; *27* B–K3 RxB; *28* PxR QxR wins (Fischer).

21	....	N–B6ch
22	BxN	NPxB
23	K–N1	BxN
24	KPxB	K–N2!
25	P–B5	R–R1
26	B–R6ch	....

A desperate attempt to stave off the inevitable.

26	....	RxB
27	RxR	KxR
28	Q–Q2ch	....

There was a pretty finish after *28* P–R6 QxP; *29* PxNP R–R1; *30* PxP K–N2; *31* P–N8(Q) R–R8ch; *32* KxR Q–R6ch; *33* K–N1 Q–N7 mate (Fischer).

28	....	P–N4
29	PxP	QxKBP
30	N–Q1	Q–R6
31	N–K3	K–N3
	Resigns	

There is no longer any defense to the long-awaited ... R–R1.

34

SARAJEVO 1967
King's Indian Defense

WHITE: KOZOMARA BLACK: R. BYRNE

"My opponent was so impressed by the piece sacrifice that the first thing he asked me after the game was whether it was prepared analysis. Not only was it not prepared analysis, it was not even prepared on my previous move! It was a clear case of shooting from the hip" (R. Byrne).

1	P–Q4	N–KB3
2	N–KB3	P–KN3
3	P–B4	B–N2
4	P–QN4	....

Santasiere's Folly Deferred!

4	....	O–O
5	B–N2	P–Q3
6	P–K3	QN–Q2
7	B–K2	P–K4
8	O–O	....

After 8 PxP N–N5, Black recovers the Pawn with a comfortable position.

8	....	P–K5
9	KN–Q2	R–K1
10	N–QB3	N–B1
11	P–QR4	P–KR4
12	P–R5	N/1–R2

"It is often difficult to decide, in cases of attacks on opposite wings, what, if any, defensive measures one ought to take time out for. Perhaps I should have played 12 ... P–R3; but in the face of White's sweeping Pawn avalanche, defensive moves usually turn out to create more weaknesses than they shield" (Byrne).

13	P–R6	P–N3

"White has scored first—Black's Queen-side Pawns have the well-ventilated look of Swiss cheese. But Black is prepared to return the compliment by ... N–N4 and ...P–R4–5–6, and the attempt to halt Black by P–R3 would only invite a dangerous sacrifice" (Byrne).

14	P–B4	PxP*e.p.*
15	BxP	B–N5

"I considered this so essential as to be obvious, but my opponent told me later that in a previous game 15 ... R–N1 was chosen and he scored quickly against it" (Byrne).

16	P–R3	....

Anticipating a useful clarification. If this move is no good, then White's position is difficult indeed.

16	....	B–R3!

Black rejects the obvious 16 ... BxB; 17 QxB N–N4; 18 Q–B4 N–K3; 19 Q–B2.

17	PxB	....

If the sacrifice is declined by 17 R–K1 BxB; 18 QxB N–N4 develops pressure against the KP.

88

Position after 16 . . . B–R3

17 . . . .   B×Pch
18 R–B2   . . . .

White does better to seek counter-
play with *18* K–R2 N–K5!; *19* P–
N3 N×N/7; *20* B×R N×Rch; *21* Q×N
Q×B; *22* P×P followed by N–Q5.

18 . . . .   N×P
19 B×N   Q–R5
20 Q–B3?   . . . .

The most demanding defense is
20 N/2–K4 P×B; *21* Q–Q3 (on *21*
Q–K1 B×P; *22* R–Q1 P–QB4; *23*
P–N3 Q–K2; *24* Q–B1 P–B4; *25*
N–Q2 Q–K6 wins) B×Rch; *22* N×B
P–N6; *23* N–R3 N–N4; *24* N–K2
(Byrne considers only *24* Q–B1
R–K3; *25* N–Q5 N×Nch; *26* P×N
QR–K1) N×Nch; *25* P×N Q×P;
26 Q×P Q×Qch (if *26* . . . Q–K3?;
27 N–B4 Q×P?; *28* N×P!); *27* N×Q
R–K6 with advantage, but there's
plenty of play left.

20 . . . .   N–N4

White turns the tables after *20* . . .
P×B?; *21* Q×Pch K–R1; *22* N–Q1!
threatening P–Q5ch.

21 Q×B   RxQ
22 N–Q5   . . . .

Position after 22 N–Q5

With three minor pieces for the
Queen, White seems to have fair
prospects. But now comes an efficient
finish.

22 . . . .   P×B!
23 N×R   Q–N6
24 R–K2   N–R6ch
25 K–B1   . . . .

Byrne gives *25* K–R1 N–B5; *26*
QR–K1 N×R; *27* R×N R–K1;
28 N/2–B1 Q–B5; *29* K–N1 Q–K5
winning.

25 . . . .   N–B5
26 N–K4   Q–R5
27 P–Q5   P–KB4
28 N–B6ch   K–B2
29 R–Q2   P–N6
30 K–K1   Q–R8ch
31 N–B1   N×Pch
32 K–Q1   . . . .

The rest needs no comment. On *32*
R×N (or *32* K–K2 N–B5ch; *33* K–
K3 P–N7) Q×R; *33* B–Q4 R–R1,
followed by R–R8.

32 . . . .   Q×Nch
33 K–B2   N–K6ch

34	K–N3	Q×Pch		37	R–R1	Q×Bch
35	K–R3	N–B7ch		38	K×Q	K×N
36	R×N	Q×R			Resigns	

35
27th U.S.S.R. CHAMPIONSHIP 1960
Nimzo-Indian Defense

WHITE: POLUGAIEVSKY   BLACK: PETROSIAN

Petrosian gets caught in the opening and is slaughtered by a twenty-six-year-old unknown, who seven years later captured the coveted Soviet crown. White prosecutes his attack with great *élan*.

1	P–Q4	N–KB3
2	P–QB4	P–K3
3	N–QB3	B–N5
4	P–K3	O–O
5	B–Q3	P–Q4
6	N–B3	P–B4
7	O–O	P×BP
8	B×P	P–QN3
9	Q–K2	....

It is hard for White to squeeze anything tangible out of this solid defense. Just for the record he has a half dozen plausible moves here; which is best is still an open question and provides a field day for theorists. 9 Q–Q3 and 9 P–QR3 are the most frequently seen alternatives. At the Piatigorsky Cup 1963, where Black's system proved itself, Gligorich and Reshevsky tried 9 B–Q3 against Najdorf. The first game continued 9 ... B–N2; 10 P–QR3 P×P; 11 P×P B–K2; 12 R–K1 QN–Q2; 13 B–B2 P–QR3; 14 Q–Q3 R–K1; 15 B–N5 P–N3; and White could

not exploit his slight initiative. The second game went 9 ... B–R3; 10 B×B N×B; 11 Q–R4 Q–B1; 12 N–QN5 P×P; 13 N/5×QP Q–N2; 14 P–QR3 B–K2; 15 P–QN4 KR–B1; and Black overcame his temporary cramp to draw.

9	....	B–N2
10	R–Q1	QN–Q2

Usual now is 10 ... P×P; 11 P×P QN–Q2 to provide the Bishop with a retreat to K2.

11	P–Q5	B×N
12	P×P	B–R4
13	P×N	Q–B2?

The innocent-looking offender. Correct is 13 ... Q–K2; 14 P–K4 QR–Q1; 15 B–N5 Q×KP; 16 Q×Q B×Q; 17 B×N P×B and Black can hold (Najdorf–Smyslov, Havana 1962).

14	P–K4!	N×QP

If 14 ... B×P (or 14 ... N×KP; 15 N–N5! is uncommonly strong); 15 B–N5 B×N; 16 Q×B N×P; 17 B–B4! Q–B1 (if 17 ... N–K4; 18 Q–KN3 wins a piece); 18 B–Q6 leaves Black in a hopeless tangle.

15	N–N5!	....

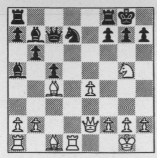

Position after 15 N–N5

15 ....   QR–Q1

Meets with a stunning refutation, but so does *15 ... N–K4; 16 B–B4 QR–K1; 17 Q–R5 P–KR3; 18 N×P! R×N; 19 B×N R×B; 20 Q×Rch!* (if *20 B×Rch? K–B1* saves the day) *Q×Q; 21 R–Q8ch K–R2; 22 B×Q* and White's material preponderance must tell.

16	B×Pch!	R×B
17	N–K6!	Q–B1
18	N×R	B–R3

The only hope, since on *18 ... Q×N; 19 P–K5* decides.

19	Q–K3	R–K2
20	Q–N3ch	P–B5
21	Q–QR3	N–B4

Black is in a sorry way. If *21 ... R×P (21 ... Q×N?; 22 B–N5); 22 Q–Q6 Q×N; 23 Q–Q5ch!* (not *23 Q×N? R–K8ch*) wins the Rook.

22	B–K3	R×P
23	B×N	Q×B
24	Q–KB3!	Resigns

On *24 ... R–K2; 25 N–K6 R×N; 26 R–Q8* mates. Black never saw daylight.

36
REYKJAVIK 1968
Nimzo-Indian Defense

WHITE: ADDISON   BLACK: SIGURJONSSON

Black tries an opening novelty, but White goes one better. Addison's sprightly Bishop sacrifice on move 15 is followed by equally energetic tactics.

1	P–Q4	N–KB3
2	P–QB4	P–K3
3	N–QB3	B–N5
4	P–K3	O–O
5	B–Q3	P–B4
6	N–B3	P–Q4
7	O–O	P×BP

8	B×P	Q–K2
9	P–QR3	B–R4
10	B–Q3	....

Geller recommends *10 B–Q2* followed by *11 R–B1.*

10 ....   P–QR3?

This loses much of its point with White's Bishop placed on Q3. Better is *10 ... N–B3.*

11	P–K4!	P×P
12	P–K5	P×N?

The best defense is *12* ... N–Q4; and if *13* B×Pch!? K×B; *14* N–N5ch K–N1; *15* Q–R5 Q×N; *16* B×Q P×N; *17* B–B6 B–Q1!

13 P×N   P×BP

Of course, not *13* ... Q×P??; *14* B–KN5.

14 Q–R4!   N–B3
15 B×Pch!   ....

Position after 15 B×Pch

15 ....   K–R1

Strangely enough, this is forced. White scores a beautiful victory after *15* ... K×B; *16* Q–R4ch K–N2 (forced); *17* Q–N4ch! K–R2; *18* Q–R3ch! K–N2 (again not *18* ... K–N1; *19* B–R6); *19* B–R6ch K–N3; *20* N–R4ch! K–R2 (*20* ... K×B; *21* N–B5ch compels mate);

21 N–B5! P×N; *22* B×Rch followed by *23* B×Q with a decisive material edge. Quite a curious triangulation of the Queen!

16 B–K4!   ....

Devastatingly accurate. Black can defend after the obvious *16* Q–R4 P–B4; *17* B–N5 P–B3.

16 ....   P–N4

Also bad is *16* ... B–B2; *17* B×N P×B; *18* Q–R4ch K–N1; *19* Q–N4ch K–R1; *20* B–R6 R–KN1; *21* Q–R5.

17 Q–Q1   R–Q1
18 N–Q4!   ....

A clearance sacrifice to give the Queen access to R5.

18	Q–B4
19 B×N	R×N
20 Q–B3	R–R2
21 Q×Pch	K–R2
22 B–K3	B–N3
23 QR–Q1	P–K4
24 B–R6	R–KN5
25 B–K4ch	**Resigns**

One last try would have been *25* ... R–N3 (or *25* ... K–N1; *26* R–Q8ch); *26* Q–N7 mate!

37

HAVANA OLYMPICS 1966
Nimzo-Indian Defense

WHITE: POMAR   BLACK: JOHANSSON

White lays a diabolical trap of uncommon beauty. It succeeds because he sees one move further than his opponent.

1	P–Q4	N–KB3
2	P–QB4	P–K3
3	N–QB3	B–N5
4	P–K3	....

This reply has been fashionable for twenty years. Earlier, *4* Q–B2 was the vogue, and before that *4* Q–N3. Occasionally sharper tries are *4* P–QR3, *4* P–B3, and Spassky's *4* B–N5.

4	....	O–O
5	B–Q3	P–Q4
6	N–B3	P–B4
7	P–QR3	....

More usual is *7* O–O. After the text White has difficulty castling.

7	....	B×Nch
8	P×B	Q–B2
9	Q–B2	....

Not *9* P×QP? P×QP, with a deadly check looming on B6.

9	....	P×BP
10	B×P	P×P

Better is *10* ... P QN3! so that if *11* O–O P×P; *12* BP×P B–R3.

11	BP×P	P–QN3

11 ... P–QN4; *12* B–Q3 Q×Q; *13* B×Q slightly favors White because

of his two Bishops in the ensuing endgame.

12	Q–Q3	B–N2
13	B–Q2	R–B1
14	R–QB1	B–K5
15	Q–K2	Q–N2
16	O–O	....

Finally! Delayed castling is also a trademark of Petrosian. Black's right move now is *16* ... P–KR3.

16	....	P–QR3
17	N–N5!	B×P

More prudent is *17* ... QN–Q2; *18* N×B N×N; *19* Q–B3 R–B2 (if *20* B×KP? N/2–B3 wins a piece).

18	B×KP!	B×R?

After *18* ... P×B! (not *18* ... R×R; *19* B×Pch Q×B; *20* R×R!); *19* R×Rch Q×R; *20* K×B P–R3 White has only a minimal edge.

19	Q–B3!	....

Position after 19 Q–B3

The demonic ultra point. Black cannot reply *19* ... Q×Q? because *20* R×R mates.

19 ....   B–N7

Inadequate, but so is *19* ... N–B3; *20* N×BP!

20 Q×Q   B×Q
21 B×R   B–Q4

On *21* ... B–B3, White has the choice of *22* R×N N×R; *23* B–N7—winning two pieces for a Rook—or, even sharper, *22* P–K4! P–R3; *23* P–Q5 B–K1; *24* P–K5 N×P; *25* B–N7, etc.

22 P–K4!   N×P
23 N×N   B×N
24 R–K1!   P–B4

Forced. On *24* ... B–B3; *25* B–N7! wins.

25 B–K6ch   K–R1

If *25* ... K–B1; *26* B–N4ch K–K1; *27* B×P wins.

26 B×P   B–B3
27 P–Q5   Resigns

After *27* ... B–N4; *28* R–K7 followed by *29* B–B3 cannot be met.

38

BEVERWIJK 1968
Nimzo-Indian Defense

WHITE: DONNER   BLACK: PORTISCH

It is rare that a grandmaster is doomed to heavy material losses already on the thirteenth move. Here is the spectacle: a sudden refutation of a recognized line and an early mating attack.

1 P–Q4   N–KB3
2 P–QB4   P–K3
3 N–QB3   B–N5
4 P–K3   P–B4
5 B–Q3   O–O

Taking the long diagonal under immediate control by *5* ... P–QN3 is desirable, but Black is in difficulty after *6* N–K2 P×P; *7* P×P B–N2; *8* O–O B–K2 (on *8* ... P–Q4; *9* P×P gives good prospects); *9* P–Q5! (O'Kelly–Portisch, Majorca 1967).

6 N–B3   P–QN3

It is more customary to contest the center with *6* ... P–Q4.

7 P–Q5!   ....

The logical reply, bottling up the center in order to cramp Black's game. An alternative is *7* O–O B–N2; *8* N–QR4 P×P; *9* P×P Q–B2!; *10* P–QR3 B–K2; *11* N–B3 P–Q4; *12* P×P N×P; *13* N×N B×N; *14* N–K5 ₁ N–Q2; *15* B–KB4= (Gligorich–Smyslov, Majorca 1967).

7 ....   B–N2

This doesn't help break White's grip. *7* ... P–QN4 offers more practical chances. But not *7* ... P×P; *8* P×P N×P?; *9* B×Pch K×B; *10* Q×N

N–B3; *11* Q–R5ch K–N1; *12* N–N5
with a mating net.

8   P–K4   ....

Position after 8 P–K4

8   ....   P–QN4!?

Sounder is *8* ... PxP; *9* BPxP
R–K1; *10* O–O! BxN (perhaps
10 ... P–Q3 must be played, with
a slight disadvantage in space);
11 PxB NxKP!?; *12* BxN RxB;
13 N–N5 R–K4; *14* Q–R5 P–KR3;
15 QxPch K–R1 (Evans–Pachman,
Venice 1967); and now *16* P–KB4!
RxP; *17* P–B4! gives White a
winning attack—*e.g.*, *17* ... B–R3
(or *17* ... PxN; *18* Q–R5ch K–N1;
19 PxP); *18* B–N2! Q–B1; *19* Q–
N6! PxN; *20* Q–R5ch K–N1; *21*
PxP Q–K1; *22* P–N6.

9   P–K5!   ....

Wasting no time in displacing the
lone defender of Black's King.

9   ....   PxBP ·
10 B–N1!   ....

Black can live after *10* PxN PxB;
11 PxNP KxP. Donner holds his
Bishop to search out Black's King
presently.

10 ....   NxP?

Not dreaming of a disastrous attack
so early, Black acts half-asleep. His
best chance is *10* ... BxP (if *10*
... PxP; *11* B–N5!); *11* B–N5 P–
KR3; *12* B–R4 Q–R4; *13* PxN
BxNch; *14* PxB QxPch; *15* Q–Q2
QxQch (not *15* ... QxR?; *16* O–O);
16 KxQ, and Black can fight on with
three Pawns for his piece.

11 BxPch!   ....

This stock combination is almost as
old as chess itself.

11 ....   KxB

Forced. Of no avail is *11* ... K–R1;
12 N–N5 P–N3; *13* Q–N4 K–N2;
14 Q–R4 R–R1; *15* NxPch BPxN;
16 Q–R6ch.

12 N–N5ch   ....

Position after 12 N–N5ch

12 ....   K–N1

Taken by surprise, Black prepares to
concede his Queen without much of a
fight. But he loses anyway after
12 ... K–N3; *13* P–KR4! NxN;
14 Q–N4 N–K5ch; *15* K–B1 NxN;
16 PxN R–R1; *17* R–R6ch! PxR;
18 PxPch K–R2; *19* Q–N7 mate.

13 Q–R5   Q×N

Now the rest is mere technique; but otherwise *13* ... R–K1; *14* Q×Pch K–R1; *15* Q–R5ch K–N1; *16* Q–R7ch leads to an easy mate.

14 B×Q   N×N
15 P–QR3   N–K5ch

Black continues his desperate resistance: *15* ... B–R4; *16* B–Q2 is even worse.

16 P×B   N–QB3
17 B–K3   N×NP
18 O–O   N–B7
19 QR–B1   N×B
20 P×N   B–Q4
21 R–B4   P–B4

22 P×P*e.p.*   R×P
23 R/1–KB1   R/1–KB1
24 R×R   N×R
25 Q–K5   N–K5
26 R×Rch   K×R
27 Q–N8ch   K–B2
28 Q×P   B–B3
29 P–R4   K–N3
30 P–KN4   K–R3
31 Q–N8   K–R2
32 Q–KB8   N–B3
33 P–N5   N–K5

Black's minor pieces can't do much. If *33* ... N–R4; *34* Q–B7 N–N6; *35* P–N6ch K–R3; *36* Q–B4ch wins a piece.

34 Q–B7   Resigns

39

UNITED STATES CHAMPIONSHIP 1959
Petrov Defense

WHITE: EVANS   BLACK: BISGUIER

An excursion into a forgotten branch of an almost forgotten defense. On move 6 Black plays with the recklessness of an angry bull charging against a locomotive.

1 P–K4   P–K4
2 N–KB3   N–KB3

The Petrov is theoretically sound but strategically limited; despite its drawish reputation it has never been too popular. The counterattack on White's KP averts the pitfalls of the Giuoco Piano, the Ruy Lopez, and other enterprising systems for White.

3 N×P   ....

After the old-fashioned *3* N–B3, B–N5 leads to the so-called Petrov Three Knights Defense, while *4* ... N–B3 produces the Four Knights Game, which was already considered too conservative to be a lethal weapon fifty years ago.

Steinitz opined that the only way for White to gain an advantage is *3* P–Q4. Fischer adopted it against German at Stockholm 1962, where play continued: *3* ... P×P; *4* P–K5 N–K5; *5* Q–K2!? (*5* Q×P P–Q4=)

N–B4? (critical and unclear is
5 . . . B–N5ch; *6* K–Q1 P–Q4; *7*
P×P*e.p.* P–KB4; *8* N–N5 O–O!;
9 N×N P×N; *10* Q–B4ch K–R1;
11 Q×B N–B3); *6* N×P N–B3; *7* N×N
NP×N; *8* N–B3 R–QN1; *9* P–B4
B–K2; *10* Q–B2 with advantage.

| *3* | . . . . | P–Q3 |

Necessary. A standard trap is *3 . . .*
N×P?; *4* Q–K2 P–Q4; *5* P–Q3, etc.

| *4* | N–KB3 | N×P |

Position after 4 . . . N×P

This position was also reached for
the first time in modern world
championship history in the thirteenth and fifteenth games of the
Spassky–Petrosian match 1969, and
Black achieved his objective by
scoring rather short draws in both.

| *5* | P–B4 | . . . . |

Playable but rather harmless, this
offbeat move was introduced by
Dr. Kaufmann of Vienna in the
1890s. White wishes to avoid his
opponent's prepared analysis after
the usual *5* P–Q4, and to steer the
game into original channels.

Spassky played *5* Q–K2 when confronted with Petrosian's "surprise,"
which amounted to a tacit admission
that he could find nothing better in
the main lines either. The fifteenth
game continued *5 . . .* Q–K2; *6*
P–Q3 N–KB3; *7* B–N5 Q×Qch;
8 B×Q B–K2; *9* N–B3 P–B3; *10*
O–O–O N–R3; *11* KR–K1 (the
supposed improvement over *11* N–
K4 of the thirteenth game) N–B2;
12 B–B1 N–K3; *13* B–Q2 B–Q2;
14 P–Q4 P–KR3; *15* B–Q3 P–Q4;
16 P–KR3 R–Q1; *17* P–R3 O–O;
18 B–K3 B–B1; *19* N–R4 KR–K1;
draw. All of which goes to prove
that this endgame is unproductive
for White.

| *5* | . . . . | P–Q4 |

Also good is *5 . . .* B–K2; *6* N–B3
(or *6* P–Q4 O–O; *7* B–Q3 P–Q4;
8 O–O N–QB3=) N×N; *7* QP×N
N–B3; *8* B–B4 B–N5 with even
chances (Teichmann–Marshall, San
Sebastian 1911).

| *6* | N–B3 | B–QB4? |

Here Black is seized by a severe
attack of daydreaming. He provokes
White's next gain of tempo in order
to win a Pawn, but he has no hold in
the center, his King is not yet castled
and he is behind in development.
Correct is *6 . . .* N–KB3.

7	P–Q4	B–QN5
8	Q–N3	P–QB4
9	B–Q3	Q–R4
10	O–O!	. . . .

"White uses his advantage energetically and with classic simplicity"
(Kmoch).

| *10* | . . . . | N×N |
| *11* | P×N | B×P |

Position after 11 . . . B×P

Black not only attacks a Rook, he also prevents a check on the King file. But it is the setting for a debacle.

It is instructive how White now maintains his initiative until the very end, through thick and thin. Black can never recover from the loss of time initiated with his reckless sixth move. Indeed, one of the major theoretical problems facing the second player is how to combine aggression with soundness. This dilemma led me some time ago to formulate Evans' Law: "White, by virtue of his first move, is allowed one minor blunder per game; for Black a slip is fatal." To this precept might be added another: "When you're not winning, you're losing." It is a strange fact that when one side fails to maintain the initiative, the other seizes it.

| 12 | B–N2 | .... |

The main point of the Pawn sacrifice.

| 12 | .... | B×B |
| 13 | QR–K1ch | .... |

The point of the point. Black must move his King (not *13 . . . B–K3?*;

14 P×P), which in turn entails the absence of his KR in the sequel.

13	....	K–B1
14	Q×B	P×QP
15	P×P	N–Q2

Trying desperately to catch up in development. Not *15 . . . Q×QP?*; *16 Q–N4ch* mates.

16	Q×QP	N–B3
17	Q–K5	Q–B4
18	N–N5	B–Q2

This meets the threat of N×Pch and frees the QR. Superficially Black's only problem is the disastrous placement of his King.

| 19 | N–K4! | N×N |

19 . . . Q×P? loses a piece to *20 N×N*.

20	R×N	R–K1
21	Q–B4	Q×P
22	KR–K1!	R×R

Unwise would be *22 . . . Q×B?*; *23 R×Rch B×R*; *24 Q–N4ch*.

| 23 | B×R | Q–K3 |

After *23 . . . Q–QB4*; *24 Q–N8ch B–K1*; *25 B×NP Q–QN4*; *26 Q–Q6ch K–N1*; *27 Q–Q8* wins.

| 24 | Q–N8ch | B–K1 |
| 25 | Q×RP | P–QN3 |

Black has defended sensibly, but his game is lost. Only *25 . . . P–KN3* offers some fighting chances. Then White's most convincing win is *26 Q×P Q×P*; *27 Q–N4ch!* (*27 B–Q5 Q–R6!*; *28 P–N3 Q–Q3* holds) K–N2 (not *27 . . . K–N1?*; *28 B×P*); *28 Q–Q4ch P–B3*; *29 B–Q5 Q–R6*;

30 R–R1 Q–Q3; *31* R–R7ch K–B1; *32* P–N3! and the threat of *33* R–QN7–N6 immobilizes Black—*e.g.,* *32* . . . B–B3; *33* R–B7ch K–K1; *34* BxBch! (not *34* Q–K4ch Q–K4) QxB; *35* RxP Q–B8ch; *36* K–N2, etc.

26 Q–R3ch   Q–K2

26 . . . K–N1; *27* BxPch leads to a hopeless ending.

27 B–B6!   Resigns

Black was hoping for *27* QxQch

KxQ; *28* BxPch, with drawing chances.

Final Position after 27 B–B6

40
U.S.S.R. 1958
Philidor Defense

WHITE: Konovalov   BLACK: Mordkovich

White's gambit on move 7 in a theoretical backwater has never received much attention. Rising to the occasion, Black makes it an old-fashioned slugfest.

1 P–K4   P–K4
2 N–KB3   P–Q3

An erstwhile favorite of Alekhine, this defense has been shunned because it leads to cramped positions —which, according to Tarrasch, "bear the germs of defeat."

3 P–Q4   N–KB3

Nothing new under the sun? Tal–Larsen, 1st Match Game 1969 went: *3* . . . PxP; *4* NxP P–KN3!?; *5* N–QB3 B–N2; *6* B–KB4 N–KB3;

7 Q–Q2 O–O; *8* O–O–O R–K1; *9* P–B3 N–B3; *10* NxN PxN; *11* P–K5 N–Q4!; *12* NxN PxN; *13* B–KN5! Q–Q2; *14* QxP R–N1; *15* B–B6 BxB; *16* PxB Q–K3; and Black managed to draw.

4 N–B3   QN–Q2
5 B–QB4   B–K2
6 PxP   . . . .

For the quiet *6* O–O see the next game. Without this preparatory exchange, the sacrifice on KB7 is not to be recommended—*e.g., 6* BxPch!? KxB; *7* N–N5ch K–N1; *8* N–K6 Q–K1; *9* NxBP Q–N3; *10* NxR QxNP; *11* R–B1 PxP!; *12* QxP (Black got a victorious attack in Rabinovich–Ilyin-Zhenevsky, Moscow 1922, after *12* Q–K2 PxN;

13 Q–B4ch P–Q4; *14* Q×Bch K–B2)
N–K4!; *13* P–B4 N/3–N5! with a
winning attack (Heidenfeld–Wolpert,
Johannesburg 1955).

6 ....   **P×P**

White maintains his grip on *6* ...
QN×P; *7* B–K2 O–O; *8* N–Q4!
followed by P–B4.

7 B×Pch!?   K×B
8 N–N5ch   ....

Position after 8 N–N5ch

8 ....   **K–N1**

Another critical variation is *8* ...
K–N3; *9* P–KR4 (if *9* N–K6 Q–N1;
10 N×BP R–N1) P–KR4; *10* P–B4
P×P; *11* N–K2 B–Q3; *12* P–K5!
(*12* B×P N–K4 gives Black a clear
advantage) N×P; *13* N×Pch K–R3;
and it is not clear how White can
make progress (*14* N–B7ch N×N;
15 N–K6ch wins the Queen but is
insufficient).

9   N–K6   Q–K1
10 N×BP   Q–N3
11 N×R   Q×P
12 R–B1   N–B4
13 P–B3!?   ....

An attempt to improve on *13* Q–K2
B–R6; *14* B–K3 Q×Rch; *15* Q×Q
B×Q; *16* K×B K–B2; *17* N–B7, with
the better ending.

13 ....   **N–N5!**

Now come the fireworks.

14 Q–K2   B–R5ch
15 K–Q2   ....

15 K–Q1 N–B7ch; *16* R×N B×R;
17 B–K3 Q–N8ch; *18* K–Q2 B×Bch;
19 Q×B Q×R; *20* Q×N K–B2; *21*
Q–B7ch would lead to a draw.

15 ....   **N–B7**
16 N–B7   ....

Not *16* Q–B4ch? B–K3; *17* Q×N
N×Pch winning the Queen. Also
inadequate is *16* R×N (or *16* N–Q1
KN×Pch!; *17* P×N N×Pch; *18* K–K3
B–N4ch!; *19* K–Q3 N–B4ch wins)
B×R; *17* N–Q1 Q–N4ch; *18* N–K3
B×Nch; *19* Q×B Q–Q1ch; *20* K–K1
P–QN3 and the stranded Knight
cannot be extricated.

16 ....   **B–R6**

Position after 16 ... B–R6

17 R×N   ....

Simplification is a wise decision. Fantastic complications arise after *17* Q–B4ch N–K3; *18* N×N N×Pch; *19* K–Q1 (too risky is *19* K–K3 N–Q3!; *20* Q–Q5 N–B4ch) N×Nch; *20* P×N Q×Rch; *21* Q×Q B×Q, and Black has all the winning prospects.

17 ....   B×R

18 N–Q1   ....

Not *18* Q–B4ch K–B1; *19* N–K2 Q×BP and wins.

18 ....   B–K8ch!
Draw

A perpetual occurs after *18* K×B Q–N8ch; *19* K–Q2 Q–Q5ch.

41
36th U.S.S.R. CHAMPIONSHIP 1969
Philidor Defense

WHITE: Tscheshkovsky   BLACK: Lutikov

Black attempts a refutation of a refutation which can be found in the books, but one more refutation restores the original judgment. *Plus ça change, plus la même chose.*

1	P–K4	P–K4
2	N–KB3	P–Q3
3	P–Q4	N–KB3

Nimzovich's move forces White to spend a tempo defending his KP, thus lessening his attacking chances.

The Hanham Variation, *3 ...* N–Q2, commits Black too soon and involves him in difficulties after *4* B–QB4 P–QB3 (necessary); *5* O–O B–K2; *6* P×P P×P (I won a quick game against Joyner in the 1956 Canadian Open Championship after *6 ...* N×P?; *7* N×N P×N; *8* Q–R5 P–KN3; *9* Q×KP); *7* N–N5! B×N; *8* Q–R5 P–KN3; *9* Q×B Q×Q;

10 B×Q with two Bishops in a superior endgame.

4 N–B3   ....

Weaker is the once popular *4* P×P, which simplifies Black's problems in the center after *4 ...* N×P. Sokolsky's *5* QN–Q2 leads to nothing because of *5 ...* N×N; *6* B×N B–K2!; *7* P×P Q×P; *8* B–B3 O–O; *9* Q×Q B×Q; *10* O–O–O B–KN5; *11* B–K2 R–K1; *12* KR–K1 N–B3, with a very drawish setting (Boleslavsky–Keres, Moscow 1962).

4	....	QN–Q2
5	B–QB4	B–K2
6	O–O	O–O
7	P–QR4	P–B3
8	Q–K2	P×P

Obviously, Lutikov is veering for a prepared variation since he had already used this against Smyslov at the Tchigorin Memorial, 1960. That game continued 8 ... P–QR4; 9 P–R3 PxP (9 ... Q–B2 maintains the tension); 10 NxP N–B4; 11 R–Q1 Q–B2; 12 B–B4, with a free and easy game for White. As shall be seen, he has a good reason for not wishing White to play P–KR3 before entering upon the following freeing combination.

9 NxP   NxP!?

Without this follow-up, Black's previous move, abandoning the center, loses much of its point.

Position after 9 ... NxP

10 NxN   ....

After *10* QxN P–Q4; *11* BxP (*11* NxQP? PxN; *12* QxP N–N3 wins a piece!) N–B3; *12* BxPch RxB; *13* Q–Q3 N–N5 with a good attack for the Pawn.

10 ....   P–Q4
11 N–KB5!   ....

Black undoubtedly had some improvement in mind over Suetin–Gusev, Tula 1950, which went: *11* B–R2 PxN; *12* R–Q1 B–B3; *13* N–B5! Q–B2; *14* QxP N–B4; *15* Q–B3 B–K4; *16* B–N5! with a clear advantage.

The noted opening authority Bernard Zuckerman commented that the text "seems to be a new move." This tempts one to wonder whether *Modern Chess Openings* (10th ed.) is ahead of its time, since this exact sequence up to move 12 can be found there on page 115. Annotators have access to such sophisticated opening material that they frequently overlook sources available at home!

11 ....   PxB

This must have been the innovation Lutikov was itching to spring. In case of *11* ... PxN, White does not have to retreat his Bishop as in the previous note, and would thus have one extra tempo for the attack. Undesirable as that may be, Black has no choice now. An old Keres analysis runs: *11* ... PxN; *12* QxP B–B3; *13* N–R6ch! PxN; *14* B–Q3 R–K1; *15* QxPch K–B1; *16* BxPch K–K2; *17* KR–K1ch K–Q3; *18* B–B4ch B–K4; *19* QxP, but Black by no means should be counted out.

12 B–R6!   ....

Probably anticipated by Black in his pregame analysis, but strong nevertheless.

12 ....   N–B3

This is the tricky resource Black was relying on. A blunder would be *12* ... B–B3?; *13* BxP! BxB; *14* Q–N4.

The justification of White's last shows up after *12* ... PxB; *13* Q–N4ch B–N4; *14* NxPch K–N2; *15* NxB! (*15* N–B5ch K–N3; *16* P–B4 P–KR4 gives Black chances for a successful defense) K×N; *16* Q–R4ch K–N3; *17* Q×Pch K×N; *18* P–B4ch K–B3; *19* P–B5 with a winning attack.

Position after 12 . . . N–B3

Suddenly White is faced with an unexpected obstacle. On *13* N×P N–N5! (the reason for preventing P–KR3, as noted on move 8); *14* QR–Q1 Q–B2 wins. And certainly not *13* B×P B×N.

13 N/4–N3! . . . .

The refutation of the refutation. Unclear is *13* QR–Q1 B×N! (not *13* . . . Q–B2; *14* N/4–N3); *14* R×Q QR×R; *15* N×Nch (or *15* N–N3 B–K3) B×N; Black has good compensation for the Queen.

The simple yet elegant retreat is precisely the kind of move one is prone to overlook in home analysis.

With one stroke White protects his Knight on B5 and renews the attack on both the Bishop and KNP.

13	. . . .	B×N
14	N×B	P×B
15	N×Bch	K–N2
16	N–B5ch	K–N3
17	N–K7ch	K–N2

Obviously White is repeating moves to gain time on the clock.

18 Q–K5! **Q–N1?**

The threat was not only *19* QR–Q1–Q6 but also *19* R–R3–N3ch. Understandably, Black is anxious to dislodge White's Queen from its dominating post; however, he could offer sturdier resistance with *18* . . . R–K1; *19* KR–K1 Q–N1, frustrating the maneuver which now follows.

19	N–B5ch	K–N3
20	N–Q6	K–N2
21	KR–K1	R–Q1
22	QR–Q1	R–Q2

Shaken by the turn of events, Black can do nothing but wait and see how his opponent applies the finishing touch.

23	R–Q4	Q–B2
24	R–N4ch	**Resigns**

In view of *24* . . . K–B1; *25* Q×N.

HAVANA OLYMPICS 1966
Pirc-Robatsch Defense

WHITE: PADEVSKY   BLACK: MATANOVICH

White gets an extremely dangerous mating attack at the cost of a Pawn. The defender returns the Pawn in an original way, then assumes the initiative himself and concludes with beautifully sharp tactics.

1	P–K4	P–Q3
2	P–Q4	N–KB3
3	N–QB3	P–KN3
4	P–B4	B–N2
5	N–B3	O–O
6	P–K5	KN–Q2

Black finds himself in an inferior ending if he tries to avoid the following wild attack by *6* ... PxP; *7* QPxP QxQch; *8* KxQ R–Q1ch; *9* K–K1 N–Q4; *10* NxN RxN; *11* B–B4 R–Q1; *12* N–N5 (Bronstein–Vasiukov, U.S.S.R. Championship 1966).

7	P–KR4	....

The only consistent follow-up, launching great complications of theoretical importance.

7	....	P–QB4
8	P–R5	PxQP
9	QxP	....

Still not fully explored is the piece sacrifice *9* PxNP!? as in the next game.

9	....	PxKP
10	Q–B2	....

All part of the master plan. White pitches a Pawn in order to switch his Queen to the KR file. *10* PxKP NxP!; *11* Q–KR4 is also difficult, but Black has an out with *11* ... B–B4!

10	....	P–K5!

Position after 10 ... P–K5

Matanovich's new idea, a vast improvement over *10* ... PxBP; *11* PxP RPxP; *12* BxP N–KB3; *13* Q–R4, when White's attack already has gathered too much momentum. Or *10* ... P–K3; *11* RPxP BPxP; *12* Q–N3 PxP; *13* BxP Q–R4; *14* B–Q2 N–KB3; *15* B–QB4 N–B3; *16* O–O–O, and again Black's prospects are sorry.

There are several points to the text. A. If *11* NxP Q–N3; *12* Q–R4 Q–R4ch!; *13* P–B3 QxKRP; *14* QxQ PxQ, and Black's problems are over. B. Black can now return his Knight to KB3 without its being driven away by PxKP. C. The diagonal for White's QB is temporarily blocked, hindering its participation in the attack.

11	N–KN5	N–KB3
12	PxP	RPxP
13	Q–R4	Q–Q5!

A vital link in Black's defensive scheme. He can now answer *14 N–R7* (or *14 QNxP*) by *R–Q1*. For example, *14 QNxP R–Q1; 15 B–Q3 N–B3; 16 P–R3 B–B4; 17 NxNch QxN; 18 BxB QxB* with a positional advantage.

14	N–N5	Q–N3
15	B–B4	....

After *15 NxKP R–K1!* Black staves off mate (*16 NxNch? PxNch*) and White's forces remain disjointed.

15	....	B–N5
16	P–B5!?	....

Throwing caution to the winds in order to get his QB into the fray. Successful or not, it is the only consistent continuation. *16 NxKP* is more prudent; yet after *16 ... QN–Q2; 17 N–B2 B–K3*, Black has snatched the initiative.

16	....	PxP
17	N–R7	QN–Q2

This exchange sacrifice puts the attack to rout.

18	NxR	NxN
19	N–B3	....

Sad but true, White can only retreat. On *19 B–R6 N–R4; 20 BxB Q–K6ch; 21 K–B1 N–N6ch* wins the Queen.

19	....	R–B1
20	B–N3	P–K3
21	Q–B2	....

The attack repulsed, White hurries to exchange Queens before Black starts his counteroffensive. The endgame, nevertheless, is lost.

21	....	QxQch
22	KxQ	N–N3
23	B–K3	....

An amusing line is *23 P–N3 B–B6; 24 R–K1 N–N5ch; 25 K–B1 B–Q5* threatening ... N–R7 mate!

23	....	P–B5
24	BxRP	P–K6ch
25	BxP	....

Hoping to resist in a long ending with Rook and Pawn for two minor pieces. *25 K–N1 N–R4; 26 K–R2 B–K4* is even less appealing.

25	....	RxN!

Position after 25 ... RxN

26	PxR	....

On *26 BxBP N–K5ch; 27 K–B1 RxB; 28 RPxR NxB*, Black would gather four minor pieces for two Rooks and Pawn—a decisive advantage.

26	....	N–K5ch
27	K–N1	PxB
28	B–B4	BxP
29	R–N1	N–Q7
30	RxP	NxB
31	R–B7	P–K7
32	K–B2	B–Q5ch

Winning a whole Rook. *32 ...*
P–K8(Q)ch; *33* RxQ BxRch; *34* KxB
would present some technical difficulties owing to White's QRP.

33 K–N3   N–K6

Again *33 ...* B–K4ch; *34* KxB
BxR; *35* K–B3 would allow resis-
tance. The text menaces *34 ...*
N–B8ch.

34	R–B8ch	K–N2
35	R–K1	B–K4ch
36	K–B2	N–Q8ch
37	K–N1	B–N6
38	RxP	BxR
	Resigns	

"Some like it hot" was the title one
annotator gave this minor masterpiece. It represents the triumph of the
counterattack.

43

U.S.S.R. (POSTAL GAME) 1968

Pirc-Robatsch Defense

WHITE: SOROKIN   BLACK: DUBORIK

Although correspondence chess takes
place far from the hurly-burly of the
tournament arena, it is not lacking in
tension, and many theoretical novelties are rigorously tested there. Here
are some fireworks!

1	P–K4	P–Q3
2	P–Q4	N–KB3
3	N–QB3	P–KN3
4	P–B4	B–N2
5	N–B3	O–O
6	P–K5	....

Less sharp, but quite playable is
6 B–Q3. A lovely miniature which
made the rounds of all the world
chess publications was Baretich–
Pirc, Yugoslav Championship 1968,
which continued: *6 ...* N–B3; *7*
B–K3 P–K4; *8* BPxP PxP; *9* P–Q5
N–Q5; *10* NxP!? NxQP!; *11* BxN
N–B5; *12* B–B1? N–K3; *13* NxNP!?
BxB!; *14* NxR Q–R5ch; *15* K–Q2?
Q–B5ch; *16* K–Q3 Q–K6ch; *17*
K–B4 BxN; *18* PxB P–N4ch; *19* KxP

R–N1ch; White Resigns. Also see
Games 44 and 45.

6	....	KN–Q2
7	P–KR4	P–QB4
8	P–R5	PxQP
9	PxNP!?	PxN
10	PxBPch	RxP
11	B–B4	....

Stronger than *11* N–N5? PxNP!;
12 B–B4 NxP; *13* Q–R5 Q–R4ch;
14 K–B1 P–Q4!; *15* BxNP RxPch;
16 N–B3 PxB; *17* QxPch K–B1, and
Black won (Bykhovsky–Bebchuk,
U.S.S.R. 1966).

| *11* | .... | P–K3 |

Although it requires testing, White
gets a strong attack after *11 ...* N–
B1; *12* N–N5 P–K3; *13* NxR KxN;
14 Q–R5ch K–N1; *15* B–Q3 P–KR3;
16 P–KN4.

| *12* | N–N5 | .... |

After *12* BxP? (or *12* QxP? Q–N3)
NxP! is adequate.

12 .... N×P!

Returning a piece to destroy the center.

Position after 12 ... N×P

13 P×N? ....

Already White goes astray in the complications. He should play *13* Q–R5 immediately. Best, then, is *13* ... P–KR3! (*13* ... Q–R4; *14* P×N transposes to the actual game); *14* P×N P×N; *15* Q–R7ch K–B1; *16* Q–R8ch! B×Q; *17* R×Bch K–N2; *18* R×Q N–B3; *19* R×P N×P; and there is no reason why Black should stand worse in this ending.

13 .... Q–R4?

Sets everything right again. Black could win with *13* ... P×NP; *14* Q–R5 Q×N!

14 Q–R5 ....

The Queen will return twice more to this square, and each time with new threats!

14 .... Q×Pch

If *14* ... P×Pch; *15* K–Q1 P×B(Q)ch; *16* R×Q R–K2 (or *16* ... R–B7; *17* Q–K8ch); *17* Q×Pch K–B1; *18* Q–N6 wins.

15 B–K2 R–B4

Worse is *15* ... R–B3; *16* Q×Pch K–B1; *17* P–QN3 N–B3; *18* Q–Q3, with a threat of *19* N–R7ch or *19* N–K4 or *19* B–R3.

16 P–KN4 P×P

Any attempt to switch to the counter-attack was *16* ... Q–N6ch; *17* K–Q1 R–Q4ch; *18* B–Q3 R×Bch; is exquisitely refuted by *19* K–K2! and the King slips out, while Black has no defense to the mating threats.

17 P×R Q–R4ch

The only move. On *17* ... Q×P (or *17* ... P×B(Q)ch; *18* R×Q Q×P; *19* B–Q3 wins); *18* B×P B×B; *19* B–Q3 is decisive.

18 K–Q1 Q–Q4ch
19 B–Q3 Q×Rch
20 Q×Q P×R(Q)

Position after 20 ... P×R(Q)

Black has found an ingenious defense. Now White is at the crossroads: to play for a win a Rook down or to take a probable draw with *21* Q×Pch K–B1; *22* Q–N6 K–K2; *23* Q–B7ch K–Q1; *24* N×Pch B×N; *25* P×B Q–B3; *26* Q×P Q×P; *27* B–N5ch B–B3; *28* B×Bch Q×B; *29* Q×R.

21 Q–R5!   . . . .

The difficulty in selecting this move is that Black has a great number of ways to defend himself.

21 . . . .   Q–B3
22 PxP   N–B3

Sorokin considers the alternatives: **A.** 22 . . . Q–K2; 23 BxPch K–B1; 24 B–B5 N–B3; 25 B–QR3 N–Q1; 26 N–K4 B–K4; 27 BxP BxB; 28 Q–R8 mate. **B.** 22 . . . BxP (or 22 . . . P–KR3; 23 B–N2!); 23 Q–K8ch B–B1; 24 BxPch K–N2 (or 24 . . . K–R1; 25 B–N2); 25 NxBch KxB; 26 NxBch K–N2; 27 N–K6ch

K–R2; 28 N–N5ch K–N2; 29 B–K3, and Black is in *zugzwang—e.g.,* 29 . . . Q–N3; 30 Q–K7ch.

23 P–K7!   B–N5ch

If 23 . . . NxP (or 23 . . . QxP; 24 B–B4ch); 24 B–N2! wins.

24 QxB   P–Q4

24 . . . N–K4 is more tenacious: but 25 BxPch K–R1; 26 Q–R3 still demolishes the defense.

25 Q–R5   Resigns

If 25 . . . QxP; 26 BxPch K–B1; 27 B–R3! QxB; 28 Q–B7 mate.

44

UNITED STATES CHAMPIONSHIP 1964
Pirc-Robatsch Defense

WHITE: FISCHER   BLACK: BENKO

Although Benko exhibits some suicidal tendencies in the management of his defense, White's nineteenth move is worth the price of admission. The opening is critically important, since Black has no clear-cut way to equalize.

1 P–K4	P–KN3
2 P–Q4	B–N2
3 N–QB3	P–Q3
4 P–B4	N–KB3
5 N–B3	O–O
6 B–Q3	B–N5

Black's path is thorny. Fischer–Perez, Havana 1965, continued: 6 . . . N–B3; 7 P–K5 PxP; 8 BPxP

N–Q4; 9 NxN QxN; 10 P–B3 B–N5; 11 Q–K2, with a pull.

7 P–KR3	BxN
8 QxB	N–B3
9 B–K3	P–K4
10 QPxP	PxP
11 P–B5	PxP

Bednarsky–Kraidman, Tel Aviv Olympics 1964, featured an important theoretical duel after 11 . . . N–Q5; 12 Q–B2 PxP; 13 PxP P–QN4; 14 O–O P–B4; 15 N–K4 P–B5; 16 NxNch QxN; 17 B–K4 QR–Q1; 18 P–B3 KR–K1; 19 K–R1 K–R1; 20 QR–K1 P–N5; 21 PxN PxP; 22 B–B1 P–Q6; 23 P–QN3!

B–R3 (not *23* . . . P–B6?; *24* BxP!);
24 BxB QxB; *25* B–B3! RxR;
26 QxR P–B6; *27* Q–K7! Q–Q3;
28 QxBP P–B7; *29* B–K4 Q–KR3;
30 Q–K7, and White prevailed
shortly.

| *12* | QxP | N–Q5 |
| *13* | Q–B2 | .... |

On *13* QxP N–N5 yields Black
counterplay. White is consistently
striving for domination of the semiopen KB file.

| *13* | .... | N–K1 |
| *14* | O–O | .... |

A worthy alternative is *14* O–O–O
N–Q3; *15* N–K2, dislodging Black's
well-posted Knight.

| *14* | .... | N–Q3 |
| *15* | Q–N3 | K–R1 |

Black enters an inferior ending after
15 . . . P–KB4; *16* B–R6 Q–B3;
17 QxBch QxQ; *18* BxQ KxB; *19*
PxP N/3xP; *20* QR–K1 QR–K1;
21 N–K4.

| *16* | Q–N4 | .... |

To prevent the freeing maneuver
with . . . P–KB4.

| *16* | .... | P–QB3 |

More active is *16* . . . P–QB4!
followed by . . . P–N4.

| *17* | Q–R5 | Q–K1? |

Either *17* . . . N–K3 or *17* . . . P–
QB4 is now essential.

| *18* | BxN | PxB |
| *19* | R–B6! | .... |

19 P–K5 P–KB4! holds for Black.

Position after 19 R–B6

| *19* | .... | K–N1 |

On *19* . . . BxR (or . . . PxN);
20 P–K5 compels mate.

| *20* | P–K5 | P–KR3 |
| *21* | N–K2! | .... |

But not *21* RxN QxP! with chances
for survival.

| *21* | .... | Resigns |

If *21* . . . N–N4 (or *21* . . . BxR;
22 QxP); *22* Q–B5 wins.

45

UNITED STATES CHAMPIONSHIP 1968
Pirc-Robatsch Defense

WHITE: ZUCKERMAN   BLACK: BENKO

Black pursues a known variation disastrously far, and his first original move gets him into trouble! Just when it looks as though he may escape with a draw, two twists seal his fate.

1	P–K4	P–Q3
2	P–Q4	N–KB3
3	N–QB3	P–KN3
4	P–B4	....

The most aggressive continuation aimed at establishing a strong center which is difficult to assail.

| 4 | .... | B–N2 |
| 5 | N–B3 | O–O |

Zuckerman–Benko, U.S. Championship 1967 continued: 5 ... P–B4; 6 B–N5ch B–Q2; 7 P–K5 N–N5; 8 P–K6 (weak is 8 N–N5 BxB; 9 QxN B–Q2; 10 P–K6 BxKP!) BxB; 9 PxPch K–Q2; 10 NxB Q–R4ch; 11 N–B3 PxP; 12 NxP BxN; 13 QxB N–QB3; with chances for both sides.

| 6 | B–Q3 | .... |

6 B–K2 P–B4; 7 PxP Q–R4 gives Black a good game.

| 6 | .... | N–R3!? |

Inferior is 6 ... P–B4; 7 PxP PxP; 8 P–K5 N–Q4; 9 NxN QxN; 10 Q–K2.

The text move has an interesting history. Valvo saw it in a game played in a New York City park. He then showed it to Benko, who proceeded to employ it in a match game against Bisguier. Although it was not successful, it became popular. 6 ... QN–Q2 is also playable: 7 P–K5 N–K1; 8 N–K4 P–QB4, with some counterplay.

| 7 | O–O | .... |

Also strong is 7 P–K5 PxP (7 ... N–K1; 8 O–O P–QB4; 9 B–K3 is favorable for White); 8 QPxP (or 8 BPxP N–Q4) N–Q4; 9 NxN QxN; 10 Q–K2.

| 7 | .... | P–B4 |

Black is now prepared to retake with his QN if White is obliging enough to capture on QB5.

| 8 | P–Q5 | .... |

Better than 8 P–K5? N–KN5!; 9 P–KR3 PxQP; 10 N–K4 N–K6; 11 BxN PxB; 12 Q–K2 Q–N3, with clear advantage (Janosevich–Benko, Belgrade 1964).

8	....	N–B2
9	P–QR4	P–QR3
10	Q–K1	B–Q2
11	P–R5	B–N4

To gain some freedom by exchanging pieces. 11 ... P–K3 is met by 12 PxP PxP; 13 P–K5.

| 12 | Q–R4 | BxB |
| 13 | PxB | P–K3 |

White's attack is already assuming proportions, but perhaps Black can continue to ignore it with *13 ...* R–N1 followed by *... P–N3* with thematic counterplay along the QN file.

14 P–B5! ....

Position after 14 P–B5

Zuckerman observed that "this move came as a disagreeable surprise—my opponent was visibly disturbed." White, of course, was merely reeling off prepared analysis and had consumed virtually no time on his clock, illustrating once more the importance of opening knowledge. Is this chess, the reader may ask, where homework takes precedence over natural ability?

14 ....   PxQP

In case of *14 ... NPxP; 15 B–N5* would prove very strong.

15 PxQP   QNxP

Leads to difficulties. So does *15 ... KNxP; 16 B–N5 P–B3* (if *16 ... B–B3; 17 N–K4*); *17 PxP PxP; 18 Q–QB4!*

Gligorich–Larsen, Beverwijk 1967, arrived at this same position after numerous transpositions. The Danish grandmaster exercised more caution with *15 ... N–Q2; 16 B–N5 P–B3; 17 B–Q2 P–KN4; 18 Q–N3 N–K4;* but White still retained an advantage with *19 P–Q4.*

16 B–N5!   ....

Stronger than *16 PxP NxN!; 17 PxRPch* (if *17 PxN BPxP; 18 N–N5 Q–Q2*) *NxP, etc.*

Also wrong is *16 NxN NxN; 17 B–N5 B–B3!; 18 BxB QxB!*

16 ....   NxN

White still gets a strong attack against *16 ... Q–Q2; 17 N–K4 NxN; 18 PxN,* followed by P–B6.

17 PxN   PxP?

A panicky decision under fire. Imperative is *17 ... P–R3* (not *17 ... P–Q4; 18 QR–N1!* intending R–N6); *18 BxP N–R2,* with chances for survival.

18 R–R4!   ....

Threatening simply *19 R–KB4* with RxP next.

18 ....   Q–Q2

Black is under the impression that White will have no better than a perpetual check, but the position is already lost in any case. Also unsatisfactory is *18 ... P–R3; 19 BxP N–N5; 20 BxB! KxB* (forced); *21 RxNch* (the quiet *21 Q–N3* also does the trick) *PxR; 22 QxPch K–R3; 23 Q–B4ch K–N2; 24 N–R4* with a winning attack.

Position after 20 ... Q×R

19	B×N	B×B
20	Q×B	Q×R
21	N–R4!	....

A rude shock. Black was braced for *21* Q–N5ch and *22* Q–B6ch with a perpetual. Now he must give up his Queen to avoid mate. Therefore—

| 21 | .... | **Resigns** |

46

HASTINGS 1968–69
Pirc-Robatsch Defense

WHITE: SMEJKAL   BLACK: SMYSLOV

Tournament winner Smyslov's only loss, against a promising young Czech player. Black makes one inadvertent move and the roof caves in.

1	P–K4	P–KN3
2	P–Q4	B–N2
3	P–QB3	....

An unpretentious system aimed at bolstering the center.

3	....	P–Q3
4	P–KB4	N–KB3
5	P–K5	N–Q4
6	N–B3	O–O

The game has the earmarks of an Alekhine's Defense, where White has abstained from driving the Knight away with P–QB4. Black has nothing to fear—yet!

7	B–B4	P–QB3
8	P–QR4	N–R3
9	O–O	QN–B2
10	Q–K1	P–B3

A handy defensive move which not only assails White's central Pawn wedge but also prevents the maneuver Q–R4 and N–N5.

| 11 | Q–R4 | B–K3 |
| 12 | N–R3 | .... |

The threat was ... N×KBP!

12	....	Q–Q2
13	B–Q2	P–QN4
14	B–Q3	N/4–N3
15	RP×P	P×NP
16	QR–K1	P–QR3?

Underestimating White's attack. Better is *16* ... QP×P; *17* BP×P

P–QR3, with a difficult game for both sides.

17 P×QP   P×P

Position after 17 . . . P×P

18 R×B!   Q×R

Of no help is *18* . . . N×R; *19* P–B5.

19 P–B5   P–N4

More resistance might be offered by *19* . . . P×P; *20* P–KN4 Q–B2; *21* B×BP P–R3. Smylsov, however, is still shaken by White's eighteenth move.

20 N×KNP!   P×N
21 B×KNP   Q–Q2
22 P–B6   B–R1

For the nonce Black has succeeded in staving off mate and holding on to his extra Rook. But White's next squelches all hope.

23 B–B5   N–K3

After *23* . . . Q–B2; *24* Q–N3 threatens a devastating discovered check.

24 Q–N4   K–B2
25 Q–R5ch   K–N1
26 Q–N4   K–B2
27 B×P!   K–K1

Forced. If *27* . . . N×B; *28* Q–R5ch K–K3; *29* B–B5ch wins.

White lost nothing by repeating moves and gained time on the clock.

28 P–B7ch   R×P
29 B–N6   N–Q1

If *29* . . . N×B; *30* Q×N regains the sacrificed material with dividends.

Position after 29 . . . N–Q1

30 Q–R5   . . . .

Intensifying the pin and hitting the Bishop as well.

30 . . . .   Q–K3

A desperate attempt to make room for the King at Q2. *30* . . . B–N2 loses to *31* B×N.

31 Q×Bch   K–Q2
32 B×R   Resigns

After *32* . . . N×B; *33* Q–N7, Black must lose a piece.

47

AMSTERDAM INTERZONAL 1964
Queen's Gambit Accepted

WHITE: FOGUELMAN   BLACK: BRONSTEIN

Black's speculative Pawn sacrifice in the opening pays dividends when White allows his Queen to be cut off from the scene of action. Such gambles, however, rarely succeed against precise defense.

1	P–Q4	P–Q4
2	P–QB4	PxP
3	N–KB3	N–KB3

Usually Black precedes his next with 3 ... P–QR3 first, for reasons apparent in the note to Black's seventh move.

4	P–K3	B–N5!?

More customary is 4 ... P–K3; 5 BxP P–B4. An interesting switch into the Gruenfeld is possible with Smyslov's 4 ... P–KN3; 5 BxP B–N2; 6 O–O O–O (more active is 6 ... P–B4; 7 PxP Q–B2); 7 N–B3 KN–Q2; 8 P–K4! N–N3; 9 B–K2 B–N5; 10 B–K3 N–B3; 11 P–Q5 BxKN; 12 BxB N–K4; 13 B–K2, with initiative (Portisch–Gheorghiu, Havana 1966).

5	BxP	P–K3
6	Q–N3	....

The acid test. Weaker is 6 P–KR3 B–R4; 7 N–B3 P–QR3; 8 P–KN4 B–N3; 9 N–K5 KN–Q2; 10 NxB RPxN; 11 Q–B3 N–QB3; 12 B–Q2 N–N3= (Borisenko–Lutikov, U.S.S.R. Championship 1968).

6	....	BxN
7	PxB	P–B4!?

Had Black interpolated 3 ... P–QR3, he could now defend his QNP with either 7 ... P–QN4 or 7 ... R–R2. Not appetizing is 7 ... Q–B1 (or 7 ... P–QN3; 8 N–B3 B–K2; 9 P–Q5 PxP; 10 NxP O–O; 11 NxBch); 8 N–B3 QN–Q2; 9 P–K4 N–N3; 10 B–K2 B–K2; 11 B–K3 O–O; 12 R–QB1 Q–Q2; 13 O–O, with two Bishops and a dominating center (Evans–Siemms, Hollywood 1954).

8	QxP	QN–Q2

Position after 8 ... QN–Q2

Should Black get away with this gambit? Admittedly White's King side is busted and his Queen has been plunged out of play; but he has the two Bishops, and a Pawn is a Pawn is a Pawn. Clearly Bronstein, since he is the stronger player, is

"Laskerizing"—selecting a doubtful variation in order to mix it up.

9 P×P   . . . .

While playable, this capture only serves to develop Black's KB with gain of time. More aggressive is 9 R–N1!

9 . . . .   B×P
10 P–B4   O–O
11 O–O?   . . . .

An inaccuracy. Much safer is *11* N–B3 to prevent Black's next.

11 . . . .   N–Q4!

Now White's Queen is barred from returning to the King side.

12 R–Q1   . . . .

But this gives Black just the tempo he needs, justifying his speculative variation. Necessary is *12* B×N (or even *12* N–B3) R–N1; *13* Q–R6 P×B; *14* Q–K2 returning the Queen where it is needed.

12 . . . .   R–N1
13 Q–B6   Q–R5
14 N–B3   . . . .

Not *14* Q×N/7? Q–N5ch; *15* K–B1 Q×Rch. This theme also lingers in the sequence.

14 . . . .   R–N3!

Equally convincing is *14* . . . N–K4!; *15* P×N (or *15* Q×B QR–B1) N×N; and if *16* P×N Q–N5ch again picks up the Rook with check.

15 Q×N/7   N×BP!

Position after 15 . . . N×BP

16 N–K2   . . . .

There is nothing better. If *16* B–B1 (*16* P×N? Q×BPch; *17* K–R1 Q–B6 mate) Q–N5ch; *17* K–R1 Q–B6ch; *18* K–N1 P–K4! and the threat of *19* . . . R–N3ch compels White to return the piece with *19* N–K2 N×Nch, etc.

16 . . . .   N–R6ch
17 K–N2   N×P
18 R–Q4   . . . .

Again forced. If *18* N–N3 N×R; *19* Q×N Q×B wins.

18 . . . .   N–N5
19 R–B4   . . . .

19 R×N Q×Rch; *20* N–N3 Q×B wins material.

19 . . . .   Q×Pch
20 K–B1   B×P
21 B–Q5   B×R
       Resigns

On *22* B×B Q–B7 mate.

48
5th MATCH GAME 1961
Queen's Gambit Declined

WHITE: RESHEVSKY   BLACK: FISCHER

For pure excitement, it is difficult to match the "desperado" combinations which predominate in the middle game. Reshevsky emerges with the better of it, but the clock then proves to be his undoing.

1	P–Q4	N–KB3
2	P–QB4	P–K3
3	N–QB3	P–Q4
4	P×P	N×P

Of course 4 ... P×P, leading to the well-known Exchange Variation, is a satisfactory alternative. But it "leads to the kind of wood pushing that always bored me" (Fischer).

5	N–B3	P–QB4
6	P–K3	N–QB3
7	B–Q3	B–K2

Another plan is 7 ... P×P; 8 P×P P–KN3; 9 P–KR4!? (or 9 O–O B–N2; 10 B–K4) P–KR3.

8	O–O	O–O
9	P–QR3	P×P
10	P×P	N–B3

R. Byrne–Bisguier, U.S. Championship 1964 continued: 10 ... B–Q2; 11 Q–B2 P–KN3; 12 B–R6 R–K1; 13 N–K4 QR–B1; 14 Q–K2 P–B4; 15 N–B3 B–B3=.

11	B–B2	....

More flexible is 11 B–K3 followed by Q–K2 and QR–Q1.

116

11	....	P–QN3
12	Q–Q3	B–N2
13	B–N5	P–N3
14	KR–K1	R–K1
15	P–KR4	R–QB1
16	QR–B1	N–Q4
17	N–K4	P–B4!?

Triggering incredible complications.

18	N–B3	B×B
19	N×B!	....

Black had expected 19 P×B N×N; 20 P×N N–R4! threatening ... B×N and ... Q×NP.

19	....	N–B5
20	Q–K3	Q×P
21	N–N5!	Q×Q

Best. Fischer gives 21 ... Q–Q4; 22 Q×N Q×N; 23 N×KP Q×P; 24 Q–R6! with an irresistible attack.

22	P×Q	N×P
23	K×N	N–Q5ch
24	B–K4!	....

Position after 24 B–K4

"I can still hear the audience gasping with each blow, thinking each of us had overlooked it in turn. 'Fischer is winning!' 'Reshevsky is winning!' The true state of affairs will crystallize in a matter of moves" (Fischer).

24	. . . .	B×Bch
25	N×B	N×N
26	N–B6ch	. . . .

White wins the exchange, but on B6 instead of Q6!

26	. . . .	K–B2
27	N×R	R×N
28	P–QR4!	. . . .

Inaccurate is 28 KR–Q1 R–K2! and the Knight clambers into the game via QB2–Q4.

| 28 | . . . . | N–Q3 |
| 29 | R–B7ch | K–B3! |

Black needs his Rook and can ill afford 29 . . . R–K2; 30 KR–QB1.

| 30 | KR–QB1! | . . . . |

To maintain control of the QB file. On 30 R×QRP R–QB1!

30	. . . .	P–KR3
31	R×P	N–K5
32	R–R6	R–Q1!
33	R–B2	. . . .

The only way to keep winning chances. Fischer gives 33 R×P R–Q7ch; 34 K–N1 P–N4; 35 P×Pch P×P; 36 R/1–B6 P–N5; 37 R×Pch K–N4; 38 R–KR6 P–B5—.

33	. . . .	R–Q6
34	R×P	R×P
35	P–QR5	P–B5
36	R–B2?	. . . .

Short of time, Reshevsky returns his material advantage and banks on his Queen-side Pawns. But he should allow a draw with 36 P–R6! P–B6ch; 37 K–B1 R–Q6, etc.

| 36 | . . . . | N×R |
| 37 | K×N | . . . . |

Position after 37 K×N

White is a Pawn down but his Queen-side Pawns look dangerous. Indeed, how can Black get his Rook back in time to stop them?

37	. . . .	R–K4!
38	P–N4	R–K6!
39	P–R6	R–QR6

Now White is stymied and Black is ready to mobilize his King-side Pawns.

| 40 | R–B6? | . . . . |

The only hope is 40 P–N5, but this was the last move of the time control and White had to rely on instinct rather than calculation.

40	. . . .	P–N4
41	P×Pch	P×P
42	P–N5	P–N5
43	R–B8	. . . .

Against 43 R–B1, Fischer gives 43 . . . P–N6ch; 44 K–N1 R–R7!;

45 R–N1 P–B6; *46* P–N6 R–N7ch; *47* K–B1 R–KR7!; *48* K–K1 R–R8ch; *49* K–Q2 RxR; *50* P–R7 P–B7; *51* P–R8(Q) P–B8(Q) and wins, since White has no perpetual.

43	....	K–B4
44	P–N6	P–N6ch
45	K–K1	....

Or *45* K–N2 R–R7ch; *46* K–N1 P–B6 with a mating net.

45	....	R–R8ch
46	K–K2	P–N7
47	R–B8ch	K–K5
48	RxPch	KxR
49	P–N7	P–N8(Q)

Sharper is *49* ... K–K5!; *50* P–N8(Q) R–R7ch; *51* K–any P–N8(Q) mate! The text also wins—by a hair.

50	P–N8(Q)ch	K–B4
51	Q–B8ch	K–K5
52	Q–R8ch	....

52 Q–B3ch K–K4; *53* Q–B3ch Q–Q5; *54* Q–N3ch K–Q4; *55* Q–B3ch Q–K5ch leads to the same fate.

52	....	K–Q5
53	Q–Q8ch	K–B5
54	Q–Q3ch	K–B4
55	Q–B3ch	K–Q3
56	Q–Q2ch	K–K4
57	Q–N2ch	K–B4
	Resigns	

After *58* Q–N5ch K–B3; *59* Q–N2ch P–K4, White no longer has any checks and Black's material superiority holds sway.

49
8th MATCH GAME 1965
Queen's Gambit Declined

WHITE: KERES   BLACK: GELLER

The hallmark of the artist is simplicity. Keres' deceptively effortless attack comes like a storm out of a still blue sky.

1	P–Q4	N–KB3
2	P–QB4	P–K3
3	N–KB3	P–Q4
4	N–B3	P–B4
5	PxQP	NxP

The Semi-Tarrasch Defense. Black recaptures with his Knight, to avoid an isolated QP. A good example of the type of play that results is Petrosian–Spassky, 18th Match Game 1969: *5* ... KPxP; *6* P–KN3 N–B3; *7* B–N2 B–K2; *8* O–O O–O; *9* B–N5 PxP; *10* KNxP P–KR3; *11* B–K3 R–K1; *12* R–B1 B–B1; *13* N–N3 B–K3; *14* N–N5 B–KN5; *15* P–KR3 B–KB4; *16* N/5–Q4 NxN; *17* NxN B–Q2; *18* Q–N3 Q–R4; and it proved impossible for White to capitalize on his slight positional advantage.

6 P–K3   ....

6 P–K4 NxN; *7* PxN PxP; *8* PxP B–N5ch permits Black to simplify, yet has been revived by Spassky.

| 6 | .... | N–B3 |
| 7 | **B–B4** | .... |

Introduced by Botvinnik against Alekhine, A.V.R.O. 1938.

| 7 | .... | N×N |

This exchange tends to give White's center a momentary stability. An alternative is 7 ... P×P; 8 P×P B–K2; 9 O–O O–O; 10 R–K1, as in the aforementioned game; now 10 ... P–QR3 (instead of Alekhine's 10 ... P–QN3) should equalize.

8	P×N	B–K2
9	O–O	O–O
10	P–K4	P–QN3
11	B–N2	B–N2
12	Q–K2	N–R4
13	B–Q3	R–B1
14	QR–Q1	P×P

Opening the game redounds to White's favor. Better is 14 ... Q–B2, awaiting further developments.

| 15 | P×P | B–N5 |

Threatening 16 ... B–B6. One way now for White to maintain tension is 16 Q–K3 B–B6; 17 B–R3. Keres chooses a more direct approach.

| 16 | **P–Q5!** | P×P |

On 16 ... Q–K2; 17 N–Q4 intensifies the pressure (17 ... P×P?; 18 N–B5).

| 17 | P×P | Q–K2? |

To meet the threat of 28 Q–K4. The obvious stopper is 17 ... B–B6 (not 17 ... R–K1; 18 N–K5! with

the added attraction of Q–R5); 18 B×B R×B; 19 KR–K1. White's control of the central files is clear, but not decisive.

| 18 | **N–K5** | P–B3 |

If 18 ... B–Q3; 19 Q–R5 P–N3 (or 19 ... P–KR3; 20 Q–B5; or 19 ... P–B4; 20 B×P B×N; 21 B–K6ch); 20 N–N4! P–B3 (forced); 21 Q–R4!

19	**Q–R5**	P–N3
20	**N×P!**	P×N
21	**B×NP**	....

Position after 21 B×NP

White's major threat is to strengthen his attack with 22 R–Q4 (or Q3).

| 21 | .... | Q–N2 |

Loses quickly. 21 ... R–QB2; 22 P–Q6! B×QP; 23 R–Q3 leaves Black's defenses in tangles. And 21 ... B–R3 allows White the option of 22 B–B5 or 22 P–Q6.

Another try is 21 ... N–B5; 22 R–Q3 N×B; 23 R–KN3 Q–N2; but 24 B–R7ch K–R1; 25 B–B5ch mates in three.

22	R–Q3	B–Q3
23	P–B4	Q–R1
24	Q–N4	B–B4ch
25	K–R1	R–QB2
26	B–R7ch!	....

In such positions combinations come of themselves.

26	....	K–B2
27	Q–K6ch	K–N2
28	R–N3ch	Resigns

50

MOSCOW CHAMPIONSHIP 1964
Queen's Gambit Declined

WHITE: AVERBACH   BLACK: ESTRIN

Prepared variations play an increasing role in modern competition. Here the novelty is White's ninth move, which poses problems.

1	P–Q4	P–Q4
2	P–QB4	P–K3
3	N–KB3	N–KB3
4	B–N5	B–N5ch
5	N–B3	PxP

The Vienna Variation gives rise to tricky complications.

6	P–K4	P–B4
7	BxP	....

The main line is 7 P–K5 PxP; 8 Q–R4ch N–B3; 9 O–O–O B–Q2; 10 N–K4 B–K2; 11 PxN PxP; 12 B–R4 R–QB1; 13 K–N1 N–R4; 14 Q–B2, where White's piece outweighs Black's Pawns (Fine–Euwe, A.V.R.O. 1938).

7	....	PxP
8	NxP	Q–B2

Meets with a stunning rebuff. Alternatives are 8 ... BxNch or 8 ...

QN–Q2 or 8 ... Q–R4; 9 BxN BxNch; 10 PxB QxPch; 11 K–B1 QxBch; 12 K–N1 O–O; 13 Q–N4 P–KN3; 14 Q–B4 N–Q2; 15 P–K5 NxB; 16 PxN K–R1; 17 R–B1 P–K4!; 18 Q–R6 QxRch; 20 QxQ PxN; 21 P–KR4 B–B4; draw agreed (Trifunovich–Gligorich, Mar Del Plata 1953).

9 Q–N3!   BxNch

On 9 ... NxP; 10 QxB NxB; 11 O–O White threatens 12 P–KR4, trapping the Knight, as well as 12 N/3–N5.

And after 9 ... Q–B4; 10 BxN PxB; 11 O–O QxN; 12 QxB N–B3; 13 Q–N3 White stands better—*e.g.*, 13 ... N–R4; 14 B–N5ch (or 13 ... O–O; 14 QR–Q1).

10 QxB   NxP?

Underestimating White's fatal reply. No better is 10 ... QN–Q2; 11 N–N5 Q–B3; 12 Q–QR3!

The best chance, is 10 ... Q–K4.

Position after 10 ... NxP

11	N–N5!	Q–B4
12	QxP	R–B1
13	B–R6	QxPch

13 ... N–Q2; *14* R–QB1 P–QR3 (*14* ... QxPch would lead to the game) is a better defensive try.

14	K–Q1	N–Q2
15	R–K1	N/5–B3

16	BxP	QxQNP

16 ... PxB allows mate in two.

17	R–QB1	Resigns

Final Position after 17 R–QB1

17 ... PxB still allows mate in two. And *17* ... QxN; *18* B–B4ch wins the Queen. Finally, *17* ... K–Q1; *18* BxN wins.

51

REYKJAVIK 1968
Queen's Gambit Declined

WHITE: SZABO   BLACK: SIGURJONSSON

A sleeping beauty. Black's pieces spring to life after the prick of his twenty-first move, which spectacularly opens diagonals for his hemmed-in Bishops.

1	P–Q4	P–Q4
2	P–QB4	P–QB3
3	N–KB3	N–B3
4	N–B3	P–K3

Diverting the game from a Slav Defense into the Gambit Declined, which contains the drawback of bottling up Black's QB. The alternative *4* ... PxP is also playable.

5	P–K3	....

White would probably prefer to develop his Bishop with *5* B–N5 first, but this could get messy after *5* ... PxP (or *5* ... P–KR3!); *6* P–K4 P–N4; *7* P–K5 P–KR3 leading to well-known complications.

5	....	QN–Q2
6	B–Q3	PxP

7	B×BP	P–QN4
8	B–K2	....

And now play has transposed into the Meran Variation. More customary is *8* B–Q3, but White has a twist in mind.

8	....	B–N2
9	P–QR3	....

This is it. After P–QN4, White hopes to render Black's QB lifeless, even if he must neglect the center temporarily to do so.

9	....	P–QR3

9 ... B–Q3 seems more natural, with the idea of meeting *10* P–QN4 with P–QR4 (thus saving a tempo). However, Black's strategy is to permit White to achieve a bind on the Queen side and counterpunch in the center.

10	P–QN4	B–Q3

Szabo–Wade, Haifa 1958, continued: *10* ... P–QR4; *11* R–QN1 P×P; *12* P×P N–Q4; *13* N×N KP×N; *14* O–O B–Q3; *15* B–Q3 O–O; *16* Q–B2 P–R3=.

11	O–O	O–O
12	B–Q2	....

Too passive. Correct is *12* P–K4 P–K4; *13* B–N5.

12	....	Q–K2
13	Q–B2	P–K4
14	QR–K1	....

White's pieces are awkwardly placed. He must be alert to the threat of ... P–QR4 as well as to a break in the center. His entire opening concept is dubious.

14	....	QR–B1

14 ... P–QR4 also merits consideration.

15	N–N5	P–R3
16	N/5–K4	B–N1
17	N–N3	....

More active is *17* P–B4!? P×QP; *18* P×P Q–Q1; but White did not care to isolate his QP in such a fashion.

17	....	KR–K1
18	N–B5	Q–K3
19	P×P?	....

Ill-conceived and relinquishing his absolute control over Black's QB4. Necessary is *19* P–B4.

19	....	N×P
20	N–Q4	Q–Q2
21	N–N3	....

Apparently all is well. White seems to have retained his grip on QB5.

21	....	P–B4!

Position after 21 ... P–B4

This surprising stroke completely refutes White's earlier strategy.

22	N×P	R×N!
23	P×R	N–B6ch!
24	B×N	....

Not *24* PxB? Q–R6.

24	....	BxB
25	N–K2	....

Forced. Again, if *25* PxB? Q–R6; *26* P–B4 N–N5 mates.

25	....	N–K5!
26	N–N3	....

Best. If *26* B–B1 N–N4!; *27* N–B4 Q–N5 is decisive. Also, on *26* N–Q4 BxPch!; *27* KxB BxP!; *28* KxB Q–N5ch; *29* K–R2 R–K4 is the finishing touch.

26	....	NxB
27	PxB	....

Of no avail is *27* R–Q1 BxR; *28* RxB R–Q1.

27	....	NxPch
28	K–N2	Q–B3!

29	P–K4	NxRch
30	RxN	BxN
31	RPxB	R–K4

This timely simplification nets a Pawn and the outcome no longer is in doubt.

32	R–Q1	RxBP
33	R–Q8ch	K–R2
34	Q–K2	P–B4
35	R–Q4	R–B5
36	RxR	QxR
37	QxQ	PxQ
38	K–B3	P–N4
39	PxP	P–R4
40	K–K4	P–B6
	Resigns	

When he stops the passed Pawn with *41* K–Q3, Black simply creates another one after *41* ... P–R5.

52
ZAGREB 1965
Queen's Gambit Declined

WHITE: LARSEN   BLACK: MATANOVICH

This serene game is typical of modern chess. Black holds his own until an oversight leads to a shattering denouement.

1	P–QB4	N–KB3
2	P–KN3	P–K3
3	B–N2	P–Q4
4	N–KB3	B–K2
5	O–O	O–O
6	P–Q4	QN–Q2
7	QN–Q2	....

By transposition, a Catalan System. Some masters prefer *7* N–B3, which could lead to sharp complications after *7* ... PxP; *8* P–K4 P–B4; *9* P–Q5 PxP; *10* P–K5 etc.

7	....	P–B3

Solid. But *7* ... P–QN3 at once is preferable, to profit from White's last, which exerted no pressure on Q5.

8	P–N3	P–QN3
9	B–N2	B–N2
10	R–B1	R–B1
11	P–K3	PxP

This position also occurred in Keres–Ragosin, U.S.S.R. Championship 1947, where Black opted for *11* ... R–B2 with the idea of ... Q–R1 followed by ... KR–B1 and ... P–B4.

12 NxP	P–B4
13 Q–K2	PxP
14 NxQP	BxB
15 KxB	N–B4
16 KR–K1	....

More natural seems *16* KR–Q1. White has a slight advantage in space, but the game has an essentially drawish character due to the symmetrical Pawn formation (2 versus 2 on the Queen side, 4 versus 4 on the King side).

16	Q–Q4ch
17 P–B3	KR–Q1
18 P–K4	Q–N2
19 N–K5	B–B1
20 R–B2	R–K1

Black may be lulled into a false sense of security by the absence of any direct threat. Better is *20* ... P–QR4 to ease the pressure. But not *20* ... N/3–Q2; *21* N/5–B6! RxN?; *22* NxR QxN; *23* P–QN4 winning the exchange.

Position after 20 ... R–K1

21 R/1–QB1	N/3–Q2
22 N–N4	....

Black has virtually equalized; only by moves like this can White maintain his small edge.

22	N–R3
23 P–QR3	N/3–N1
24 R–B4	P–QR3
25 Q–QB2	RxR
26 QxR	P–QN4
27 Q–B3	....

White has won the struggle for control of the QB file, but it is doubtful that this has any great significance. After *27* Q–B7 QxQ; *28* RxQ B–Q3, a draw could be agreed upon.

27	P–N5
28 PxP	BxP

More prudent is *28* ... QxP. Black slowly drifts into trouble.

29 Q–K3	B–K2

Not *29* ... R–B1?; *30* Q–N5! with an attack from out of the blue— *e.g.*, *30* ... RxR (or *30* ... P–B3; *31* N–R6ch K–R1; *32* NxP!); *31* NxP! R–B7ch; *32* K–R3 B–B1; *33* N–R6ch K–R1; *34* QxPch mates.

30 R–B4	....

Planning to resume control of the file with the Rook in front of the Queen. It is understandable that Black busies himself with this positional threat, overlooking the combinative point which it contains.

30	R–QB1?

Tired of prolonged defense, Black misses the right move *30* ... N–KB3.

Position after 30 . . . R–QB1

31 N×P! . . . .

"This is one of the most difficult two-move combinations ever seen in a practical game; not only because *31 . . . P×N; 32* Q–B3 would win, but because of the alternative variation which actually comes about" (*Chess*, a British magazine).

31 . . . . **R×R**
32 N–R6ch! **Resigns**

Mate is unavoidable after *32 . . .* P×N (or *32 . . .* K–R1; *33* B×Pch); *33* Q×P.

53
UNITED STATES CHAMPIONSHIP 1967
Queen's Gambit Declined

WHITE: D. BYRNE   BLACK: BISGUIER

"When you don't know what to do, wait for your opponent to get an idea," advised the wily Dr. Tarrasch; "it's sure to be bad!" Here White's fixation with winning a pinned piece proves to be his undoing.

1	P–QB4	N–KB3
2	P–KN3	P–K3
3	N–KB3	P–Q4
4	B–N2	B–K2
5	P–Q4	O–O
6	O–O	QN–Q2
7	P×P	. . . .

Black's stodgy setup has led, by transposition into the Catalan System. Better is 7 P–N3, since the text frees Black's "problem child," his QB.

| 7 | . . . . | P×P |
| 8 | N–B3 | P–B3 |

| 9 | Q–B2 | R–K1 |
| 10 | P–QR3 | P–QR4 |

And now the game has assumed the characteristics of the Exchange Variation.

11	B–N5	N–N3
12	QR–Q1	N–B5
13	N–K5!?	. . . .

White should now strive for P–K4 by playing *13* KR–K1 first.

| 13 | . . . . | N–Q3 |

Perfectly good is *13 . . .* N×N; *14* P×N N–N5; *15* B–B4 P–KN4; *16* B–B1 N×KP; *17* P–K4 P–Q5.

| 14 | P–B3 | N–Q2 |
| 15 | B–B4? | . . . . |

More consistent is *15* B×B Q×B; *16* N×N Q–K6ch; *17* R–B2 B×N;

18 R–Q3 Q–K2 (if *18* ... B–B4;
19 RxQ BxQ; *20* RxRch RxR;
21 P–K4); *19* P–K4 with chances for
initiative.

15	....	NxN
16	PxN	Q–N3ch
17	K–R1	N–B5
18	N–R4	Q–N4
19	P–K4	PxP
20	KR–K1	....

The die is cast. White prepares the
seemingly devastating threat of B–
KB1.

20	....	B–K3

More forcing is *20* ... PxP; *21*
B–KB1 B–K3, transposing into the
game.

21	B–KB1	....

Consistent. The consequences of
21 RxP NxRP; *22* PxN B–N6 are
ramified, but seem to favor Black.

21	....	PxP
22	R–K4	....

Winning the Knight, but now Black's
counterplay begins in earnest. *22*
R–Q4 would have been met by P–B7.

Position after 22 R–K4

22	....	QR–Q1!
23	R–N1	....

Not *23* RxR RxR; *24* BxN BxB;
25 RxB QxR! (the saving clause);
26 QxQ R–Q8 mates.

23	....	P–N4
24	RxN	....

The point is *24* B–B1 NxRP! wins.

24	....	PxB
25	PxP	....

There is no hope after *25* RxP QxKP.

25	....	Q–Q4!

Avoiding the snare *25* ... BxR?;
26 BxB R–Q7; *27* Q–K4 QxN;
28 BxPch winning the Queen.

26	N–N6	Q–Q7
27	Q–K4	Q–KB7
28	R–B2	....

To prevent ... R–Q7, but now he
loses the Knight.

28	....	QxN
29	B–Q3	RxB
30	QxR	B–Q4
31	P–R3	K–R1
32	R–KB1	R–KN1

Black's Bishops are just too powerful.
White could resign here.

33	R/2–B2	R–N6
34	K–R2	R–N7ch
35	RxR	PxR
36	R–KN1	QxRch!
	Resigns	

Of course, *37* KxQ B–B4ch leads to
mate.

54

VARNA OLYMPICS 1962
Queen's Indian Defense

Sheer fantasy! Tal keeps finding an array of bewildering and unpredictable moves. His opponent finally drops from sheer exhaustion.

1	P–Q4	N–KB3
2	P–QB4	P–K3
3	N–KB3	P–QN3
4	N–B3	B–N5
5	B–N5	B–N2
6	P–K3	P–KR3
7	B–R4	BxNch

Also played frequently is *7* . . . P–KN4; *8* B–N3 N–K5; *9* Q–B2 BxNch; *10* PxB P–Q3, with chances for both sides.

8	PxB	P–Q3
9	N–Q2	P–K4
10	P–B3	Q–K2
11	P–K4	QN–Q2
12	B–Q3	N–B1

Intending . . . P–KN4 and . . . N–N3 with the initiative.

13 P–B5!?   ....

Ultrasharp. If now *13* . . . P–KN4; *14* B–N5ch! P–B3; *15* PxQP QxP; *16* N B4 transforms the position drastically. A steadier course is *13* N–B1.

13 ....   QPxP

On *13* . . . NPxP! Tal said he was considering *14* P–Q5, with control of QB4 and QN5, and possibilities of exploiting the open QN file. This is extremely unclear.

14	PxKP	QxP
15	Q–R4ch	....

Surprising moves follow each other with increasing regularity. Tal is determined to keep the initiative come hell or high water.

15 ....   P–B3

Tal said that on the better *15* . . . N/1–Q2 he intended *16* Q–B2—the two Bishops plus the mobile center would be compensation for the Pawn. But his assessment is too optimistic.

16 O–O   N–N3

If *16* . . . QxBP; *17* N–B4 (or *17* B–R6) QxB; *18* QR–Q1 P–QN4; *19* RxQ PxQ; *20* N–Q6ch K–K2; *21* N–B5ch! with Black's King in a vise.

17 N–B4   ....

Tal had an acute problem choosing the best order of moves. On *17* B–N3 Q–K2; *18* N–B4 P–QN4 follows.

17	....	Q–K3
18	P–K5!	P–N4
19	PxN!	....

Position after 19 P×N

An unexpected Queen sacrifice—only the beginning.

19 ....   **P×Q**

If *19* ... O–O, Tal considered *20* QR–K1 strongest, as after *20* ... Q×R; *21* R×Q P×Q; *22* B×N P×B; *23* R–K7, Black cannot go in for *23* ... R–B2, because of *24* N–Q6!

If *19* ... O–O; *20* QR–K1 Q–Q4; *21* Q–B2 N×B; *22* N–K5 leads to a powerful attack.

20 P×P   **R–KN1**

Now how is Tal to continue? By *21* QR–K1?

21 B–B5!   ....

With only a Bishop as material compensation for the Queen, White gives that away as well!

21 ....   **N×B**

Black rightly goes about his business and captures everything in sight. If *21* ... Q×N; *22* KR–K1ch Q–K3; *23* R×Qch! P×R; *24* B×Nch K–Q2; *25* R–Q1ch K–B2; *26* B–N3ch with a decisive attack—*e.g.*, *26* ... K–B1; *27* B–KB7! or *26* ... K–N3; *27* R–N1ch winning the Bishop.

If *21* ... Q×B; *22* N–Q6ch K–Q2; *23* N×Q defends the Bishop and keeps the initiative.

22 B×Q   **B–R3!**

22 ... P×B; *23* N–Q6ch K–K2; *24* N×B R×P; *25* P–N3 leaves Black's Pawns scattered and weak.

23 N–Q6ch   **K–K2**
24 B–B4   ....

White saves his piece in the nick of time. Incredible.

24 ....   **R×P**
25 P–N3   **K×N**
26 B×B   **N–B4?**

It is a pity that after defending so well Black falters in the absence of a threat. After *26* ... R–QN1 he could hardly lose; his extra Pawn, though weak and doubled, is a safety factor.

27 QR–N1   **P–B3**
28 KR–Q1ch   **K–K2**
29 R–K1ch   **K–Q3**
30 K–B2   **P–B5**

Returning the Pawn in order to squirm out of a potential mating net.

31 P–N4   **N–K2**
32 R–N7   **QR–KN1**
33 B×P   **N–Q4**
34 B×N   **P×B**
35 R–N4   **R–QB1**
36 R×P   **R×BP**
37 R–R6ch   **K–B4**

37 ... R–B3; *38* R×Rch K×R; *39* R–K6ch with *40* R×P next wins.

Position after 37 . . . K–B4

| 38 | R×BP | P–KR4 |
| 39 | P–KR3 | P×P |

40	RP×P	R–R2
41	P–N5	R–R4
42	R–B5	R–B7ch

The sealed move. White's connected Pawns are decisive.

43	K–N3	K–B5
44	R/1–K5	P–Q5
45	P–N6	R–R8
46	R–B5ch	K–Q6
47	R×R	K×R
48	K–B4	R–KN8
49	R–N5	Resigns

55

UNITED STATES CHAMPIONSHIP 1968
Reti Opening

WHITE: BENKO   BLACK: HOROWITZ

Black single-mindedly pursues a consistent strategical idea—the exploitation of White's weak square QN3. This obsession proves to be his downfall, since White's beautiful tactics prevail on the other wing.

1	P–QB4	P–QB3
2	N–KB3	P–Q4
3	P–QN3	N–B3
4	P–N3	P–K3

A similar position arose in Reti–Emanuel Lasker, New York 1924, where Black chose the more enterprising 4 . . . B–B4. Black, of course, rejects 4 . . . B–N5; 5 B–N2 B×N; 6 B×B P×P; 7 P×P Q–Q5; 8 Q–N3 Q×R; 9 Q×P K–Q1 (forced); 10 O–O etc.

The text is extremely passive. 4 . . . P–KN3 comes into consideration.

5	B–KN2	B–K2
6	B–N2	O–O
7	O–O	P–QR4
8	P–QR3	P–B4!?

An obvious loss of time, since the Pawn has taken two moves to reach a square it could have reached in one. But Black has a plan to exploit the supposed weakness on White's QN3; he manages to do so, but at heavy cost.

Better is 8 . . . QN–Q2. (But not 8 . . . P–R5; 9 P–QN4 P×P; 10 N–K5, regaining the Pawn favorably.)

9	PxP	PxP
10	P–Q4	N–R3

A strange place for the Knight, but consistent. *10 . . . P–QN3* is more flexible.

| 11 | N–B3 | B–B4 |

In a roundabout way the opening has transposed into a sort of Tarrasch Defense to the Queen's Gambit, with the difference that Black's QN is on R3 instead of QB3.

12	N–K5!	PxP
13	QxP	N–B4

Apparently White has fallen into the trap and left his QNP vulnerable. If he is obliged to retreat with *14 Q–Q1*, Black would have every reason to be satisfied with his game after *14 . . . Q–N3; 15 NxP NxN; 16 BxN QR–Q1.*

Position after 13 . . . N–B4

14	NxQP!	NxP
15	Q–KB4!	. . . .

Interesting but insufficient is *15 NxBch QxN; 16 Q–KB4 NxR; 17 QxB N–N6; 18 N–N4 NxN!; 19 QxN P–KN3; 20 Q–KB4 KR–K1; 21 B–Q5 P–R5* (Benko).

| 15 | . . . . | NxN? |

Black's last chance to avoid the combination is *15 . . . B–B7; 16 NxBch (16 QR–Q1!? BxR; 17 RxB K–R1! holds) QxN; 17 QR–K1 KR–Q1,* with fair chances of survival.

16	QxB	NxR
17	NxP!	. . . .

The killer. After this unexpected sortie, Black has no valid defense. He was hoping for *17 R–Q1? N–K6!*

Position after 17 NxP

| 17 | . . . . | Q–B1 |

17 . . . N–B2 is refuted by *18 B–K4!* (bringing the fianchettoed Bishop to the center to strengthen the King-side attack is an Alekhine trademark and appears in a number of his famous games) *R–R3; 19 Q–R5! R–R3; 20 QxR!* with a convincing advantage.

17 . . . RxN; 18 BxN is equally hopeless, so Black decides to die with his boots on.

18	N–R6ch!	K–R1
19	QxN	N–B7

Not that it matters at this point, but *19 . . .* Q–K1; *20* R×N would have thwarted the primitive sequel.

20 Q–N8ch!   **Resigns**

The banal smothered mate after *20 . . .* R×Q; *21* N–B7.

56
SOUSSE INTERZONAL 1967
Ruy Lopez

WHITE: FISCHER   BLACK: STEIN

A violent clash of wills between the American and Soviet champions. Fischer's prosecution of the attack is crowned by the brilliant offer of a Bishop, which is declined, carrying the struggle into the endgame.

1	P–K4	P–K4
2	N–KB3	N–QB3
3	B–N5	P–QR3
4	B–R4	N–B3
5	O–O	B–K2
6	R–K1	P–QN4
7	B–N3	P–Q3
8	P–B3	O–O
9	P–KR3	. . . .

The attempt to dispense with this prophylactic move, which prepares P–Q4 by preventing the pin on KN5, has not fared too well. Fischer–Korchnoi, Stockholm 1962, went: *9* P–Q4 B–N5; *10* B–K3 P×P (also good is *10 . . .* P–Q4); *11* P×P N–QR4; *12* B–B2 N–B5 (also playable is *12 . . .* P–B4); *13* B–B1 P–B4; 14 P–QN3 N–QR4; *15* P–Q5 N–Q2; *16* QN–Q2 B–B3, and Black's Queen-side counterplay is sufficient.

9	. . . .	B–N2

An unusual sideline. The better known sequence is *9 . . .* N–QR4; *10* B–B2 P–B4, etc. The text possibly commits the Bishop prematurely.

10	P–Q4	N–QR4
11	B–B2	N–B5
12	P–QN3	N–N3
13	QN–Q2	QN–Q2

More active is *13 . . .* P×P; *14* P×P P–B4.

14	P–QN4!	. . . .

Prevents . . . P–B4 and prepares a dominating buildup with *15* B–N2 followed by P–B4.

14	. . . .	P×P
15	P×P	P–QR4
16	P×P	P–B4

Inferior is *16 . . .* R×P; *17* P–Q5! P–B4; *18* P×Pe.p. B×P; *19* N–Q4, after which White has a target against the isolated QNP.

17	P–K5	P×KP

It is hard to say whether Black would do better with *17 . . .* N–K1 in order to liquidate both White's center Pawns.

| 18 | P×KP | N–Q4 |
| 19 | N–K4 | N–N5! |

Not *19* . . . R×P; *20* N/4–N5! P–R3; *21* Q–Q3 P–N3; *22* N–K6! wins (Fischer).

Position after 19 . . . N–N5

"The idea is to force the Bishop to retreat and thereby hem in White's QR" (Fischer).

| 20 | B–N1 | R×P |
| 21 | Q–K2 | .... |

"Increasing the pressure. Not *21* P–K6 P×P; *22* N/4–N5? (or *22* N/3–N5 B–Q4; *23* N×RP R–B4! holds) QB×N!; *23* N×B B–B3 wins" (Fischer).

| 21 | .... | N–N3? |

Black should take time out to safeguard his King side with *21* . . . R–K1 followed by . . . N–B1. Stein commits the strategical error of so pressing on the Queen side as to allow White to become entrenched on the opposite wing. (Unfortunately Black's King lives there.)

| 22 | N/3–N5 | QB×N |

Fischer gives *22* . . . P–N3 (or *22* . . . P–R3; *23* N–R7! R–K1; 24

N/7–B6ch! B×N; *25* N×Bch Q×N; *26* P×Q winning the exchange); *23* P–K6! P–B4; *24* N–B7! followed by B–N2 with a crushing attack.

23	Q×B	P–N3
24	Q–R4	P–R4
25	Q–N3	N–B5
26	N–B3?	....

Keres recommends *26* N×P!? R×N; *27* B×P, but Black might hold after *27* . . . R–N2; *28* B–R6 Q–B1.

More forcing is Fischer's suggestion *26* P–K6! P–B4; *27* N–B3, transposing into the actual game. The point becomes apparent in the note to Black's move 28.

| 26 | .... | K–N2 |

Keres again recommends *26* . . . N–Q6; *27* B×N (not *27* R–Q1 N×B! and White has nothing) Q×B; but again Fischer points out that after *28* B–N5! White penetrates decisively on the weak dark squares.

| 27 | Q–B4 | R–KR1 |
| 28 | P–K6! | .... |

"This blow rocks the remnants of the tower around the Black King" (Gligorich). Most commentators were impressed by this struggle, and it was voted the best game of 1967 by the jury of the prestigious *Chess Informant*.

| 28 | .... | P–B4? |

Fischer maintains Black could offer stiffer resistance with *28* . . . B–B3!; *29* P×P B×R; *30* P–B8(Q)ch! Q×Q; *31* Q–QB7ch K–N1; *32* B×P N–Q4; *33* Q–N7 N–B3; *34* B–B4 R–KR2!; *35* B×Rch N×B; *36* Q–Q5ch Q–B2;

37 QxQch KxQ; *38* RxB with an
extra Pawn—but a tough ending to
win.

29 BxP!   ....

Position after 29 BxP

29 ....   **Q–KB1**

The only reasonable way to decline
the offer. R. Byrne points out that
29 ... B–Q3 is refuted by *30* P–K7!
BxQ (or *30* ... BxP; *31* Q–N3
R–QR3; *32* N–N5); *31* PxQ(Q)
RxQ; *32* BxB PxB; *33* B–B7! wins.

On *29* ... PxB, White wins rapidly
with *30* Q–N3ch K–R2 (if *30* ...
K–B1; *31* Q–N6 Q–K1; *32* B–R6ch);
31 N–N5ch! BxN; *32* BxB Q–Q6;
33 Q–B7ch K–N3; *34* Q–B7ch! KxB;
35 Q–N7ch K–B5; *36* QR–Q1!
(Fischer).

30 B–K4?   ....

In the heat of battle White misses the
clincher *30* N–R4! BxN; *31* QxB
QxB; *32* Q–K7ch K–N1; *33* Q–
Q8ch K–N2; *34* Q–B7ch K–N1;
35 P–K7, etc.

30 ....   **QxQ**
31 BxQ   **R–K1?**

A better try is *31* ... RxP, but
Black was in extreme time trouble.
Now White wins material and the
rest, though still difficult, enters the
realm of technique.

32	QR–Q1	R–R3
33	R–Q7	RxKP
34	N–N5	R–KB3

Also lost is *34* ... R–R3; *35* B–N1
K–B3; *36* N–K4ch K–B2; *37* NxP.

35	B–B3!	RxB
36	N–K6ch	K–B3
37	NxR	N–K4
38	R–N7	B–Q3
39	K–B1	N–B7

Also insufficient is *39* ... NxB;
40 RxR N–Q7ch; *41* K–K2 BxN;
42 R–B8ch K–N4; *43* RxB KxR;
44 KxN.

40	R–K4	N–Q5
41	R–N6	R–Q1
42	N–Q5ch	K–B4
43	N–K3ch	K–K3
44	B–K2	K–Q2
45	BxPch	NxB
46	RxN	K–B3
47	P–QR4	B–B2
48	K–K2	P–N4
49	P–N3	R–QR1
50	R–N2	R–KB1
51	P–B4	PxP
52	PxP	N–B2
53	R–K6ch	N–Q3

If *53* ... B–Q3; *54* R–B6! puts an
end to all resistance.

54	P–B5	R–QR1
55	R–Q2	RxP
56	P–B6	**Resigns**

57

1st MATCH GAME 1968
Ruy Lopez

WHITE: TAL BLACK: GLIGORICH

Tal is still dangerous, although he has lost a lot of his old fire. Here he tries to land a roundhouse blow but is frustrated by a ruthlessly precise defense.

1	P–K4	P–K4
2	N–KB3	N–QB3
3	B–N5	P–QR3
4	B–R4	N–B3
5	O–O	B–K2
6	R–K1	P–QN4
7	B–N3	P–Q3
8	P–B3	O–O
9	P–KR3	P–R3

This and the following were introduced by Smyslov. Black's idea is to hold the center by ... R–K1 and ... B–B1, while preventing the reply N–N5.

10	P–Q4	R–K1
11	QN–Q2	B–B1
12	N–B1	B–N2
13	N–N3	N–QR4
14	B–B2	N–B5
15	P–QR4	....

This idea was adopted in the 1st Match Game, Evans–Lombardy, 1962. An alternative is *15* B–Q3 N–N3; *16* B–Q2, awaiting developments.

15	....	P–Q4
16	P–N3	....

After *16* PxQP PxQP, Black draws without difficulty (Stein–Spassky, Amsterdam 1964).

16	....	PxKP
17	QNxP	NxN
18	BxN	....

Stein–Reshevsky, Los Angeles 1968, went: *18* RxN!? BxR! (*18* ... P–KB4?; *19* R–K1 P–K5; *20* PxN PxN; *21* RPxP with a great advantage); *19* BxB N–N3; *20* BxR NxB; *21* PxNP PxNP; *22* B–K3 PxP; *23* NxP Q–Q4; and the game was shortly drawn.

18	....	BxB
19	RxB	Q–Q4
20	R–N4	....

A wild try for an advantage. On *20* R–K1 N–R4; *21* PxNP NxP; *22* RxP PxP! equalizes.

20	....	N–R4
21	BxP	NxP

Position after 21 ... NxP

22	R–R3!?	....

Mixing it up. The 5th Match Game was quickly drawn after *22* R–N1 P×RP; *23* N×P Q–K3!; *24* Q–B3 P–QB4, etc.

22 ....   P×RP

The Rook is untouchable—*22* ... B×R?; *23* R×Pch K–R1; *24* N–N5 R–K2; *25* Q–R5 wins. But *22* ... N–B4; *23* P×NP P–B4 merits attention.

23 R×P   QR–N1
24 R×P   ....

Not best. After the game Gligorich suggested *24* Q–KB1, and Tal thought that *24* B–K3 was right.

24 ....   P×P

Possibly stronger is *24* ... R–R1.

25 P×P?   ....

After *25* N×P N×N; *26* Q×N Q×Q; *27* P×Q, White is a Pawn ahead in the ending, but Tal thought there were too many technical difficulties to force a win; however, that was the path he should have taken.

25 ....   P–QB4

Much stronger is *25* ... R–R1! when White must address himself to the threat of ... R–R8 as well as ... P–QB4 and ... P–KB4.

26 B–K3   R–N5
27 R–N5   Q–N2
28 R–R6!   N×P

Simpler was *28* ... P–N3; White then must sacrifice a Rook on KN6 to obtain a draw.

29 N×N   R–N8
30 B–B1   Q–N7

Finally Black starts playing for the win. On *30* ... P×N; *31* Q–R5! R×Bch; *32* K–R2 B–Q3ch; *33* R×B Q–B2; *34* Q–R6! retains the edge.

31 Q–R5?   ....

A faulty combination, which nearly succeeds. Correct is *31* N–N3 Q–K7 (*31* ... Q×N allows *32* Q–R5!); *32* Q–Q5, with a keen struggle.

31 ....   Q×Bch
32 K–R2   B–Q3ch
33 R×B   Q–B5ch
34 R–N3   Q×R
35 N–B5   ....

Position after 35 N–B5

White's attack looks formidable. Alas, fortune does not always favor the brave.

35 ....   R/1–K8!

This is what Tal must have overlooked. The mate threat compels White to engage in unfavorable simplifications.

36 Q×Pch   K×Q
37 N×Qch   K–K3
38 R–N6ch   K–Q4
39 N–B5   R–N2
40 N–K3ch   R×N!

Very pretty. Black eliminates all technical problems.

41 PxR	R–QB2
42 K–N3	P–B5

43 K–B4	P–B6
44 P–K4ch	K–B5
45 R–QR6	P–B7
46 R–R1	K–Q6
Resigns	

58

HAVANA 1965
Ruy Lopez

WHITE: IVKOV   BLACK: DONNER

"This is the kind of game that I always admire: a new idea in the opening, an excellent conception of the middle game and, finally, a spectacular King-side attack involving some sacrifices" (Rossolimo).

1 P–K4	P–K4
2 N–KB3	N–QB3
3 B–N5	P–QR3
4 B–R4	N–B3
5 O–O	NxP

After a long interment the Open Defense has achieved sporadic popularity. One reason is that the Closed Variation has been analyzed to death.

6 P–Q4	P–QN4
7 B–N3	P–Q4
8 PxP	B–K3
9 Q–K2	N–B4
10 R–Q1	NxB
11 BPxN!?	....

An original idea, good for surprise value. A thwarted brilliancy with important theoretical implications occurred in Rogoff–Tarjan, U.S. Junior Championship 1968, after the usual *11* RPxN Q–B1; *12* P–B4 QPxP; *13* PxP BxP; *14* Q–K4 N–N5; *15* N–R3 B–N6; *16* NxP!? R–QN1 (an improvement over *16* ... BxR; *17* NxPch QxN; *18* QxRch K–Q2; *19* B–N5—Gipslis–Haag, Asztalos Memorial 1964); *17* N–Q6ch PxN; *18* PxPch Q–K3; *19* P–Q7ch K–Q1; *20* B–N5ch P–B3; *21* Q–KB4 Q–N3! (and not *21* ... R–N2?; *22* N–Q4!) with Black on top.

11	B–K2

Perhaps Black should regroup with *11* ... N–N1; *12* B–N5 B–K2; *13* BxB QxB; *14* N–B3 P–QB3.

12 N–B3	O–O
13 B–K3	N–R4
14 QR–B1	N–N2
15 N–K4	B–KN5

Black's problem is the inability to enforce ... P–QB4. If *15* ... R–B1; *16* N–B5 NxN; *17* BxN P–QB3; *18* N–Q4 is too powerful.

16 P–KR3	BxN

Weak is *16 ... B–R4; 17 N–N3
B–N3; 18 Q–Q2 B–K5; 19 N×B P×N;
20 Q–B2* etc.

17 Q×B   P–QB3?

Hoping for *18 R×BP? Q–K1* winning
a piece. However, he should hasten
to simplify with *17 ... P×N; 18
R×Q P×Q; 19 R×QR R×R; 20 R×P
B–Q3!; 21 P×B N×P; 22 P×P N–B4;
23 P–QR4 P–N3; 24 R–N7 N×B;
25 P×N R–QB1; 26 P×P P×P;
27 R×NP R–B7*, with a theoretically
drawn ending.

18 N–N3   R–B1
19 N–B5   P–N3?

The last chance to defend was with
18 ... K–R1; 19 Q–N3 R–KN1;
although White has a firm grip,
there would be no immediate way to
win. The text allows a brilliant
conclusion.

Position after 19 ... P–N3

20 R×QP!   Q–K1

Hopeless, as is *20 ... P×R; 21
R×R Q×R; 22 N×Bch.*

21 B–R6   Resigns

He's had enough.

59
MOSCOW 1967
Ruy Lopez

WHITE: TAL   BLACK: KERES

Despite the firm advocacy of Tarrasch and Euwe, the Open Defense
to the Lopez has never enjoyed a
wide following. Here Black uncorks
an improvement that gives him a
won game before Tal can even get
his pieces out.

1	P–K4	P–K4
2	N–KB3	N–QB3
3	B–N5	P–QR3
4	B–R4	N–B3
5	O–O	N×P
6	P–Q4	P–QN4
7	B–N3	P–Q4

It is not advisable for Black to vary
from the ordained sequence. Trifunovich tried to rehabilitate *7 ...
P×P*, against Fischer at Bled 1961,
and met with a rebuff after *8 R–K1
P–Q4; 9 N–B3 B–K3; 10 N×N P×N;
11 R×P B–K2; 12 B×B P×B; 13 N×P
O–O; 14 Q–N4 N×N; 15 R×N Q–B1;
16 R–K4 R–B3; 17 B–K3.* Black's
neurotic KP could not be cured.

8	P×P	B–K3
9	Q–K2	B–K2
10	P–B3	O–O
11	B–B2?	....

Bronstein has had some success with this rare attempt to dislodge the Knight, avoiding the simplifications of the usual *11* QN–Q2.

11 ....   **Q–Q2!**

A Pawn sacrifice originally recommended by Dr. Euwe. After *12* BxN PxB; *13* QxKP B–Q4, there is no good way for White to keep his Pawn. If *14* R–Q1 (or *14* Q–K2 BxN; *15* PxB!? Q–B4; *16* P–KB4 P–B3 with advantage) BxQ; *15* RxQ QR–Q1; *16* RxR RxR; *17* QN–Q2 BxN; *18* PxB NxP, and White is badly off.

12 **R–Q1**   **P–B4**
13 **QN–Q2**   ....

Black obtains great activity after *13* PxPe.p. NxP/3; *14* N–N5 B–KN5; *15* P–B3 B–B4ch; *16* K–R1 QR–K1.

13 ....   **K–R1!**

Position after 13 . . . K–R1

Anchoring the Knight on K5. The game reaches its climax right here. White's last two moves were to eliminate the powerfully posted Knight; but the text all but refutes this strategy and sets his game tumbling downhill.

14 **N–N3**   ....

If *14* NxN BPxN; *15* BxP PxB!; *16* RxQ PxN; *17* Q–Q1 BxR; *18* QxB QR–Q1, and White must remain a piece down after returning the Queen. With Black's King still in N1, he could have broken up this combination by *19* Q–K6ch and *20* B–K3.

14 ....   **B–B2!**

This move may look quiet, but it is deadly, since White must now cope with the vicious pin . . . B–R4.

15 **QN–Q4**   ....

15 KN–Q4 NxKP; *16* P–B3 B–R4; *17* Q–K1 P–B4 leaves White busted.

15 ....   **B–R4**
16 **NxBP!?**   ....

A desperate attempt to fish in troubled waters. The passive *16* NxN QxN; *17* Q–Q3 Q–KN3! leaves White all tied up; but he still has a chance to live after *18* R–K1 P–B5; *19* N–Q2.

16 ....   **QxN**
17 **RxP**   **B–N3**

Not only defending the Knight but threatening the brutal . . . NxQBP.

18 **Q–K3**   **QR–Q1**
19 **RxR**   **RxR**
20 **N–Q4**   **NxN**
21 **PxN**   **P–B4!**
22 **P–Q5**   ....

It's all over after *22* P–B3 PxP!; *23* Q–K1 (if *23* QxN Q–QB1!) P–Q6; *24* PxN QxP/5; *25* QxQ BxQ; *26* B–N1 P–Q7.

22	....	QxP
23	P–B3	B–N4!
24	P–B4	QxQP
25	BxN	BxB
26	PxB	....

Position after 26 PxB

Finally White has reestablished material equality—at the cost of his

King. The next few moves are forced.

26	....	Q–Q8ch
27	K–B2	Q–B7ch
28	Q–K2	R–B1ch
29	K–K1	Q–R5
30	P–QN3	....

There is no defense, but the longest go at it is *30* B–Q2 Q–Q5; *31* B–K3 Q–N5ch; *32* B–Q2 (or *32* Q–Q2 Q–B5; *33* B–B2 BxP; *34* Q–K2 Q–N5ch; *35* Q–Q R–K1ch; *36* B–K3 Q–KB5 wins) QxP; *33* R–B1, and the end is not long in coming.

30	....	Q–Q5

Resigns

On *31* B–N2 Q–N8ch; *32* K–Q2 R–Q1ch; *33* K–B3 Q–Q5 mate. A pleasing and forceful Black effort.

60

MARIANSKE LAZNE 1962

Ruy Lopez

WHITE: GUFELD   BLACK: KAVALEK

This combines unusual theoretical value with a setting unique in the annals of chess history—Bishop and Pawns slaying two Rooks!

1	P–K4	P–K4
2	N–KB3	N–QB3
3	B–N5	B–B4
4	P–B3	P–B4!?

Riskier but more aggressive than *4* ... KN–K2; *5* O–O B–N3; *6* P–Q4, etc.

5	P–Q4	PxKP

5 ... PxQP; *6* P–K5 PxP; *7* NxP offers White good perspectives, but has not been tested sufficiently in modern play.

6	N–N5	....

Probably best is *6* PxB PxN; *7* QxP. Unclear is *6* BxN QPxB; *7* NxP B–Q3; *8* O–O Q–R5.

6	....	B–N3

One of the shortest master games on record is Vasiukov–Giterman,

U.S.S.R. Championship Preliminaries 1960: *6* . . . B–K2; *7* P×P N×P?; *8* N–K6 Resigns!

7   P–Q5   . . . .

Barden suggests *7* N×KP. There is nothing wrong with the text either.

7   . . . .   P–K6!
8   N–K4   . . . .

Better than *8* P×N NP×P; *9* B×KP B×B; *10* N–K4 Q–R5; *11* B–Q3 B–N3; *12* QN–Q2 P–Q4 (Trappl–Rhiha, Prague 1962).

8   . . . .   Q–R5

Possibly stronger is Bondarevsky's suggestion *8* . . . N–B3; *9* P×N NP×P.

9   Q–B3   N–B3

Not *9* . . . P×Pch; *10* K–B1 N–Q1?; *11* B–N5 winning the Queen.

10   N×Nch   P×N
11   P×N   . . . .

This is White's last chance to avoid complications with *11* B×P B×B; *12* Q×B N–K2.

11   . . . .   P×Pch

Position after 11 . . . P×Pch

12   K–Q1   . . . .

White might try to pick off the bone in his throat on KB2 if possible, but *12* K–B1 QP×P; *13* B–K2 R–KN1!; *14* B–K3 (weaker is *14* Q–R5ch Q×Q; *15* B×Qch K–K2; *16* N–Q2 B–R6!; *17* B–B3 QR–Q1 with a bind) B–N5; *15* Q×P/2 Q×Qch; *16* K×Q B×B; *17* K×B R×Pch; *18* K–B3 R×NP gives Black four Pawns for the piece, with a continuing initiative.

12   . . . .   QP×P
13   B–K2   B–K3
14   Q–R5ch   Q×Q
15   B×Qch   K–K2
16   P–QN3   . . . .

This doesn't work, but it is already difficult for White to organize his forces efficiently. An alternative is *16* N–Q2 followed by K–K2, although Black still remains for choice.

16   . . . .   B–Q4
17   B–R3ch   K–K3
18   B–N4ch   P–B4
19   B–R3   KR–KN1
20   N–Q2   B×P
21   B×B   R×B
22   R–KB1   . . . .

If *22* N–B4 (*22* K–K2? P–B8ch) R–N8ch; *23* K–K2 QR–KN1; *24* N×B R×KR!; *25* R×R R–N8 wins.

22   . . . .   R–Q1
23   K–K2   R×Nch!
24   K×R   P–K5
25   B–B8   P–B5
26   P–N4   R–N4!
27   B–B5   R×B!
28   P×R   B×P

Position after 28 ... BxP

Black still has all eight Pawns after twenty-eight moves!

This setting is so rare that it deserves a picture—White is helpless against the Pawn steamroller.

29	QR–N1	K–B4
30	R–N4	P–B6
31	R–Q4	BxR
32	PxB	K–B5
33	RxP	P–K6ch
34	K–K1	PxRch
35	KxP	

And White lost by overstepping the time limit.

61
ZURICH 1959
Sicilian Defense

WHITE: TAL   BLACK: NIEVERGELT

Rather than yield the initiative, Tal embarks on a typically speculative sacrifice. One surprise follows another until Black cracks under the pressure.

1	P–K4	P–QB4
2	N–KB3	N–QB3
3	P–Q4	PxP
4	NxP	N–B3
5	N–QB3	P–Q3
6	B–KN5	P–K3

Larsen has experimented with *6 ... B–Q2.*

7	Q–Q2	P–KR3

Tal–R. Byrne, Havana Olympics 1966, continued: *7 ... P–QR3; 8 O–O–O B–Q2; 9 P–B4 B–K2; 10 N–B3 P–N4; 11 BxN PxB; 12 P–B5! Q–R4 (12 ... P–N5; 13 N–K2*

P–K4 is probably necessary); 13 K–N1 O–O–O; 14 P–KN3 K–N1; 15 B–R3 with lasting pressure.

8	BxN	PxB
9	O–O–O	P–R3
10	P–B4	B–Q2
11	B–K2	....

Superficial. Much more forceful is *11 P–KN3* followed by B–R3 and P–B5, as in the above-quoted game.

11	....	P–KR4
12	K–N1	Q–N3
13	N–N3	O–O–O
14	KR–B1	B–K2
15	R–B3	....

The Rook hopes to find employment on the third rank, where it is free to shuttle to either wing. The immediate threat is R–R3.

15	....	QR–N1
16	B–B1	K–N1
17	R–Q3	B–QB1
18	P–QR3	P–R5
19	Q–K1	R–N5
20	N–Q5!?	....

Position after 20 N–Q5

The first of several unexpected ripostes. Black is forced to capture, but the resulting position is by no means unfavorable for him.

20	....	P×N
21	P×P	N–K4
22	P×N	BP×P

The net result is that Black has straightened out his Pawns and opened diagonals for his two Bishops. White must attack now or sustain the disadvantage.

| 23 | N–R5 | B–Q1 |

Safer is *23* ... K–R1.

| 24 | N–B6ch! | K–R1 |

Not *24* ... P×N; *25* R–QN3 winning the Queen.

| 25 | R–QN3 | Q–B2 |

An error is *25* ... Q–B4?; *26* N×P! P×N; *27* R–QB3, and *28* R×Bch next.

| 26 | R–QB3!? | .... |

Tal writes: "After *26* N×B Q×N, White has no attack, and Black would be in a better position. Therefore I decided to sacrifice a piece. Because of this sacrifice I was criticized considerably and heard: 'It was incorrect' ... 'Tal was lucky' ... 'It was a bluff' ... 'Tal was dead lost'—but I did not see at what point I was dead lost; and concerning the other accusations of the wise critics, I console myself with pleasure that the chess fan, the spectator, and the reader are happy only when the grandmaster *risks*, rather than just 'pushes wood.' "

26	....	P×N
27	R×P	Q–N2
28	R×P	....

Black gets too much for the Queen after *28* B×P Q×B; *29* R×Qch B×R. So White decides to capture a second Pawn and keep up the pressure.

| 28 | .... | R–R5? |

Stronger is *28* ... Q–K2; *29* R–QB6 B–N2; *30* P–Q6 Q–Q2; *31* R–B3 P–K5.

| 29 | R–Q3 | B–B2 |
| 30 | R–KB6 | B–Q1 |

If *30* ... P–K5; *31* R–QB3 B–K4; *32* R/6–B6 B×R; *33* Q×B R–Q1; *34* R–B7 Q–N1 (not *34* ... R×P?; *35* Q–B5); *35* Q–B6ch B–N2; *36* R×B Q×R; *37* Q×R Q×P; *38* Q×Pch K–N1, White has at least a draw by perpetual.

| 31 | R–B6 | P–K5 |

After *31* ... R–K1! White has no immediately decisive continuation.

32 R–QN3   B–R4

Not *32* ... Q–Q2?; *33* Q–B3!

33 Q–K3   Q–R2

Position after 33 ... *Q–R2*

34 Q–R6!   ....

The final bolt. Had Tal not risked, such a complex setting would not have arisen. Of course, the Queen is immune, because of *35* R×Bch.

34	....	R–Q1
35	B×P	B–Q7
36	Q–B6	Q–Q2
37	B×B	Resigns

On *37* ... R×B; *38* R–R6ch forces mate. A startling climax.

62

VARNA OLYMPICS 1962
Sicilian Defense

WHITE: TAL   BLACK: MOHRLOK

"This was the only game I played in 1962 which I felt satisfied about," Tal has said. Yet like many of his vintage brilliancies it has a murky quality and one cannot help wondering how he would have fared had his nemesis, Korchnoi, conducted the defense.

1	P–K4	P–QB4
2	N–KB3	N–QB3
3	P–Q4	P×P
4	N×P	N–B3
5	N–QB3	P–Q3
6	B–KN5	....

The once feared but now seldom seen Rauzer Variation. When Tal played this against Larsen, 6th Match Game 1969, his opponent wrote: "A pleasant surprise!" How fashions change! *6* B–QB4 is all the rage now.

6	....	P–K3
7	Q–Q2	B–K2
8	O–O–O	O–O
9	N–N3	....

"This gives a more interesting game than *9* P–B4 N×N; *10* Q×N Q–R4; *11* P–K5, which usually results in an early draw" (Tal). To avoid this prospect, Tal varied with *11* B–B4 in the above-quoted game, and Larsen equalized with *11* . . . B–Q2; *12* K–N1 B–B3; *13* KR–B1 P–KR3; *14* B–R4 Q–R4!

9 . . . .   Q–N3

9 . . . P–QR3!?; *10* BxN PxB (or *10* . . . BxB; *11* QxP BxN; *12* PxB Q–B3; *13* Q–N3 with advantage— Tal–Kramer, Varna Olympics 1962); *11* B–K2 K–R1; *12* B–R5 B–Q2; *13* P–B4 P–N4 is double-edged (Tal– Larsen, 4th Match Game 1969).

10 P–B3   P–QR3

"Preferable to *10* . . . R–Q1; *11* B–K3 Q–B2; *12* Q–B2 (holding up Black's Queen-side advance because of *12* . . . P–QR3?; *13* B–N6) N– Q2; *13* N–N5 Q–N1; *14* P–N4! and White's attack with the KNP and KRP proceeds very fast" (Tal).

11 P–N4   . . . .

"If *11* BxN BxB; *12* QxP B–N4ch with a good attack; I don't like to win such Pawns" (Tal).

11 . . . .   R–Q1
12 B–K3   Q–B2
13 P–N5   . . . .

"If here *13* Q–B2 N–Q2 and, in contrast to the note to Black's tenth, White does not have the strong N–N5 available" (Tal).

13 . . . .   N–Q2
14 P–KR4   P–N4
15 P–N6!?   . . . .

Position after 15 P–N6

15 . . . .   BPxP

"I had played this Pawn sacrifice in previous games," Tal has written, "and Mohrlok was obviously prepared for it, for he replied very quickly. In a radio game with Stoltz in 1960, Black went *15* . . . N–B4; *16* PxBPch KxP; *17* B–R3 N–R5; *18* P–B4 N–N5; *19* P–B5! P–K4; *20* NxN NxPch; *21* K–N1 PxN; *22* N–R5!, and White won.

"In a practice game a few years ago, my chess trainer Koblentz took with the KRP here; but then White quickly breaks through along the KR file with *15* . . . RPxP; *16* P–R5 PxP; *17* RxP N–B3; *18* R–R1 P–Q4; *19* P–K5! NxP; *20* Q–R2 K–B1; *21* Q–R8ch! (I actually played *21* B–KB4 B–Q3; *22* Q– R8ch, when Black could have got away with *22* . . . K–K2!) N–N1; *22* B–KB4 B–Q3; *23* R–R7."

16 P–R5   PxP
17 RxP   N–B3
18 R–N5   . . . .

"White wants to switch the attack between the KR and KN file according to Black's defense; so he posts one Rook on each file, with the Queen supporting from behind" (Tal). Now *18* . . . P–N5!; *19* N–R4 R–N1 has the merit of denying the Knight later access to Q5.

18	. . . .	N–K4
19	Q–N2	B–B1

"Up to here, everything has followed a game between Spassky and Boleslavsky in the 1958 Soviet Championship. I couldn't remember this game while I was playing, and afterward asked Spassky for the continuation; he didn't know either!" (Tal).

20	B–K2	. . . .

"Mohrlok had played very rapidly up to here, but now thought for twenty minutes; so I guessed that *20* B–K2 must be a new move. Afterward he told me that he had expected *20* B–Q4, but then comes *20* . . . P–R3!; *21* R–N3 N–R4; *22* R–R3 N–B5 winning the exchange" (Tal).

20	. . . .	N–B5
21	B×N	P×B
22	N–Q4	. . . .

"I looked at *22* R–N1, but it's good only if Black overlooks the trick of *23* B–N6. With *22* . . . R–N1; *23* N–R5 (threatening N–B6) K–R1!, Black halts the attack, after which White's QR is misplaced on the KN file" (Tal).

22	. . . .	R–N1

"If *22* . . . P–K4 White can choose between the simple and positional *23* N–B5 B×N; *24* R×B and the sacrificial *23* R–R1 P×N; *24* B×P Q–B2; *25* Q–R2!" (Tal).

23	R–R1	R–N2
24	R–R6!	. . . .

Position after 24 R–R6

"The strongest move in the game. White's main idea is to play P–KB4–5 to create a Knight outpost at Q5, or alternatively to go P–KB4 and P–K5 to drive Black's Knight from the protection of his KRP" (Tal).

24	. . . .	K–B2

"The main variation I calculated was *24* . . . P–N3 (apparently a logical way of enabling Black's Queen and Rook to defend his second rank); *25* R/6×Pch! P×R; *26* R×Pch K–B2 (if *26* . . . K–R1; *27* R×N Q–R2; *28* N×P with two Pawns for the exchange and a continuing attack); *27* Q–N5 N–R2 (*27* . . . Q–K2?; *28* N–B6); *28* Q–R5! N–B3; *29* R×Nch! K×R; *30* N–B5!! and despite his huge material plus of two Rooks for a minor piece, Black is helpless. The immediate threat is *31* B–N5ch K–K4; *32* P–B4 mate. If *30* . . . P×N; *31* N–Q5ch mates;

after *31* ... K–K4; *32* P–B4ch! KxP; *33* Q–R1—or *31* ... K–K3; *32* QxP—or *31* ... K–N2; *32* B–Q4ch. Again, if *30* ... P–K4; *31* N–Q5ch K–K3; *32* N–Q4ch! (White is not satisfied with winning the Queen) K–Q2 (*32* ... PxN; *33* Q–B5 mate); *33* Q–B7ch mates.

"Another possibility is *24* ... Q–B2; *25* N–B6 (or at once *25* P–K5) R–K1; *26* P–K5! N move; *27* N–K4 and the attack is overwhelming" (Tal).

25 R–R4   ....

"The threat of P–KB4 and P–K5 has become stronger, since after the Knight moves Black's KRP is *en prise*" (Tal).

25 ....   Q–N3

Tal makes no comment on this move, and Black's task is by no means easy. If *25* ... P–R3; *26* R–N6 K–K1 (*26* ... P–K4; *27* N–B5 BxN; *28* PxB P–Q4; *29* BxP PxB; *30* RxNch! KxR; *31* Q–N6ch K–K2; *32* Q–K6 mate); *27* P–B4, Black is curiously tied up, despite his Pawn.

26 N–Q1   ....

"The Knight goes on the defense, but only temporarily; Black's Queen has to move again" (Tal).

26 ....   Q–B2
27 P–B4   P–R3
28 R–N6   R–K1

"If *28* ... P–K4; *29* N–B5 BxN; *30* PxB, and White returns to the attack against Q5 with his remaining Knight" (Tal).

Black's only chance is *28* ... K–K1; though *29* P–B5 P–K4; *30* N–K6 BxN; *31* PxB (threatening RxN) continues the attack with full force.

29 P–B5   P–K4
30 N–QB3   ....

"*30* RxNch is less exact; *30* ... PxR; *31* Q–N6ch K–K2; *32* N–QB3 K–Q1; and Black escapes" (Tal).

30 ....   Q–Q1

"There's nothing to be done. If *30* ... PxN; *31* RxNch PxR; *32* N–Q5 threatens both the Queen and Q–N6 mate" (Tal).

31 N–B6   Resigns

After the Queen moves, *32* RxNch wins.

63
10th MATCH GAME 1965
Sicilian Defense

WHITE: TAL   BLACK: LARSEN

Tal in the saddle! His reckless and profound Knight sacrifice triggers a ferocious struggle; the soundness of the ploy baffles analysts to this day.

1 P–K4   P–QB4
2 N–KB3   N–QB3

3	P–Q4	PxP
4	NxP	P–K3
5	N–QB3	P–Q3
6	B–K3	....

In the eighth game of the match Tal adopted the positional 6 P–KN3; although he got some slight pressure, Larsen managed to draw without too much effort.

6	....	N–B3
7	P–B4	B–K2
8	Q–B3	O–O

Since White obviously intends Queen-side castling, it is possible that Black should prepare to follow his example with *8* ... B–Q2; ... P–QR3; ... Q–B2, etc.

9	O–O–O	Q–B2
10	N/4–N5	....

Although temporarily displacing White's Queen, this move should not alter the position in any significant way, since the Knight will be driven back at once. It does, however, tempt Larsen to save a tempo by not bothering to return his Queen to B2 and it thus plays its part in preparing the combination which wins the game.

10	....	Q–N1
11	P–KN4	P–QR3
12	N–Q4	NxN
13	BxN	P–QN4

Exciting tactics ensue after *13* ... P–K4; *14* P–N5 PxB (not *14* ... B–N5; *15* Q–N3 BxR; *16* PxN BxKBP; *17* N Q5 PxB; *18* NxBch K–R1; *19* R–N1 wins); *15* PxN PxN (or *15* ... BxP; *16* N–Q5 B–Q1; *17* P–B5, and White's attack should prevail); *16* PxB PxPch; *17* K–N1

R–K1; *18* P–K5! RxP; *19* PxP R–Q2; *20* Q–K4! and Black is helpless.

14	P–N5	N–Q2
15	B–Q3	P–N5
16	N–Q5!	....

"The lightning bolt that shatters open a veritable Pandora's box of combinative havoc" (R. Byrne).

Position after 16 N–Q5

This sacrifice is so electrifying that it deserves a diagram.

16	....	PxN

The way to refute a sacrifice begins by accepting it; an old maxim, but true nonetheless.

Black cannot decline by *16* ... B–Q1, because *17* N–B6ch! PxN; *18* PxP BxP; *19* KR–N1ch K–R1; *20* P–K5 B–KN2; *21* RxB! KxR; *22* Q–N4ch K–R1; *23* R–N1, and mate next.

17	PxP	P–B4

It is very hard to decide on the best defense—even in post-mortem analysis. In fact, one of Black's problems is that he has so many plausible replies! For example, *17* ... R–K1 loses outright to *18*

BxPch KxB; *19* Q–R5ch K–N1; *20* P–N6 PxP; *21* QxP, etc.

Perhaps *17* . . . P–N3 is the sturdiest try. It has the drawback of allowing White to pry open the KR file by P–KR4–5; but in the time it takes to do that, Black might be able to mobilize his Queen-side pieces for defense.

18 QR–K1   R–B2

If *18* . . . B–Q1, then *19* Q–R5 sets up the menace of a Bishop sacrifice on KN7. Tal gives *19* . . . N–B4; *20* BxNP! NxBch; *21* K–N1. However, as R. Byrne points out, Black's strongest is *21* . . . Q–B2! (not the acquiescent *21* . . . NxR; *22* P–N6! KxB; *23* QxPch K–B3; *24* P–N7 R–K1; *25* R–N1! N–N7!; *26* P–N8(Q) RxQ; *27* QxR wins); *22* BxR NxR; *23* RxN Q–B2!; *24* QxQch KxQ; *25* BxP P–QR4; and, with White's three Pawns balanced by Black's piece, the ending will be no walkaway for either side.

19 P–KR4   B–N2

All things considered, Larsen has defended reasonably, and the contest could still go either way.

Position after 19 . . . B–N2

20 BxBP   . . . .

Picking up a second Pawn for the piece. Perhaps *20* P–R5 is sharper.

20 . . . .   RxB
21 RxB   N–K4?

This returns the piece. A tougher resistance is offered by *21* . . . R–B2; *22* RxR KxR; but after *23* R–K1, White's attack has by no means abated.

22 Q–K4   Q–KB1

22 . . . R–B2 now fails against *23* RxR NxR; *24* P–N6 PxP; *25* QxP Q–KB1; *26* R–N1.

23 PxN   R–B5

Better was *23* . . . QxR; *24* QxR BxP, which at least denies White a strong passed Pawn in the center.

24 Q–K3   R–B6

Finally Black weakens irretrievably in this colossal struggle of nerves. This was his last chance to put up a fight with *24* . . . BxP; *25* PxP RxB; *26* QxR BxR; *27* QxP—even though White's three Pawns and dominating position outweigh the piece, the issue is still somewhat in doubt.

Black also had the choice of *24* . . . BxP; *25* PxP BxR; *26* RxPch QxR; *27* BxQ R–B8ch; *28* K–Q2 KxB obtaining two Rooks and Bishop for the Queen. Despite this material advantage, White smartly forces the win here by *29* P–Q7 R/8–B1; *30* P–R5! K–B2 (or *30* . . . QR–Q1; *31* Q–K7ch K–N1; *32* P–R6); *31* Q–K5 QR–Q1; *32* Q–B6ch K–N1; *33* Q–K6ch R–B2; *34* P–N6.

25	Q–K2	Q×R
26	Q×R	P×P
27	R–K1	R–Q1
28	R×P	Q–Q3
29	Q–B4	R–KB1
30	Q–K4	P–N6
31	RP×P	R–B8ch
32	K–Q2	Q–N5ch

33	P–B3	Q–Q3
34	B–B5	Q×B
35	R–K8ch	R–B1
36	Q–K6ch	K–R1
37	Q–B7!	Resigns

A pretty finish.

64
BELGRADE 1964
Sicilian Defense

WHITE: VELIMIROVICH   BLACK: NIKOLICH

A germinal game which brought young Velimirovich and his novel attacking system to the attention of the chess world. White sacrifices a Rook and a Knight in order to rip open the position, an exhibition of daring and ingenuity.

1	P–K4	P–QB4
2	N–KB3	N–QB3
3	P–Q4	P×P
4	N×P	N–B3
5	N–QB3	P–Q3
6	B–QB4	P–K3
7	B–K3	B–K2
8	Q–K2	O–O

Fischer–Pascual, Philippines 1967, continued: *8* . . . P–QR3; *9* O–O–O Q–B2; *10* B–N3 B–Q2; *11* P–N4 N×N; *12* B×N (stronger is R×N) P–K4; *13* P–N5 P×B; *14* P×N P×N; *15* P×B P×Pch; *16* K–N1, and now . . . B–K3 would have equalized.

9	O–O–O	Q–B2
10	B–N3	P–QR3
11	P–N4	N×N

11 . . . N–QR4 is more stubborn.

| 12 | R×N! | . . . . |

Velimirovich–Gajovich, in Belgrade 1966, featured a curious finish: *12* B×N P–QN4? (. . . P–K4 is quite sufficient); *13* P–N5 N–Q2; *14* Q–R5 N–B4; *15* KR–N1 B–N2; *16* B–B6! P–N5; *17* Q–R6! Black Resigns.

| 12 | . . . . | P–QN4 |

Tal gives a crucial variation: *12* . . . P–K4; *13* R–B4! Q–Q1; *14* P–N5 N–K1; *15* R×B!? R×R; *16* P–KR4 N–B2; *17* P–R5 with a terrific attack.

13	P–N5	N–Q2
14	Q–R5	N–K4?

A time-consuming maneuver. It is better to try to remove the KB by *14* . . . N–B4.

15	P–B4	N–B3
16	R–Q3	N–N5
17	R–Q2	R–Q1
18	P–B5	P–N3
19	PxP	RPxP
20	Q–R4	. . . .

More precise is *20* Q–Q1, preparing P–KR4–5.

| 20 | . . . . | N–B3 |

Black's game already is seriously compromised. For example, the plausible *20* . . . B–N2 is speedily refuted by *21* B–Q4 P–K4; *22* BxP! PxB; *23* BxPch! KxB; *24* Q–R7ch K–K1; *25* QxPch K–B1; *26* R–B1ch and mates.

21	Q–N3	N–K4
22	P–KR4	B–N2
23	P–R5	P–N5
24	PxP!	NxP

Not *24* . . . PxN; *25* R–R8ch! KxR; *26* Q–R4ch K–N2; *27* Q–R7ch mates.

25	R/2–R2!	PxN
26	B–Q4!	P–K4
27	R–R8ch!	NxR
28	P–N6!	. . . .

Position after 28 P–N6

White's forceful maneuvers have all been based on the power of his KB (which his opponent should have taken pains to eliminate long ago). Black no longer has any defense.

28	. . . .	B–KB3
29	PxPch	K–B1
30	R–R7!	NxP

Of no avail is *30* . . . QxP; *31* BxQ NxB; *32* Q–N6 B–N4ch; *33* K–Q1 R–Q2; *34* Q–N7ch K–K1; *35* Q–N8ch mates.

| 31 | Q–N6 | B–N4ch |

If *31* . . . P–Q4 (or *31* . . . R–Q2; *32* QxB wins); *32* B–B5ch K–K1; *33* B–R4ch etc.

32	K–N1	R–Q2
33	Q–N7ch	K–K1
34	Q–N8ch	Resigns

65

YUGOSLAV CHAMPIONSHIP 1966
Sicilian Defense

WHITE: VELIMIROVICH   BLACK: SOFREVSKY

Piece sacrifices for the sake of rapid development are common in many sharp variations of the Sicilian, but White's innovation here was so unexpected that it sent the theoreticians scurrying back to the drawing board.

1	P–K4	P–QB4
2	N–KB3	N–QB3
3	P–Q4	PxP
4	NxP	P–K3
5	N–QB3	P–Q3
6	B–K3	N–B3
7	B–QB4	B–K2
8	Q–K2	....

This system is largely Velimirovich's contribution to opening theory.

8	....	P–QR3
9	O–O–O	Q–B2
10	B–N3	N–QR4
11	P–N4	P–QN4

Naturally, Black keeps the option of Queen-side castling open as long as possible.

12	P–N5	NxBch

Not *12 ... N–Q2?; 13 BxP! PxB; 14 NxKP Q–B3; 15 NxPch,* with a stock attack. The second player must always be alert to this possibility.

13	RPxN	N–Q2
14	N–B5!	....

The only try for an advantage, otherwise Black's solid position coupled with the two Bishops would be assessed as favorable. The Trojan horse must be accepted. If *14 ... B–B1* (or *14 ... P–N5;* see game 66); *15 B–Q4! PxN; 16 PxPch K–Q1; 17 KR–K1 Q–R4; 18 N–Q5* wins.

14	....	PxN
15	N–Q5	Q–Q1

Velimirovich gives *15 ... Q–N2* (not *15 ... Q–R4; 16 PxP B–N2; 17 NxB KxN; 18 B–N6ch*); *16 PxP N–K4; 17 P–KB4 BxKBP; 18 PxN B–K5; 19 PxP BxN; 20 B–B5! BxR; 21 P–Q7ch QxP; 22 RxQ KxR; 23 QxBch K–B3; 24 Q–Q6ch* and mates.

16	PxP	....

Position after 16 PxP

16	....	O–O?

The only defense is *16* . . . B–N2!;
17 P–B6! (*17* KR–K1 BxN; *18* RxB
O–O; *19* P–B6 NxP! was drawn—
Hindle–Hamann, Vrnjacka Banja
1967) PxP; *18* KR–K1 BxN; *19*
RxB R–KN1! (not *19* . . .O–O;
20 PxP BxP; *21* R–N1ch K–R1;
22 R–R5! B–N2; *23* RxB! KxR;
24 Q–N4ch K–R1; *25* Q–B5 N–B3;
26 B–Q4 wins); *20* P–KR4 (better is
20 PxP) R–QB1, and White's attack,
not conducted forcefully enough,
subsided (Gheorghiu–Hamann, Vrnjacka Banja 1967).

This illustrates the growing importance of prepared analysis. In great
secrecy players vivisect whole variations at home. The last word,
however, still has not been uttered on
this remarkable line. It will be tested
further in tournaments and correspondence until laid to rest by a foot-
note in the next edition of *Modern
Chess Openings*.

17 P–B6	PxP

Unfortunately, there is no way to
return the piece gracefully. If *17*
. . . NxP; *18* PxN BxP; *19* B–N6
Q–Q2; *20* NxBch PxN; *21* KR–N1
yields a winning attack.

18 B–Q4	N–K4
19 PxP	BxP
20 KR–N1ch	B–N2
21 BxN	PxB
22 QxP	P–B3
23 N–K7ch	K–B2

A prettier finish is *23* . . . K–R1;
24 RxQ PxQ; *25* RxRch BxR;
26 R–N8 mate.

24 Q–R5ch	Resigns

66
MALAGA 1969
Sicilian Defense

WHITE: MEDINA   BLACK: POMAR

A testimony to the infinite richness of
chess. Black's refinement on move
14, designed to deny the attack of the
previous game, spawns a host of new
complications.

1 P–K4	P–QB4
2 N–KB3	P–Q3
3 P–Q4	N–KB3
4 N–B3	. . . .

The scant experience with *4* PxP
NxP; *5* PxP P–K3; *6* Q–Q3 NxQP;
7 N–B3 indicates White holds the
edge.

4	PxP
5 NxP	N–B3
6 B–QB4	Q–B2

6 . . . B–Q2; *7* B–N3 P–KN3 produces a last-minute switch to the
Dragon Variation. Black's setup is
quite flexible.

7 B–N3	P–QR3

And so Black, unwillingly it seems, is
dragged back into this well-known
theoretical sequence.

8 B–K3	P–K3

9	Q–K2	B–K2
10	O–O–O	N–QR4
11	P–N4	NxBch
12	RPxN	P–QN4
13	P–N5	N–Q2
14	N–B5!	P–N5!?

Apparently Pomar has no taste for *14 . . . PxN; 15 N–Q5* as in the preceding encounter. But his medicine may turn out to be even more bitter.

15 NxPch!?   . . . .

An imaginative gamble. The prudent course *15 NxB PxN; 16 NxB RxN* (not *16 . . . PxPch; 17 KxP RxN; 18 R–Q2*) gives Black some counterplay despite the abysmal weakness of his QP.

15	. . . .	K–B1
16	Q–R5!	. . . .

Now Black can capture either Knight —he has to choose between two equally attractive moves—this is the insidious start of time pressure. White is playing *va banque* and need not trouble himself with these niceties. If there is an outright refutation, of course, he will pay the penalty. But if the defense should prove unclear and tortuous, then White will be aided by the relentless ticking of the clock.

16 . . . .   KxN

The complications are monstrous. After *16 . . . PxN; 17 Q–R6! Q–R4! (17 . . . K–N1?; 18 N–R5 B–B1; 19 N–B6ch NxN; 20 PxN! BxQ; 21 BxB forces mate); 18 PxP K–N1; 19 N–R5 B–B1; 20 N–B6ch NxN; 21 PxN! BxQ; 22 BxB Q–R4*

(forced); *23 KR–N1ch Q–N3; 24 P–R4! B–N2; 25 P–R5!* (25 P–B3 P–Q4 is easier for Black) *BxP; 26 PxQ RPxQ; 27 B–N7 R–R7; 28 RxP RxP; 29 R–Q4!* forces B–B6 (*29 . . . RxPch?; 30 K–Q1 B–B4; 31 R–R1 wins) 30 R–KB4!* followed by RxB and R–R1 wins.

17 B–Q4ch   N–K4

Again "the lady or the tiger." An alternative is *17 . . . K–N1 (17 . . . P–K4?; 18 N–Q5); 18 BxR KxB; 19 N–K2 (19 QxP? N–K4!) B–N2.* The game could still go either way, but Black's chances are not worse.

18 P–B4!   . . . .

Saving the Knight with *18 N–R4* would lose all the momentum of the attack after *18 . . . B–N2* followed by *. . . R–QB1.*

18	. . . .	PxN
19	BxP	B–N2?

No better is *19 . . . K–N1; 20 PxN PxP; 21 KR–B1 B–B1; 22 BxP!*

Saidy says that Black can hope to weather the storm by returning the piece with *19 . . . P–R3; 20 PxN BxPch; 21 K–N1 PxP;* but *22 P–R4!* (instead of his *22 KR–N1 P–B3; 23 P–R4 Q–B2*) regains the piece favorably—if *22 . . . B–B5; 23 KR–B1! P–B3; 24 RxB! PxR; 25 R–N1ch K–B1; 26 B–N4ch wins.*

And *19 . . . R–B1; 20 PxN PxP; 21 R–Q3* is also difficult to meet.

Ivkov suggests simply *19 . . . R–R2;* but *20 PxN PxP; 21 KR–B1* keeps the embers glowing. If desperate measures are needed, the answer is *19 . . .* Q×B!; *20* P×Q N–N3, with three pieces for the Queen. If *21* KR–B1 (or *21* Q–R6ch K–N1; *22* KR–B1 B–B1; *23* Q–R5 P–R3; *24* P–B5 RP×P; *25* Q×P? B–R3) P–R3! repulses the attack.

20	P×N	P×P
21	R–Q7!	Q×R

21 . . . Q–B4; *22* R×QB Q–K6ch; *23* K–N1 Q×KP; *24* R–KB1 wins.

22	Q–R6ch	K–N1
23	B×P	P–B3

Even worse is *23 . . .* B–KB1; *24* Q–B6.

24	P×P	B–B4

Or *24 . . .* B–KB1; *25* R–N1ch K–B2; *26* Q–R5 mate.

25	Q–N7ch!	Q×Q
26	P×Q	....

Rarely does one Pawn win two Rooks!

26	....	K–B2
27	P×R(Q)	R×Q
28	B×R	B×P
29	R–B1ch	....

With an exchange and a Pawn ahead, White won easily in twenty-five more moves; for the record they were:

29	....	B–B4
30	B–K5	B–K6
31	K–N1	K–N3
32	B–B4	B–Q5
33	R–K1	K–R4
34	K–B1	K–N5
35	B–K5	B–B7
36	R–B1	B–K6ch
37	K–Q1	B–B4
38	R–B4ch	K–R6
39	R–B3ch	K–N7
40	R–N3ch	K–B7
41	K–Q2	P–KR4
42	R–N8	P–R4
43	P–B4	P–KR5
	(finally)	
44	R–QB8	B–K6ch
45	K–B3	K–K7
46	P–N4	B–Q7ch
47	K–N3	B×P
48	P–B5	B–K5
49	P–B6	K–K6
50	K–R4	B–Q4
51	K–N5	K–K5
52	B–B6	P–R6
53	R–Q8	K–K6
54	R×B	Resigns

67
HAVANA OLYMPICS 1966
Sicilian Defense

WHITE: TAL BLACK: BOLBOCHAN

In a position replete with attacking themes we expect Tal to prevail, but the unique twist he gives the task each time is truly marvelous. The "quiet" maneuver at White's twenty-fifth turn is the straw that breaks the camel's back.

1	P–K4	P–QB4

"It is more advisable to try *1 . . .*

P–K4 against Tal, but Bolbochan is a hardheaded opponent who steps aside for no one" (R. Byrne).

2	N–KB3	N–QB3
3	P–Q4	PxP
4	NxP	P–K3
5	N–QB3	P–Q3
6	B–K3	N–B3
7	B–QB4	....

The system with 7 P–B4 B–K2; 8 Q–B3 has met with the solid rebuff 8 ... P–K4!; 9 NxN PxN; 10 PxP PxP; 11 B–QB4 O–O; 12 O–O N–N5!= (R. Byrne–Panno, Havana Olympics 1966).

7	....	B–K2
8	Q–K2	O–O
9	B–N3	....

Once Black castles ... NxP becomes a threat.

9	....	P–QR3

The immediate 9 ... N–QR4 is the right way to get into the fight.

10	O–O–O	Q–R4

Once again it is better to leave this square free for the Knight. 10 ... Q–B2 is preferable.

11	K–N1	R–K1

More active is 11 ... B–Q2 and ... P–QN4. Black mistakenly supposes that the breakthrough will come with P–KB4–5 and braces himself against that.

12	KR–N1	B–Q2
13	P–N4	NxN
14	BxN	B–B3
15	P–N5	N–Q2
16	R–Q3	P–KN3

Necessary to parry the threat of R–R3 and Q–R5. The disadvantage of 16 ... N–B1 is its abysmal passivity.

17	P–KR4	....

"The prospect of an open KR file is enough to make White's mouth water!" (R. Byrne).

17	....	N–B4
18	P–R5!	....

Position after 18 P–R5

Daring Black to capture the Rook which would allow White's Bishops to rake the King side.

18	....	NxB

The kind offer is declined for the sake of removing one of the two lethal Bishops. The principal variation is 18 ... NxR; 19 QxN BxNP (or 19 ... P–K4; 20 PxP PxP; 21 Q–B3! R–KB1; 22 Q–R3 PxB; 23 R–R1 mates); 20 PxP BPxP; 21 P–K5 B–Q1; 22 RxPch! PxR; 23 QxPch K–B1; 24 B–K3! QxP; 25 B–R6ch K–K2; 26 Q–R7ch K–B3; 27 B–N7ch K–N4; 28 Q–R6ch K–B4; 29 Q–R3ch K–N3; 30 BxQ PxB; 31 BxP—and Black, a Pawn down with an exposed King, must lose (R. Byrne).

19	RP×N	P-K4
20	B-K3	Q-B2
21	B-Q2	QR-Q1
22	R-R1	B-B1
23	Q-N4	P-N4
24	Q-R4	P-N5

Julio Bolbochan is a very stubborn, indefatigable defender, and he has managed to prime a promising counterattack.

| 25 | N-Q1! | .... |

"It is amazing that White can spare the time for this Knight maneuver" (R. Byrne).

25	....	P-Q4
26	N-K3!	P×KP
27	N-N4!	....

Position after 27 N-N4

The Knight's mission is revealed. Not now 27 ... P×R; 28 N-B6ch K-R1; 29 P×NP P×Pch; 30 K-B1 P×P; 31 Q×Pch mates.

| 27 | .... | P-B4 |

27 ... B-N2 also fails against 28 R×R R×R; 29 B×P with the winning threat of 30 P×P BP×P; 31 Q×Pch K-B2; 32 N-R6ch.

| 28 | N-B6ch | K-B2 |
| 29 | P×Pch | K-K3 |

Also bad is 29 ... P×P; 30 Q-R7ch B-N2; 31 Q×Bch! K×Q; 32 R-R7ch K-B1; 33 B×Pch R-K2; 34 R×R/2, emerging a full Rook ahead.

| 30 | N×R | R×N |
| 31 | P×P | .... |

It seems as though White would like to leave his Rook *en prise* forever.

| 31 | .... | B-N2 |
| 32 | R/3-R3 | .... |

Finally.

32	....	B-Q4
33	Q-R5	K-Q2
34	Q×Rch	Resigns

Brilliant to the very end. On 34 ... K×Q; 35 P-R8(Q)ch B×Q; 36 R×Bch K-K2; 37 B×Pch nets a Rook.

68

EAST GERMAN CHAMPIONSHIP 1967
Sicilian Defense

WHITE: HENNINGS   BLACK: MOEHRING

It is amazing how much hot water a master can wade into in the first dozen moves. Black's defensive setup undergoes another mauling, even though every one of his moves is plausible.

| 1 | P-K4 | P-QB4 |
| 2 | N-KB3 | N-QB3 |

3	P–Q4	PxP
4	NxP	P–Q3
5	N–QB3	P–K3
6	B–K3	N–B3
7	B–QB4	....

Since the Bishop "bites on granite," this move was considered inferior before Fischer rehabilitated it. Black must institute active countermeasures.

| 7 | .... | B–K2 |

7 ... NxP; 8 QNxN P–Q4; 9 NxN PxN; 10 B–Q3 PxN; 11 BxP gives White the better Pawn structure. The text is sound yet passive. 7 ... P–QR3 is more flexible.

| 8 | Q–K2 | .... |

This entire system is so recent that it is not covered in the 10th edition of *MCO* (1965).

| 8 | .... | O–O |

While not an error here, castling generally should be delayed in favor of rapid Queen-side action.

| 9 | O–O–O | Q–B2 |
| 10 | B–N3 | P–QR3 |

Now 10 ... N–QR4 is indicated.

| 11 | P–N4 | P–QN4 |
| 12 | P–N5 | NxN |

An emergency measure, since 12 ... N–Q2?; 13 N–Q5! PxN; 14 NxN QxN; 15 BxP gains material.

| 13 | BxN | N–Q2 |
| 14 | KR–N1 | N–B4? |

If such a natural move can lead to trouble, then Black is already walking a tightrope. After 14 ... B–N2, a hard fight would still lie ahead.

The *Deutsche Schachzeitung* gives an interesting variation: 14 ... P–N5; 15 N–Q5! PxN; 16 BxQP B–N2; 17 P–N6 N–K4 (if 17 ... RPxP; 18 RxP! B–KB3; 19 BxKB NxB; 20 RxN wins); 18 BxN PxB; 19 Q–R5 P–R3; 20 PxPch K–R1; 21 R–N6 B–N4ch; 22 RxB BxB; 23 PxB QxP; 24 QxQ RxQ; 25 RxP RxP; 26 P–Q6 R–QB1; 27 P–B3 PxP; 28 P–Q7! wins.

| 15 | Q–R5 | P–N5 |

Black can hardly be blamed for overlooking White's rejoinder. But he still loses after 15 ... N–Q2; 16 P–N6! RPxP; 17 RxP.

15 ... P–N3; 16 Q–R6 NxBch; 17 RPxN P–B3 is barely tenable.

| 16 | B–B6! | .... |

This elegant coup threatens the still more elegant 17 Q–R6!

Position after 16 B–B6

| 16 | .... | R–K1 |
| 17 | R–N3 | .... |

Now the threat is 18 R–R3 P–R3; 19 PxP BxB; 20 PxP BxP; 21 R–N1 K–B1; 22 RxB.

17	....	PxN
18	R–R3	PxPch
19	K–N1	BxB

20	P×B	K–B1
21	P–K5	N–K5

On *21* ... P×KP; *22* Q–N5 P×P;
23 Q×BP N–Q2; *24* R×N wins.

22	P×Pch	K–K2
23	Q–R4ch	P–B3
24	Q×N	P–Q4
25	P–N8(Q)	R×Q
26	R×Pch	Resigns

69

SKOPJE 1967
Sicilian Defense

WHITE: FISCHER   BLACK: GELLER

A flawed masterpiece. Fischer's ultrasharp attack meets with a stunning
refutation after a momentary lapse.

1	P–K4	P–QB4
2	N–KB3	P–Q3
3	P–Q4	P×P
4	N×P	N–KB3
5	N–QB3	N–B3
6	B–QB4	P–K3
7	B–K3	B–K2

Black should start rapid action on
the Queen side with *7* ... P–QR3;
8 B–N3 Q–B2; *9* Q–K2 P–QN4;
10 O–O–O N–QR4 (or ... B–N2).

8	B–N3	O–O
9	Q–K2	Q–R4

An attempt to improve on the
customary *9* ... P–QR3; *10* O–O–O
Q–B2; *11* P–N4.

10	O–O–O	N×N
11	B×N	B–Q2
12	K–N1	B–B3

Fischer–Sofrevsky, Skopje 1967, continued: *12* ... QR–Q1; *13* Q–K3!
P–QN3 (if *13* ... P–QN4!?; *14*
P–QR3 is safest); *14* B×N P×B (Black
should reconcile himself to *14* ...

B×B; *15* R×P B–B1); *15* N–Q5!
KR–K1 (if *15* ... P×N; *16* R×P
Q–R3; *17* R–KR5! uncorks a
winning attack); *16* N×Bch (*16* Q–
R6! is an even quicker kill) R×N;
17 R×P R–QB1; *18* Q–B4 B–K1;
19 Q×BP, and Black Resigns.

13	P–B4	QR–Q1
14	KR–B1	....

Also good is *14* P–B5 (or *14* P–N4)
P×P; *15* P×P KR–K1; *16* Q–B2 with
lasting pressure.

14	....	P–QN4
15	P–B5!	....

The die is cast. The more prudent
15 P–QR3 would lose a tempo, which
is not to Fischer's taste.

15	....	P–N5
16	P×P	P×N
17	P×Pch	K–R1
18	R–B5!	Q–N5
19	Q–B1!	....

Fischer says this was the hardest
move to find (forty-five minutes).
Black must meet the threat of *20*
R×N.

19	....	N×P

Who can quarrel with success?
Objectively better is *19* ... N–N5;
20 BxP Q–N2; *21* Q–B4, but White
has three Pawns for a piece and an
attack still brewing.

Position after 19 ... NxP

20 P–QR3?   ....

A pity that White loses his way in the
labyrinth. Fischer gives *20* Q–KB4!
as the winning move, with the following substantiation: *20* ... PxP (or

20 ... N–Q7ch; *21* RxN PxR;
22 P–B3 QxKB; *23* BxPch! KxB;
24 Q–N4ch K–R1; *25* Q–Q4ch
mates); *21* R–KR5! N–B6ch (if
21 ... B–KB3; *22* Q–B5 P–KR3;
23 RxPch! PxR; *24* Q–N6! forcing
mate); *22* KxP NxRch (again on
22 ... RxP; *23* QxR NxRch; *24*
K–N1! QxB; *25* RxPch! KxR;
26 Q–R5 mate); *23* K–B1 RxP;
24 BxR! (menacing RxPch) B–Q2;
25 BxPch winning Black's Queen.

20 ....   Q–N2
21 Q–KB4   B–R5!

Turnabout is fair play. Now White's
attack has boomeranged.

22 Q–N4   B–KB3
23 RxB   BxB!
**   Resigns**

On *24* R–B4 (or *24* PxB NxR)
B–R7ch!; *25* KxB QxP mate.

70

SKOPJE 1967
Sicilian Defense

WHITE: FISCHER   BLACK: DELY

A crisp miniature. Black tries to
solve his opening problems superficially, and ends up receiving two
fatal jolts.

1 P–K4   P–QB4
2 N–KB3   P–Q3
3 P–Q4   PxP
4 NxP   N–KB3
5 N–QB3   N–B3
6 B–QB4   P–K3
7 B–N3   P–QR3

8 P–B4   Q–R4

Also interesting is *8* ... N–QR4;
9 P–B5! NxB; *10* RPxN B–K2;
11 Q–B3 O–O; *12* B–K3 B–Q2;
13 P–KN4 P–K4; *14* N/4–K2 with
good attacking prospects (Fischer–
Bielicki, Mar Del Plata 1960).

9 O–O   NxN

A better solution is *9* ... P–Q4;
10 NxN PxN; *11* P–B5 with a slight
initiative, but nothing serious.

10 QxN   P–Q4

Naïvely attempting to free his game
with . . . B–B4. The lesser evil is
10 . . . Q–QB4; *11* QxQ PxQ; although White has an endgame
advantage after *12* P–QR4.

11 B–K3   NxP

Better but far from good is *11* . . .
PxP; *12* NxP B–K2; *13* N–Q6ch etc.
Fischer gives *11* . . . N–N5; *12* K–
R1! NxB; *13* QxN PxP; *14* QxP!
B–K2; *15* QR–K1 P–KN3; *16* N–
Q5! B–Q1; *17* Q–K5 O–O; *18* N–
K7ch wins.

12 NxN   PxN
13 P–B5!   . . . .

No rest for the weary. The obvious
recapture with *13* QxP would give
Black time for *13* . . . P–KN3.

13 . . . .   Q–N5

Fischer gives *13* . . . PxP; *14* P–N4!
B–K3 (if *14* . . . Q–N5; *15* B–R4ch!
P–N4; *16* Q–Q5); *15* PxP BxB; *16*
RPxB Q–N5; *17* R–R4! QxQ;
18 RxQ B–K2; *19* RxP K–B1;

20 P–B6! BxP; *21* RxB! PxR; *22*
B–R6ch and mates.

14 PxP   BxP?

Overlooking the concluding combination. *14* . . . PxP is the only
hope of survival.

15 BxB   PxB

Position after 15 . . . PxB

16 RxBch!   QxR
17 Q–R4ch!   Resigns

Mate or heavy material loss is un-
avoidable: *17* . . . P–N4; *18* QxKP
R–Q1; *19* Q–B6ch R–Q2; *20* R–Q1
Q–K2; *21* B–N6! and the threat of
Q–B8ch is devastating.

71

CANDIDATES' TOURNAMENT 1959
Sicilian Defense

WHITE: FISCHER   BLACK: BENKO

In an equal position Black commits
an inexactitude which ordinarily
might go unpunished. He sidesteps
some beautiful losing variations but
gets crushed nevertheless.

1	P–K4	P–QB4
2	N–KB3	N–QB3
3	P–Q4	PxP
4	NxP	N–B3
5	N–QB3	P–Q3

6 **B–QB4   Q–N3**

A roguish way to throw White off balance.

7 **KN–K2   ....**

Probably White should pursue rapid development with *7* N×N P×N; *8* O–O. Fischer also got very little against Saidy in the 1967 U.S. Championship with *7* N–N3 P–K3; *8* O–O B–K2; *9* B–K3 Q–B2; *10* P–B4 O–O, etc.

7 **....   P–K3**
8 **O–O   ....**

Better is *8* B–N3 to reserve the option of castling long. Now Black has no trouble equalizing.

8 **....   B–K2**
9 **B–N3   O–O**
10 **K–R1   ....**

If *10* B–K3 Q–B2; *11* P–B4 N–KN5! The text prepares a retreat for the Bishop to KN1.

10 **....   N–QR4**
11 **B–N5   Q–B4**

"A finesse aimed at provoking *12* B–K3 Q–B2 after which White's initiative is blunted" (Fischer).

12 **P–B4   P–N4**
13 **N–N3   P–N5?**

Strangely enough, Black never gets another chance to capture the Bishop. Correct is *13* ... N×B; *14* RP×N B–N2; *15* N–R5 K–R1, with even chances.

14 **P–K5!   P×P**

If *14* ... P×N (or *14* ... N×B; *15* KP×N P×P; *16* B–R6 threatens

Q–N4ch); *15* P×N B×P; *16* B×B P×B; *17* N–K4 Q–B4; *18* N×QP Q–N3; *19* R–B3 K–R1; *20* R–N3 Q–R3; *21* Q–N4 (threatening Q–N8ch!) Q–N3; *22* Q–R4 wins (Fischer).

15 **B×N   P×B**

Also bad is *15* ... B×B; *16* QN–K4 Q–K2 (if *16* ... Q–Q5; *17* N×Bch K–R1; *18* Q–N4ch K–R1; *19* QR–Q1 Q×NP; *20* N–R5 R–KN1; *21* Q×Rch! K×Q; *22* R–Q8 mate); *17* N–R5! K–R1; *18* N/4×B P×N; *19* P×P P×P; *20* N–B6 (threatening Q–R5) wins (Fischer).

Best is *15* ... P×N; *16* N–K4 Q–N5; *17* Q–N4 B×B; *18* N×Bch K–R1; *19* Q–R4 P–KR3; *20* N–N4 P×NP, with defensive possibilities despite the threat of N×RP.

16 **QN–K4   ....**

Position after 16 QN–K4

16 **....   Q–Q5**

It is too late for Black to save himself, but he could have made White look better by succumbing with *16* ... Q–B2; *17* N–R5! P–B4; *18* N/5–B6ch K–N2; *19* Q–R5 B×N (not *19* ... P–KR3; *20* R–B3 R–R1; *21* R–N3ch K–B1; *22* Q×RPch!);

20 N×B P–KR3 (or 20 . . . R–R1;
21 Q–N5ch K–B1; 22 Q R6ch
K–K2; 23 Q–R4 K–B1; 24 N×Pch);
21 R–B3! R–R1; 22 N–K8ch! R×N;
23 R–N3ch K–B1; 24 Q×RPch
K–K2; 25 Q–R4ch K–Q3 (if 25
. . . K–B1; 26 R–R3! Q–Q1; 27
Q–R6ch K–K2; 28 Q–N5ch K–Q3;
29 R–Q3ch wins the Queen); 26
R–Q3ch K–B3 (if 26 . . . K–B4;
27 B–R4! threatens Q–B2ch); 27
B–R4ch K–N2; 28 B×R winning the
exchange, while Black still remains
all tied up (Fischer).

17 Q–R5   N×B

No better is 17 . . . P×P; 18 N–B5!

P×N; 19 R×P Q×N; 20 R×Q P×R;
21 Q×N.

18 Q–R6!   P×P

On 18 . . . P–B4; 19 P–B3! P×QBP;
20 P×BP followed by N–R5 forces
mate.

19	N–R5	P–B4
20	QR–Q1	Q–K4
21	N/4–B6ch	B×N
22	N×Bch	Q×N
23	Q×Q	N–B4
24	Q–N5ch	K–R1
25	Q–K7	B–R3
26	Q×N	B×R
27	R×B	Resigns

72

VARNA OLYMPICS 1962

Sicilian Defense

WHITE: O'KELLY   BLACK: PENROSE

Black's superlative defensive play is
rewarded. The final position, although drawn, is one of the most
unusual on record.

1	P–K4	P–QB4
2	N–KB3	N–QB3
3	P–Q4	P×P
4	N×P	P–K3

This old move has achieved new
popularity after having been considered inferior on account of 5 N–
N5 P–Q3; 6 B–KB4, forcing Black
to play . . . P–K4 and thus be saddled
with a hole on his Q4. However, this
hole is compensated by White's loss

of time with his Knight maneuver
which violates the principle "Don't
move the same piece twice in the
opening."

5 N–QB3   . . . .

After 5 P–QB4 N–B3; 6 N–QB3
B–N5 White cannot prevent . . .
P–Q4 followed by simplifying ex-
changes.

5 . . . .   Q–B2

Black refrains from 5 . . . P–Q3, to
afford his KB a freer sphere of
activity on QN5, QB4, or Q3, as
circumstances demand.

6 B–K2   ....

6 B–K3 allows more choice.

6 ....   P–QR3
7 O–O   ....

If *7* P–QR3 P–QN4; *8* NxN PxN,
with a satisfactory position.

7 ....   N–B3
8 B–K3   B–N5
9 NxN   ....

The pressure against his KP compels
White to simplify—or to speculate
with *9* N–R4!? (see next game).

9 ....   NPxN
10 B–Q3   ....

Now the drawback of having developed the Bishop to K2 can be
seen more clearly—White loses a
tempo. *10* Q–Q4 P–B4; *11* Q–B4
B–N2; *12* B–B3 Q–K4!; *13* B–Q2
O–O is slightly better for Black
(Gligorich–Taimanov, Buenos Aires
1960).

10 ....   P–Q4

Also playable is *10* ... P–K4; *11*
P–B4 P–Q3.

11 PxP   BPxP
12 B–Q4   B–K2

Best. If *12* ... B–Q3 (not *12* ...
Q–KB5?; *13* P–KN3! QxB??; *14*
B–N5ch); *13* R–K1! BxPch; *14*
K–R1 leaves Black desperately be-
hind in development.

13 R–K1   O–O

Castling into it *"sans peur ni re-
proche"* (O'Kelly).

14 Q–B3   B–N2
15 R–K3   KR–K1

16 QR–K1   QR–Q1
17 Q–R3   ....

White is preparing a massive attack
and only timely countermeasures
will save his opponent.

17 ....   N–K5!

The only move, since if *17* ...
P–N3; *18* R–B3 N–K5; *19* QxPch!
KxQ; *20* R–R3ch K–N1; *21* R–R8
mate.

18 Q–R5!   ....

Insufficient is *18* BxNP KxB; *19*
R–N3ch K–R1; *20* Q–R6 R–KN1
etc.

Also inadequate is *18* NxN PxN;
19 BxKP BxB; *20* RxB QxP with
good counterplay.

The key defense arises after *18* P–B3
P–B4!; *19* PxN QPxP, regaining the
piece with advantage.

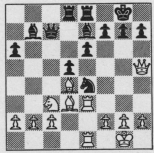

Position after 18 Q–R5

18 ....   B–KB3!

Again the only move, but a sufficient
one; the redoubtable Bishop on Q4
is eliminated. *18* ... P–N3? would
permit the stock mate starting with
19 QxRPch. And *18* ... P–B4 loses

to *19* R–R3 P–R3; *20* BxNP N–N4; *21* Q–N6!

19   NxN   ....

White has nothing better than a draw after *19* RxN PxR; *20* BxB NPxB; *21* BxKP P–B4 (Penrose).

19   ....   BxB
20   QxRPch!   ....

"This sacrifice leads only to a draw, as I had seen when making it; but I entertained two hopes at that moment: that Black would not accept it, or that, despite everything, there might yet prove to be a winning line" (O'Kelly).

"White must go in for this sacrifice since if *20* N–N5 P–R3; *21* R–R3 Q–B5 and Black has the initiative" (Penrose).

20   ....   KxQ

Black does not fear ghosts. Not *20* ... K–B1?; *21* N–N3 BxR; *22* RxB K–K2; *23* QxP with a virulent attack taking shape.

21   N–B6ch   K–R3
22   R–R3ch   K–N4
23   N–R7ch   K–N5!

Not *23* ... K–B5?; *24* R–R4 mate.

24   B–K2ch   K–B5
25   B–Q3   ....

White has nothing better than to repeat moves, since if *25* R–R4ch? K–K4 and the King escapes. *25* B–R5? is refuted by BxPch; *26* KxB QxPch; *27* K–N1 QxN!

25   ....   K–N5
26   B–K2ch   K–B5
27   B–Q3   K–N5!

27 ... BxPch; *28* KxB Q–B4ch; *29* K–B1 Q–K2; *30* R–B3ch gives White at least a draw.

Draw

Final position after 27 ... K–N5

This draw is more fascinating than many a decisive game, and it is hard to believe that White has nothing better than a repetition after *28* B–K2ch K–B5; *29* B–Q3 etc.

If *28* K–B1 (threatening *29* P–B3ch) BxBP!; *30* KxB Q–B5ch is the saving clause.

73

U.S.S.R. TEAM CHAMPIONSHIP 1962
Sicilian Defense

WHITE: LUTIKOV   BLACK: KLAVINS

Black is stalked unrelentingly after one rather minor slip in the opening. The result is a textbook model on the strength of the initiative.

1	P–K4	P–QB4
2	N–KB3	N–QB3
3	P–Q4	PxP
4	NxP	P–K3
5	N–QB3	Q–B2
6	B–K3	P–QR3
7	P–QR3	P–QN4
8	NxN	....

The alternative 8 B–K2 B–N2; 9 P–B4 NxN; 10 QxN N–K2!; 11 O–O N–B3; 12 Q–Q2 B–K2; 13 QR–Q1 P–Q3 renders only an equal game, where Black's delaying the customary ... N–KB3 shows itself to advantage.

8	....	QxN

Gligorich–Darga, Sarajevo 1962, continued: 8 ... PxN; 9 B–K2 B–N2; 10 O–O P–QB4; 11 P–B4 B–K2; 12 B–B3 N–B3; 13 P–K5 R–Q1; 14 Q–K1 N–Q4=.

9	B–K2	B–N2
10	B–B3	Q–B2
11	P–K5	R–B1
12	O–O	BxB
13	QxB	P–Q3

If 13 ... QxP; 14 Q–N7 regains the Pawn advantageously.

14	PxP	BxP
15	B–Q4	BxPch?

Snapping at the bait. Black can maintain parity with 15 ... N–B3; 16 P–R3 (if 16 BxN PxB; 17 QxP BxPch; 18 K–R1 B–K4) B–K2.

16	K–R1	B–K4
17	N–Q5!	Q–N1

Not 17 ... PxN?; 18 BxB QxB; 19 KR–K1 winning the Queen. The next few moves are forced.

18	BxB	QxB
19	N–N6	R–Q1
20	QR–Q1	RxR
21	RxR	P–B4
22	N–Q7	Q–K5
23	Q–KN3	Q–K7
24	Q–N8ch	K–B2
25	N–K5ch	K–B3

Position after 25 ... K–B3

Black's King seems to gave reached safety and he has some nasty threats of his own. However, he still has no time to draw a free breath—as the sequence shows.

26	Q–B8ch!	K×N
27	Q×NPch	N–B3
28	Q–N3ch	K–K5

Of no avail is *28 . . .* P–B5; *29* Q–N5ch K–K5; *30* P–B3ch K–K6; *31* Q–B5 mate.

29	P–B3ch	K–K6
30	R–K1	P–B5
31	R×Qch	K×R
32	Q×P	Resigns

74

UNITED STATES NATIONAL OPEN 1968
Sicilian Defense

WHITE: KOEHLER   BLACK: EVANS

After a brief theoretical skirmish, Black essays the speculative sacrifice of an exchange, proving once again that even in well-trodden paths ingenuity will out. A remarkable endgame blooms after only fifteen moves.

1	P–K4	P–QB4
2	N–KB3	P–K3
3	P–Q4	P×P
4	N×P	N–QB3
5	N–QB3	....

Should White try for the more ambitious Maroczy Bind? After *5* N–N5 P–Q3; *6* B–QB4 (*6* B–KB4 P–K4; *7* B–K3 N–B3; *8* B–N5!? is Bronstein's idea) N–B3; *7* QN–B3 P–QR3; *8* N–R3 B–K2; *9* B–K2 O–O; *10* O–O P–QN3; *11* B–K3 B–N2; *12* R–B1 N–K4; *13* Q–Q4 N/4–Q2 (Reshevsky–Matulovich, Sousse Interzonal 1967); *14* KR–Q1 keeps a slight spatial advantage which is difficult to exploit.

5	....	P–QR3
6	B–K3	Q–B2
7	B–K2	N–B3
8	O–O	....

It is debatable whether White should stop for *8* P–QR3. Definitely inferior, however, is *8* P–B4 B–N5; *9* O–O!? B×N; *10* P×B N×P; *11* B–Q3 P–Q4; *12* N×N Q×N; *13* B–Q4 O–O; *14* Q–R5 P–B3, and Black's extra Pawn tells in the long run (Formanek–Benko, U.S. National Open 1968).

8	....	B–N5
9	N–R4	....

Sharpest. *9* N×N NP×N is easy for Black.

Position after 9 N–R4

9	....	B–Q3

Black has a welter of interesting choices here.

9 . . . NxP; 10 NxN QxN; *11* N–N6 R–QN1; *12* B–B3 P–B4; *13* BxN PxB; *14* Q–R5ch offers unclear attacking prospects.

Portisch tried the novelty *9 . . . B–K2!?* against the Brazilian prodigy Mecking at the Sousse Interzonal 1967, and play continued: *10* NxN NPxN; *11* N–N6 R–QN1; *12* NxB QxN; *13* P–K5 N–Q4; and now Matulovich's *14* B–B1! B–B4; *15* P–B4 N–K2; *16* P–QN3 maintains the advantage.

At the U.S.S.R. Championship 1966, Lepeshkin–Furman, Black tried the queer-looking *9 . . . N–K2!?; 10* P–QB4 NxP; *11* B–B3 N–B4 (but not *11 . . . N–B3; 12* P–B5!); *12* P–QR3 NxN; *13* PxB NxP; *14* NxP QPxN; *15* Q–Q4 O–O; *16* QxN, and now . . . N–B4 followed by . . . B–Q2 would have given him a comfortable position.

I had won a nice game against Garcia at the Havana Olympics 1966 with *9 . . . O–O!?; 10* NxN QPxN; *11* P–QB4? (correct is *11* B–N6! Q–B5; *12* B–Q3) B–Q3; *12* B–N6 (too late) BxPch; *13* K–R1 Q–B5; *14* P–KN3 Q–R3; *15* K–N2 P–K4!; *16* R–R1 Q–R6ch; *17* K–B3 B–N5ch; *18* K–K3 Q–R3ch; *19* K–Q3 KR–Q1ch; *20* BxR RxBch; *21* K–B2 RxQ; *22* QRxR P–KN3; *23* P–B3 Q–K6; *24* RxB BxP; *25* N–B3 BxPch; *26* NxB NxN; *27* R–N2 N–B7; *28* RxN QxR; White Resigns.

10 P–KN3   . . . .

Again considered theoretically sharpest. Duller is *10* NxN NPxN; *11* N–N6 R–QN1; *12* NxB RxN; *13* BxP R–R1; *14* B–Q3 BxPch; *15* K–R1 B–B5; *16* Q–Q2 BxB; *17* QxB Q–K4= (Kotz–Taimanov, U.S.S.R. Championship 1962).

10 . . . .   P–QN4

The first salvo. More usual is *10 . . . NxP; 11* NxN QxN (not *11 . . . QPxN; 12* Q–Q4 P–KB4; *13* B–R5ch); *12* N–N6 R–QN1; *13* B–B3 P–B4; *14* BxN PxB; *15* Q–R5ch, again with unclear attacking chances. The point of the text becomes apparent after Black's twelfth.

11 NxN?   . . . .

A slight transposition which proves harmful. Correct is *11* N–N6! upon which I intended *11 . . . QxN* (necessary may be *11 . . . R–QN1; 12* NxB RxN; *13* P–QR4!); *12* NxNP (later, while analyzing this position with me, Fischer suggested *12* NxKP! followed by NxPch, with a terrific and probably winning attack) B–B4; *13* BxB QxB; *14* N–B7ch K–K2, and Black shortly wins two pieces for a Rook.

11 . . . .   QxN
12 N–N6   B–N2!

The real point. White keeps the upper hand after *12 . . . R–QN1; 13* NxB RxN; *14* B–Q3. The next few moves are forced.

13 NxR   QxKP
14 B–B3   QxKB
15 QxQ   BxQ

Now the contest starts in earnest.

16 **N–N6** ....

Rejecting *16* P–QR4 BxN; *17* PxP K–K2; *18* PxP P–KR4! when Black's initiative outweighs White's Queen-side Pawns.

16 .... **P–KR4!**

Position after 16 ... P–KR4

Black has a Pawn for the exchange, and his minor pieces are stationed magnificently. The immediate threat is ... P–R5. Even so, his combination contains an element of risk, since White has a multitude of defenses which could not be examined thoroughly over the board.

17 **P–KR4** ....

Not *17* P–KR3 P–R5; *18* P–KN4 NxP!; *19* PxN P–R6, followed by P–R7 mate!

Perhaps White should try either *17* P–QR4 or *17* P–QB4.

17 .... **N–N5**
18 **P–R4** ....

If *18* N–B8 B–K4; *19* B–B5 P–N4!; *20* N–Q6ch BxN; *21* BxB PxP; *22* PxP P–K4 followed by ... R–N1 wins.

18 .... **K–K2**
19 **PxP** **PxP**
20 **P–N4** ....

Koehler suggested *20* P–B4, but Black stays on top with *20* ... NxB; *21* PxN B–B3; *22* PxP BxQNP; *23* KR–B1 BxP; *24* R–B5 B–B3; *25* R–R7 B–N1! ·

20 .... **NxB**
21 **PxN** **B–B3**
22 **P–B4** **BxKNP**
23 **PxP** **BxNP**
24 **KR–B1** **R–QN1**
25 **N–B8ch** **K–B3**
26 **N–R7** **BxP**
27 **R–B7** **B–N6**
28 **NxB** **BxR**

More efficient than *28* ... RxN; *29* RxP followed by R/1–R7 with drawing chances.

29 **NxB** **RxP**
30 **N–K8ch** **K–K2!**
31 **R–R8** ....

If *31* NxP R–N5ch wins the stray Knight.

31 .... **P–R5**
32 **K–B2** **P–N4**

The rest is a visit to the butcher shop. The Knight is no match for four Pawns.

33 **N–N7** **R–N7ch**
34 **K–B3** **P–B4**
35 **N–R5** **P–K4**
36 **P–K4** **P–N5ch**
37 **K–K3** **P–B5ch**
38 **NxP** **PxNch**
39 **KxP** **P–N6**
40 **R–R1** **R–KR7**
Resigns

75

BLED 1961
Sicilian Defense

WHITE: TAL   BLACK: OLAFSSON

Tal's intuition leads him into an unsound combination, but he has the clock on his side and luck—the luck of the strong. Indeed, how many players in the world would have found the refutation over the board?

1	P–K4	P–QB4
2	N–KB3	N–QB3
3	P–Q4	PxP
4	NxP	P–K3
5	N–QB3	Q–B2
6	B–K3	P–QR3
7	P–QR3	N–B3
8	P–B4	P–Q3

Transposing into the cramped but solid Scheveningen Variation. This is a crucial moment; Black's move here determines the character of the game. Against Yanofsky, at Stockholm 1962, Olafsson decided to simplify with 8 ... NxN; 9 QxN (would Tal have chosen the speculative 9 BxN!? QxP; 10 P–KN3 Q–B2; 11 P–K5 N–Q4; 12 N–K4?) N–N5; 10 B–Q2 Q–B4; 11 QxQ BxQ; 12 N–Q1 P–Q3; 13 B–K2 N–B3; 14 N–B3 B–Q5=.

9	Q–B3	B–K2

An alternative is 9 ... P–K4 (inferior is 9 ... NxN; 10 BxN P–K4; 11 PxP PxP; 12 Q–N3!); 10 NxN PxN; 11 PxP PxP (or Taimanov's 11 ... N–N5!?); 12 B–QB4 R–QN1.

10	B–Q3	O–O
11	O–O	B–Q2
12	QR–K1	P–QN4
13	Q–N3	K–R1
14	NxN	BxN
15	P–K5	N–N1

Black has the faulty idea of bringing this Knight to KB4 via R3. Natural and better is 15 ... N–K1. White would still have attacking prospects, to be sure, but it would be hard to crash through, since Black's King side contains no organic weaknesses.

16	Q–R3	N–R3
17	P–B5!?	....

In the tournament book Tal himself says he should have played 17 K–R1 instead of this premature sacrifice. He spent forty minutes on this move, which was still not sufficient to analyze completely all the possibilities arising from it. He was therefore depending upon his intuition and luck. This attitude is not unique. Najdorf, for example, confesses: "Often I sacrifice intuitively, without fully seeing the possible continuation."

17	....	NxP
18	RxN	....

There is no turning back. Bad is 18 BxN PxB; 19 PxP BxP; 20 RxP B–Q2.

18	....	PxR
19	BxBP	P–N3
20	B–Q4	....

Position after 20 B–Q4

This is the point of Tal's combination, but unfortunately it is not correct.

20	....	K–N1?

In his calculations Tal most feared *20 ... Q–Q1!* since he saw *21 P–K6ch B–B3; 22 Q–R4 PxP; 23 RxP*, the fine reply *23 ... B–K4!*, whereupon *24 RxB* (or *24 R–K7 QxR*) *QxQ; 25 R–K4ch Q–B3* loses for White.

But then he found *20 ... Q–Q1; 21 PxPch B–B3; 22 Q–R4* which he assessed as favorable, counting on either *22 ... BxBch?; 23 QxBch K–N1; 24 B–K4 R–K1; 25 R–Q1* or *22 ... K–N2; 23 B–Q7! BxB; 24 N–Q5 BxBch; 25 QxBch K–R3; 26 R–K7* with at least a draw. Two months later, however, some Moscow amateurs found the simple resource *22 ... B–KN2!* which forces simplification and causes the collapse of Tal's whole combinational buildup.

21	P–K6	B–N4

If *21 ... P–B3; 22 BxP! PxB 23 Q–R6 B–Q1* (or *23 ... B–K1; 24 N–Q5 and N–B4 next); 24 P–K7 QxP; 25 RxQ BxR; 26 QxPch K–R1; 27 P–KN4!* with a winning attack.

22	PxPch	RxP
23	BxP	R–N2

Black could offer more resistance with *23 ... R–B3*. The plausible *23 ... R–K2* is met by *24 R–KB1*. One possibility is *24 ... R–KB1; 25 RxRch KxR; 26 Q–B5ch K–N1; 27 N–Q5 BxN; 28 QxBch K–B1; 29 Q–R8ch* mates.

24	Q–K6ch	K–R1
25	B–K8!	P–R3
26	BxB	QxB
27	N–K4	R–K1
28	Q–N6	....

Even simpler is *28 Q–B7 R/1–KN1; 29 NxB PxN; 30 Q–R5* mate.

28	....	R–K2
29	P–KR4	Q–Q4
30	BxRch	RxB
31	QxP	QxQ
32	NxQ	BxP
33	R–K8ch	R–N1
34	N–B7ch	K–N2
35	RxRch	KxR
36	NxPch	K–R2
37	N–B5	B–N4
38	P–QN3	Black lost on time.

Commentators are fond of saying at this point, "A typical Tal game."

76

STOCKHOLM INTERZONAL 1962
Sicilian Defense

WHITE: STEIN   BLACK: PORTISCH

Black overlooks a sparkling twist, and one careless move costs him the game. Remarkable.

1	P–K4	P–QB4
2	N–KB3	P–K3
3	P–Q4	PxP
4	NxP	P–QR3

It should be noted that Black's order of moves is quite deliberate. The "forcing" *4* . . . N–QB3 allows White to set up a Maroczy Bind after *5* N–N5 P–Q3; *6* P–QB4, which many players using the Taimanov Variation would rather not face.

5	B–Q3	. . . .

Spassky employed this against Petrosian in their title match, 1969. *5* N–QB3 N–QB3; *6* B–K3, etc., allows a transposition into the main line. The point is *5* P–QB4 N–KB3; *6* N–QB3 B–N5 equalizes rather readily (if *7* P–K5 N–K5; *8* Q–N4 NxN; *9* P–QR3 B–B1; *10* PxN Q–R4 or . . . P–Q3).

White does not seem to have any powerful waiting move here.

5	. . . .	N–KB3
6	O–O	. . . .

Of course not *6* P–K5? Q–R4ch.

6	. . . .	Q–B2
7	N–Q2	N–B3

More flexible is *7* . . . P–Q3, reserving Q2 for the QN.

8	NxN	NPxN

8 . . . QPxN; *9* P–KB4 B–B4ch; *10* K–R1 still gives White attacking possibilities.

9	P–KB4	B–B4ch
10	K–R1	P–Q3

More consistent is *10* . . . P–Q4— but that's another story.

11	N–B3	P–K4
12	PxP	PxP
13	N–R4	O–O
14	N–B5	B–K3
15	Q–K2	P–QR4
16	B–QB4	K–R1
17	B–KN5	N–Q2

Virtually forced. Not *17* . . . N–K1; *18* BxB PxB; *19* Q–B4! PxN; *20* QxB, etc.

18	QR–Q1	N–N3?

White gets a lucky break. After *18* . . . BxN; *19* PxB (*19* RxB P–B3; *20* B–B1 N–N3 gives White nothing) P–B3 White would retain a slight advantage, but whether it's enough to win would remain to be seen.

19	NxP!	BxB

Forced. On *19* . . . NxB (or *19* . . . KxN; *20* B–B6ch K–N1; *21* Q–R5); the reply is the same as the game—

Position after 19 . . . B×B

20 B–B6!   **B–K2**

There's nothing else. Black is itching to play 20 . . . B×Q; but he can't, because of *21* N–B5ch K–N1; *22* N–R6 mate. Also futile is *20* . . . N–Q2; *21* R×N!

21 Q–B3   **Resigns**

If *21* . . . B×B; *22* Q×B N–Q2; *23* R×N *finis.*

77

YUGOSLAVIA v. U.S.S.R. MATCH GAME 1967

Sicilian Defense

WHITE: BOGDANOVICH   BLACK: SUETIN

Blow and counterblow—a violent struggle of wills from start to finish. Striving to avoid a draw, and exhausted by complications, Black falls into a deadly snare.

1 P–K4	P–QB4
2 N–KB3	P–K3
3 P–Q4	P×P
4 N×P	N–QB3
5 N–QB3	Q–B2
6 P–B4	P–QR3
7 B–K3	P–QN4

The popularity of the Taimanov System is due largely to the great latitude it offers the second player. Here Black neglects his King-side development to start a diversion on the other wing.

8 N×N	Q×N
9 B–K2	B–R6!

Position after 9 . . . B–R6

An ingenious innovation designed to improve on *9* . . . P–N5; *10* B–B3! P×N; *11* P–K5 P×P; *12* R–QN1 Q–B6ch; *13* B–Q2 Q–R6; *14* B×R, winning material.

10 B–Q4	B×P
11 N×P	B×R
12 B×B	P×N

If *12* . . . K–B1; *13* N–Q6 yields a strong bind.

13 BxKNP	QxKP
14 O–O	RxP
15 B–Q3	Q–K6ch
16 K–R1	B–N2
17 BxR	N–R3

17 . . . N–K2 looks better, but the text gives the Knight access to N5.

18 BxNP	B–Q4
19 R–B3	. . . .

An irresponsible annotator recommended "*19* B–Q3, threatening Q–R5." However, Black wins neatly by *19* . . . Q–KR6!; *20* Q–K2 N–N5. '

19	Q–B4

Black seems justified in playing for the win. He spurns *19* . . . N–N5; *20* RxQ N–B7ch; *21* K–N1 NxQ; *22* R–Q3 RxP; *23* RxN RxPch; *24* K–B1 RxP with a draw in view.

20 P–B4	B–B3

Still not *20* . . . BxR??; *21* QxPch mates. *20* . . . N–N5 looks good, though.

21 BxB	QxB
22 Q–QN1	R–K7?

Still with an eye on the main chance. After *22* . . . R–R1; *23* P–R3 P–B4 Black has a comfortable game.

23 Q–N8ch	K–K2

Position after 23 . . . K–K2

24 B–B6ch!	. . . .

Satan never sleeps. Now White has a mate in three.

24	KxB
25 Q–Q8ch	Resigns

If *25* . . . K–B4; *26* Q–N5ch K–K5; *27* Q–K5 mate.

78

MOSCOW 1967
Sicilian Defense

WHITE: SPASSKY   BLACK: SUETIN

An object lesson in how to sustain the initiative. Each time Black is on the verge of equalizing, Spassky finds an ingenious way to prevent it.

1 P–K4	P–QB4
2 N–KB3	N–QB3
3 N–B3	P–K3

3 . . . P–K4 is also playable.

4 P–Q4	PxP

5	NxP	Q–B2
6	B–K3	P–QR3
7	N–N3	....

A dubious attempt to improve on either 7 P–QR3 or 7 B–Q3.

7	....	N–B3
8	P–B4	B–N5
9	B–Q3	O–O

Black's reply lacks vitality. Much better is 9 ... P–Q4; 10 P–K5 P–Q5!; 11 NxP N–Q4.

| 10 | O–O | BxN |

Better is 10 ... P–Q4. Unless provoked, Black should not give up his good Bishop just to double the QBP.

| 11 | PxB | P–Q3 |

In accordance with classical theory, Black attempts to keep the center closed in order to minimize the scope of White's two Bishops. More forcing, however, is 11 ... P–Q4; 12 P–K5 N–Q2 (not 12 ... N–K5; 13 BxN PxB; 14 N–B5); followed by an eventual ... P–B4.

12	R–B3	P–K4
13	P–B5	P–Q4
14	R–N3!	K–R1

14 ... PxP would be met by 15 B–R6.

| 15 | PxP | N–K2 |

15 ... NxP allows the powerful stroke 16 Q–R5 NxB; 17 P–B6 P–KN3; 18 Q–R6 R–KN1; 19 RxN Q–Q1; 20 N–K4 Q–B1; 21 Q–R4 with a bind.

16	B–B5	N/3xP
17	Q–N4	R–KN1
18	R–R3	N–KB3
19	Q–N5	N/2–Q4

Virtually forced. Not 19 ... P–QN3?; 20 BxN QxB; 21 RxPch!

| 20 | R–KB1 | P–QN3 |
| 21 | B–K4! | B–N2? |

Black could ease the pressure somewhat with 21 ... PxB; 22 BxN R–N1 (but not 22 ... NxB?; 23 RxPch KxR; 24 Q–R5 mate).

| 22 | BxN | BxB |
| 23 | B–K7! | .... |

No rest for the weary. 23 ... QxB? is impossible, because of 24 RxPch.

| 23 | .... | Q–B3 |
| 24 | R–R6! | .... |

Position after 24 R–R6

The threat of 25 RxN compels Black's reply, which in turn lands him in a difficult ending.

24	....	N–K5
25	RxQ	NxQ
26	R–Q6!	....

Again Black is allowed no breathing space. After 26 RxP N–K5, Black would regain the Pawn. The text forces him to relinquish drawing chances arising from opposite-colored Bishops.

| 26 | .... | BxN |

27	RP×B	N–K5
28	R×P	N×P
29	P–B6	....

Material is even, but White has managed to preserve his initiative despite the disappearance of Queens.

29	....	KR–K1

The ending is lost after 29 ... N–Q4; 30 R–N7 P×P; 31 B×Pch N×B; 32 R×N R–N2; 33 R/1×BP R×R; 34 R×R R–QB1; 35 R–B2 followed by K–B1, etc.

30	P×Pch	K×P
31	R–N7	N–K7ch
32	K–R1	N–B5
33	P–N3	N–N3

If 33 ... N–K3; 34 B–Q6 (not 34 B–B6ch K–N1; 35 B×P? N–B4) N–Q1; 35 R–Q7 P–K5; 36 B–B7 wins at least a Pawn.

34	B–Q6	N–R1
35	P–B4	K–N3
36	P–KN4	R–K3
37	P–B5	K–N4
38	P–R3	P–K5
39	K–N2	P–K6
40	B–B4ch	K–N3
41	R–N6!	....

This insures the win of a Pawn and, with it, the game. Note the power of the Bishop contrasted with the immobile Knight.

41	....	P–K7
42	R–K1	R–QB1
43	P–N4	P–QR4
44	R×P	P×P
45	R/2×Rch	P×R
46	B–K5	....

Good technique. 46 R×Pch K–B2; 47 R–K5 N–N3; 48 R–B5ch K–K3 puts Black back in the ball game.

46	....	P–R4
47	R×Pch	K–B2
48	R–QN6	P×P
49	P×P	K–K2
50	B×N	R×B
51	R×P	K–K3
52	R–QB4	K–Q4

Position after 52 ... K–Q4

Black plays on because he is hoping for a miracle. At Havana 1952, one of my first great international tournaments, I learned at first hand the full meaning of Tartakower's dictum that "you can't win by resigning." The Dutch master Prins was a piece down against one of the Cuban lesser lights, Quesada; his position was obviously hopeless, but he insisted on adjourning the game. When I asked Prins why he didn't resign immediately, he replied that anything can happen. Sure enough, his opponent obliged the next day by dying of a heart attack. Such drastic solutions to the problem of saving a lost game do not readily present themselves. Nor does such a stubborn attitude endear a master to his colleagues.

53	R–B1	R–KN1
54	K–N3	K–B3
55	K–B4	R–B1ch

56	K–K5	R–KN1
57	K–B5	R–B1ch
58	K–K6	R–KN1
59	R–KN1	Resigns

White's smooth transition from a superior middle game to a won ending illustrates once again that a chess game is an organic whole.

79

34th U.S.S.R. CHAMPIONSHIP 1961
Sicilian Defense

WHITE: NEZHMETDINOV   BLACK: TAL

Tal falls prey to some of his own dazzling tricks. It is a unique experience to watch him on the receiving end, and his opponent never lets up.

1	P–K4	P–QB4
2	N–KB3	P–Q3
3	P–Q4	PxP
4	NxP	N–KB3
5	N–QB3	P–K3
6	B–K2	....

This tame developing move now seems old-fashioned.

6	....	P–QR3
7	O–O	Q–B2
8	P–B4	QN–Q2
9	P–KN4!?	....

It is clear that White's intentions are anything but tame. Objectively better is 9 B–B3, but it is a sound psychological ploy to play aggressively against opponents who like to attack.

9	....	P–QN4
10	P–QR3	....

If 10 P–N5 P–N5.

10	....	B–N2
11	B–B3	N–B4?

The Knight is misplaced here. Correct is 11 ... P–R3! (12 P–N5? PxP; 13 PxP P–Q4) followed possibly by ... O–O–O. Black must remove his King from the danger zone before undertaking counteraction in the center.

12	Q–K2	P–K4
13	N–B5	P–N3
14	PxP	PxP
15	N–R6!	....

The Knight is curiously well posted, mainly because of the pressure exerted against B7. Not the least of its merits is the prevention of castling.

15	....	N–K3
16	B–N2	B–N2

The text anticipates meeting 17 P–N5 with BxN. No better is 16 ... N–B5; 17 BxN PxB; 18 P–K5 BxN; 19 PxNch K–B1; 20 Q–K7ch winning a piece.

16 ... N–Q5 doesn't work because of 17 Q–B2 BxN; 18 QxN, etc. Perhaps Black should try 16 ... BxN; 17 BxB N–Q5; 18 Q–Q1 Q–N3 (if 19 K–R1 O–O–O) with nuclear complications.

Position after 16 . . . B–N2

17 RxN!   . . . .

This sacrifice is far from obvious and requires some intricate tactics to justify it. But not *17 P–N5?* BxN.

17	. . . .	BxR
18	N–Q5	Q–Q1

Black rejects *18 . . .* BxN; *19* PxB N–Q5; *20* Q–B2, because of the dual threats P–Q6 and QxB—*e.g.*, *20 . . .* Q–N3; *21* B–K3! or *20 . . .* Q–Q3; *21* P–N5.

19	Q–B2	N–B5
20	BxN	PxB
21	P–K5!	. . . .

Position after 21 P–K5

Possibly Black was hoping to save himself after *21* QxP BxN; *22* PxB Q–N3ch; *23* K–R1 O–O–O; *24* NxP BxP; *25* R–QN1 KR–B1; *26* RxB R–Q2, etc.

21   . . . .   **BxP**

If *21 . . .* BxN (or *21 . . .* B–N2; *22* N–B6ch! BxN; *23* PxB, with R–K1ch to follow); *22* PxB B–K3; *23* B–B6ch K–B1; *24* Q–B5ch mates.

The question is whether *21 . . .* B–R5 holds. White appears to have nothing better than *22* N–B6ch (if *22* Q–B5 R–QB1) QxN; *23* PxQ BxQch; *24* KxB BxB (*24 . . .* O–O–O fails to *25* BxBch KxB; *26* NxP R–Q7ch; *27* K–K1) *25* R–K1ch K–B1; *26* KxB R–K1; *27* R–Q1 with a winning bind.

22	R–K1	P–B3
23	NxPch!	QxN
24	Q–Q4!	. . . .

Each blow is more powerful than the last.

24   . . . .   **K–B1**

The point appears after *24 . . .* BxB; *25* RxBch K–B1; *26* R–KB5!

25 RxB   **Q–Q1**

If *25 . . .* R–Q1; *26* R–K8ch.

26	R–B5ch!	PxR
27	QxRch	K–K2
28	Q–N7ch	K–K3
29	PxPch	**Resigns**

80

SANTA MONICA 1965
Sicilian Defense

WHITE: EVANS   BLACK: BLACKSTONE

A Donnybrook in which neither side is afforded the luxury of castling. Noteworthy is the Knight's tour to the edge of the board—QR8!—one of the most curious winning moves in history.

1 P–K4	P–QB4
2 N–KB3	P–Q3
3 P–Q4	PxP
4 NxP	N–KB3
5 N–QB3	P–QR3
6 B–K2	P–K3

White was rather expecting *6* ... P–K4 instead of this belated transposition into the Scheveningen.

7 P–B4	Q–B2
8 B–B3	B–Q2

The game is already out of the books. Now White is tempted to exploit the fact that Black's KN cannot retreat to Q2.

9 P–KN4	P–R3

This is generally a good reaction, since Black gets control of the KR file after the inevitable P–N5.

10 P–N5	PxP
11 PxP	N–N1
12 B–K3	....

Perhaps White ought to speculate on *12* P–N6!? PxP; *13* B–N4, although he has no clear-cut continuation after *13* ... Q–B1 followed by ... N–KB3. After the text Black hastens to sink his Knight on K4.

12	N–K2
13 P–KR4	QN–B3
14 N–N3	....

Better is *14* Q–K2 followed by O–O–O.

14	N–N3
15 P–R5	KN–K4
16 B–K2	P–N4
17 Q–Q2	N–B5
18 BxN	PxB
19 N–Q4	N–K4
20 Q–N2	....

After *20* O–O–O R–QN1, White's King is not entirely secure.

20	R–QN1!

This compels both sides to forgo castling and is the best practical chance. On *20* ... O–O–O; *21* O–O–O, the board belongs to White, and P–N6, properly timed, will smash Black's structure.

Position after 20 ... R–QN1

Black has two Bishops, a dominating Knight on K4 and pressure along the QN file; White, on the other hand, will seek to mobilize his forces along the KB file and swap off the Knight. It is interesting to see how tactics are wedded to these strategical concepts in the double-edged sequence. White's immediate problem is how to defend his NP. He rejects *21 O–O–O Q–N2; 22 P–N3 P–R4*, because Black's attack comes first.

21	R–QN1	Q–R4
22	K–K2	....

Black was threatening . . . R×P.

22	....	K–Q1
23	N–B3	B–B3
24	N×N	Q×N
25	Q–B3	R–N2
26	B–B4	Q–B4
27	KR–Q1	R–Q2
28	R–Q2	B–K2

The game is rapidly approaching its climax. The apparently strong *28 . . . P–Q4* is refuted by *29 B–K3! P–Q5?; 30 B×P R×B; 31 R×Rch Q×R; 32 R–Q1.*

29	QR–Q1	B×P

Losing patience. Safer is *29 . . . K–B1; 30 B–K3 Q–K4.*

30	B×P	Q–N3?

The best chance is *30 . . . Q–R4; 31 R–Q4 B–B3; 32 R×P B–QN4; 33 N×B Q×N; 34 P–N3 Q×RP; 35 Q×Q R×Q; 36 R–B6 P–R4; 37 R–R6 K–B1; 38 R–N6 R–N2; 39 R–B6ch K–Q2; 40 R–R6* with some winning prospects.

31	B–B4	B×B

32	Q×B	K–K1

Not *32 . . . R×P?; 33 R×Rch B×R; 34 R×Bch K×R; 35 Q×Pch* and *36 Q×R* next.

33	Q–K5	R–KR2

Not *33 . . . Q×P?; 34 R–QN1.*

34	R×R	B×R
35	N–Q5!	Q–B3

Better is *35 . . . Q–N2;* but *36 N–K3* keeps the advantage.

36	Q–N8ch	Q–B1

Forced. If *36 . . . B–B1; 37 N–N6 Q×Pch; 38 K–Q2* White escapes the perpetual then wins the Bishop.

37	N–B7ch	K–Q1

Again forced. If *37 . . . K–B1 (37 . . . K–K2; 38 Q–N4ch); 38 Q×Qch B×Q; 39 R–Q8ch* cleans up.

38	N×P	R×P
39	Q–N6ch	K–K2
40	Q–Q6ch	K–K1
41	N–B7ch	K–Q1
42	N–R8!	Resigns

Final Position after 42 N–R8

The threat of *43 Q–B8* mate or *43 N–N6* is horrendous.

81

CANDIDATES' TOURNAMENT 1959

Sicilian Defense

WHITE: TAL   BLACK: PETROSIAN

A master of attack versus a genius of defense. The outcome is a stupendous draw marked by mutual give-and-take.

1	P–K4	P–QB4
2	N–KB3	P–Q3
3	P–Q4	P×P
4	N×P	N–KB3
5	N–QB3	P–QR3
6	B–N5	QN–Q2
7	B–QB4	Q–R4
8	Q–Q2	P–K3
9	O–O	....

Also sharp is *9* O–O–O P–N4; *10* B–N3 B–N2; *11* KR–K1 N–B4; *12* B×N P×B; *13* Q–B4 B–K2; *14* Q–N4! with advantage (Stein–Tal, U.S.S.R. Championship 1962).

9	....	P–R3
10	B–R4	P–KN4!?

Safer is *10* ... B–K2; *11* QR–Q1 N–K4; *12* B–K2 (or *12* B–QN3 N–N3; *13* B–N3 N–R4) and now either *12* ... P–QN4 or *12* ... P–KN4 produces a stiff fight.

11	B–KN3	N–R4
12	B×KP!	....

Where there's a will there's a way. Gufeld–Petrosian, U.S.S.R. 1959, went: *12* QR–Q1 N–K4; *13* B–N3 N×B; *14* RP×N P–N5, with good play.

180

12	....	P×B
13	N×P	N×B
14	BP×N	N–K4
15	R×Bch!	....

The only way to refresh the attack. Not *15* N×B Q–B4ch; *16* K–R1 R×N.

15	....	R×R
16	Q×QP	R–B3

But not *16* ... B×N?; *17* Q×Bch K–Q1; *18* R–Q1ch K–B2; *19* Q–Q6ch wins.

Position after 16 ... R–B3

17	N–B7ch?	....

White falters at a crucial moment. The correct continuation is *17* Q–B7! P–N3 (on *17* ... Q–N5; *18* N–Q5); *18* N–N7ch K–B1; *19* N–R5! and White regains his material or mates.

17	....	K–B2
18	R–KB1	R×Rch
19	K×R	N–B5!

Energetic. If Black stops to protect his Rook, then *20* N/3–Q5 exposes his King to hideous threats.

20 QxKRP   ....

Position after 20 QxKRP

Again White finds a way to nourish his attack. Now *20* ... QxN?; *21* Q–R7ch wins the Queen. And if

20 ... R–R2; *21* N/3–Q5 is unpleasant.

20 ....   Q–QB4!
21 NxR   ....

On *21* N/3–Q5 N–K6ch forces simplifications.

21 ....   N–Q7ch
22 K–K2   B–N5ch
23 K–Q3   ....

23 KxN Q–Q5ch; *24* K–K1 leads to the same result.

23 ....   Q–B5ch
24 K–K3   Q–B4ch

A mistake would be *24* ... N–B8ch; *25* K–B2.

Draw

82

26th U.S.S.R. CHAMPIONSHIP 1959
Sicilian Defense

WHITE: TAL   BLACK: POLUGAIEVSKY

Black survives a ferocious attack and seems well on his way to drawing after forcing the exchange of Queens. However, he is beguiled by this calm setting and underestimates the extent of Tal's initiative.

1 P–K4   P–QB4
2 N–KB3   P–Q3
3 P–Q4   PxP
4 NxP   N–KB3
5 N–QB3   P–QR3
6 B–N5   QN–Q2

7 B–QB4   Q–R4
8 Q–Q2   P–K3
9 O–O   B–K2

9 ... P–N4 allows *10* B–Q5! PxB; *11* N–B6 Q–N3; *12* PxP N–K4; *13* QR–K1 B–N2; *14* B–K3 Q–B2; *15* P–B4 with advantage (Mnatsakian–Zurakhov, U.S.S.R. Championship Preliminaries 1959).

10 QR–Q1   N–B4

Safer is *10* ... P–R3; *11* B–R4

N–K4; *12* B–K2 (or *12* B–QN3 N–N3; *13* B–N3 N–R4=) P–KN4; *13* B–N3 P–N4; *14* P–QR3 B–QN2; *15* P–B4 PxP; *16* RxP N–N3; *17* R/4–B1 Q–N3; *18* K–R1 NxP; *19* NxN BxN; *20* B–R5 P–Q4 with an extra Pawn (Olafsson–Evans, Buenos Aires 1960).

11 KR–K1	B–Q2
12 P–QR3	Q–B2

If *12* . . . KNxP; *13* NxN QxQ; *14* BxQ NxN; *15* RxN P–Q4; *16* BxQP PxB; *17* R–K2 K–B1; *18* B–N4 BxB; *19* PxB, with a superior ending.

13 P–QN4	N–R5

Unsatisfactory is *13* . . . P–N4 (or *13* . . . QNxP; *14* NxN NxN; *15* RxN QxB; *16* BxB KxB; *17* N–B5ch wins); *14* N/4xNP! PxN; *15* NxP BxN; *16* BxBch QN–Q2; *17* P–K5!

14 NxN	BxN

Not *14* . . . QxB?; *15* N–N6.

15 BxKP!	. . . .

A stock sacrifice in an unusual setting.

15	PxB
16 NxP	QxP

Position after 16 . . . *QxP*

How is White to sustain his attack? *17* QxQ BxQ; *18* R–QB1 B–R5; *19* N–B7ch K–B2; *20* NxR RxN; *21* R–B7 B–B3; *22* P–K5 PxP; *23* RxKP R–K1 (threatening . . . N–Q4) is obviously in Black's favor.

17 Q–Q4	K–B2
18 R–QB1	Q–R7
19 P–K5!	PxP

An understandable attempt to simplify, since *19* . . . QxN; *20* PxN BxP; *21* BxB QxB; *22* Q–Q5ch K–B1; *23* R–K6 keeps up the pressure.

20 QxP	QxPch!
21 KxQ	. . . .

Else *21* K–R1 B–B3.

21	N–N5ch
22 K–N1	NxQ
23 RxN	BxB
24 NxBch	K–N3

If *24* . . . K–B3; *25* QR–B5! KR–K1; *26* N–K4ch K–N3; *27* R–N5ch K–B2; *28* N–Q6ch wins material.

25 N–K6	KR–K1?

Plausible but disastrous. The only chance is *25* . . . QR–B1 (in order to prevent R–B7 and gain time for . . . P–R3). *26* R–B1 can be met by B–N4! The text loses a tempo.

26 R–K3	QR–B1

Too late now. White's Rook has fatal access to KN3.

27 R–B1	B–N4
28 R–N3ch	K–R3
29 NxP	R–B1

Position after 27 ... B–N4

30	R–K1	R–KB3
31	P–R3	R–QB7
32	R–K5	R–QB8ch
33	K–R2	Resigns

A good illustration of lulling an opponent into a false sense of security.

83
SOLINGEN 1968
Sicilian Defense

WHITE: PARMA   BLACK: SZABO

Black provokes a familiar sacrifice for the sake of refuting it. The result is a stinging loss which reconfirms the judgment that he is ill-advised to tamper with the standard order of moves in this variation.

1	P–K4	P–QB4
2	N–KB3	P–Q3
3	P–Q4	PxP
4	NxP	N–KB3
5	N–QB3	P–QR3
6	B–N5	P–K3
7	P–B4	QN–Q2

7 ... B–K2 or 7 ... P–KR3 are the most solid continuations; 7 ... Q–N3 and 7 ... P–N4 are sharper and still unrefuted tries. Because of the sifting sands of theory, the Najdorf Variation is a risky but promising way of playing for a win nowadays.

| 8 | B–B4 | P–N4!? |

This works no better here than it ever has, but there is no easy way to discourage the pending sacrifice on K6. An alternative is 8 ... Q–R4.

| 9 | BxKP! | .... |

The exclamation is not for originality, but merely to indicate its great strength. After 9 B–N3 B–N2, Black can hold his own.

| 9 | .... | PxB |
| 10 | NxKP | Q–N3? |

10 ... Q–R4!; 11 NxB (or 11 O–O!?) RxN; 12 QxP is unclear. But not 10 ... Q–K2; 11 N–Q5! QxN; 12 N–B7ch K–B2; 13 NxQ KxN; 14 Q–Q4 B–N2; 15 O–O–O with a dangerous attack before Black consolidates.

| 11 | N–Q5 | NxN |
| 12 | QxN | Q–K6ch |

The point is *12 ... B–N2?*; *13 N–B7ch!* QxN; *14* Q–K6ch mates.

13	K–B1	N–N3
14	N–B7ch	K–Q2
15	Q–B7ch	K–B3
16	NxR	....

More pertinent is *16* N–Q5! QxP; *17* Q–B7ch KxN; *18* R–Q1ch K–K3; *19* R–K1 QxRch; *20* KxQ P–R3 (or *20 ...* N–Q4; *21* Q–B6, followed by K–B2 and R–K1ch); *21* P–B5ch! K–Q4; *22* QxN PxB; *23* K–B2 R–R5ch; *24* R–Q1ch K–K4; *25* Q–B6 R–N1; *26* Q–K8ch Black resigns. (Matanovich–Gufeld, Yugoslavia *vs.* U.S.S.R., 1969.)

16	....	NxN
17	Q–Q5ch	K–B2

Position after 17 ... K–B2

A moment of truth. This position was known to theory, which awarded a plus to White after *18* QxN. But this judgment is hazardous—*e.g.*, *18 ...* B–K3 (not *18 ...* B–R6?; *19* P–K5!); *19* P–QN3 P–Q4 (threatening ... B–QB4); *20* Q–Q8ch K–N2; *21* R–K1 Q–Q7; *22* P–B5 QxP; *23* PxB Q–Q6ch; *24* R–K2 Q–Q8ch; *25* R–K1 Q–Q6ch; and White must be content with a draw.

18	R–K1!	....

Here is Parma's new move. He forgoes the win of the Knight in order to consolidate, while he retains Rook and two Pawns for two pieces. White is able to force favorable simplifications before the enemy can activate his minor pieces.

18	....	Q–R2
19	P–K5	PxP
20	QxPch	K–N2
21	B–K7!	N–B2
22	Q–Q6!	BxB
23	RxB	Q–N3
24	QxQch	KxQ
25	RxP	N–Q4?

Black could put up a whopping fight with *25 ...* N–K3!; *26* R–KB7 R–Q1.

26	P–KN3	N–K6ch
27	K–B2	N–N5ch

If *27 ...* NxP; *28* R–Q1 keeps the Knight locked up while the Kingside Pawns advance. After the text White must avoid *28* K–B3? because of R–K1.

28	K–K2	B–N2
29	R–K1	NxP
30	K–B2	....

Position after 30 K–B2

30	....	R–Q1

30 ... P–KR4; *31* R–K6ch B–B3;
32 R/7–N6 N–N5ch; *33* K–K2
R–QB1; *34* P–B5 is no better.

31	R–K6ch	B–B3
32	P–KN4	R–Q7ch
33	R–K2	R–Q3

34	P–B5	R–Q5
35	K–N3	N–B8ch
36	K–R4	N–Q7
37	P–B6	N–B6ch
38	K–N3	P–KR4
39	PxP	R–Q8
40	P–B7	N–Q5
41	P–B8(Q)	Resigns

84
MOSCOW 1963
Sicilian Defense

WHITE: TAL   BLACK: GLIGORICH

Since Gligorich himself is one of the arch exponents of the White side, it is interesting to see how he conducts the defense. Tal, however, on move fifteen introduces a piece sacrifice which takes everyone by surprise.

1	P–K4	P–QB4
2	N–KB3	P–Q3
3	P–Q4	PxP
4	NxP	N–KB3
5	N–QB3	P–QR3
6	B–N5	P–K3
7	P–B4	B–K2
8	Q–B3	Q–B2
9	O–O–O	QN–Q2
10	P–KN4	P–N4
11	BxN	....

Fischer (as Black) writes: "Gligorich and I have a standing feud with this position, which we've reached no less than three times. I've lost twice and drawn once." Bernstein–Fischer, U.S. Championship 1958, continued:

11 B–N2 B–N2; *12* KR–K1 (better is P–QR3) P–N5; *13* N–Q5!? PxN; *14* PxP K–B1; *15* N–B5 R–K1; and Black (for a change) won.

11	....	NxB
12	P–N5	N–Q2
13	P–QR3	....

Careless is *13* B–R3? P–N5!; *14* N/3–K2 B–N2; and Black already assumes the initiative with an early ... P–Q4 (Fischer–Smyslov, Candidates' Tournament 1959).

13	....	B–N2

13 .. R–QN1 is a sharper alternative.

14	B–R3	....

Sherwin–Fischer, U.S. Championship 1960, continued: *14* P–KR4 P–Q4; *15* PxP N–N3; *16* P–B5 NxP; *17* PxP O–O–O; *18* B–N2 NxN; *19* QxBch QxQ; *20* BxQch KxB; *21* PxN BxRPch; *22* K–N1 PxP;

23 NxKP K–QB1 and was drawn shortly.

14	....	O–O–O
15	BxP!?	....

Possibly a prepared variation. Gligorich-Fischer, Candidates' Tournament 1959, went: *15* P–B5!? BxPch; *16* K–N1 P–K4; *17* N/4xP PxN; *18* NxP, and now Fischer gives *18* . . . Q–N3! (instead of his . . . Q–B4); *19* NxPch K–B2; *20* NxP B–KB3 as roughly equal.

15	....	PxB
16	NxKP	Q–B5?

Flustered, Gligorich finds a second-best move. Here the Queen is maladjusted. It would have been interesting to follow the course of the game after Keres' recommendation *16* . . . Q–N3!

17	N–Q5	BxN
18	PxB	K–N2

To meet the threat of P–N3, winning the Queen. Wrong is *18* . . . N–B4; *19* P–N3 Q–K5; *20* Q–B3! with the double threat of *21* KR–K1 or P–N4.

Slightly better seems *18* . . . K–N1; *19* P–N3 Q–B1; and if *20* N–Q4 K–R1 holds.

19	P–N3	Q–B1
20	R–Q3!	N–N3
21	R–B3	Q–Q2
22	R–B7ch	QxR
23	NxQ	KxN

Position after 19 . . . Q–B1

24	Q–B3ch	K–N1
25	QxP	N–B1

Black would be all right materially if it weren't for the Pawn deficit. As it is, he can offer only token resistance.

26	R–K1	QR–N1

On *26* . . . KR–N1; *27* QxP R–R1; *28* RxB is good enough to win.

27	Q–Q4	B–Q1
28	R–K6	R–B1
29	P–KR4	P–R3
30	P–N6	KR–N1
31	P–R5	R–B4
32	Q–K4	RxRP
33	R–K8	RxR
34	QxR	B–B3
35	P–B4	PxP
36	PxP	R–R6
37	K–Q2	B–B6ch
38	K–K2	B–Q5
39	P–KB5	RxP
40	P–B5	PxP
41	P–Q6	R–R7ch
42	K–Q3	R–R6ch
43	K–B4	Resigns

85

33rd U.S.S.R. CHAMPIONSHIP 1965
Sicilian Defense

WHITE: KHOLMOV   BLACK: BRONSTEIN

White's sacrifices are so startling that one is left with the impression that he stumbled into them by accident. Actually, his concept is incredibly profound.

1 P–K4	P–QB4
2 N–KB3	N–KB3
3 N–B3	....

Eschewing *3* P–K5 N–Q4; *4* N–B3, etc., as in games 95 and 96.

3	P–Q3
4 P–Q4	PxP
5 NxP	P–QR3

The Najdorf Variation, by transposition. The fancy footwork is over.

6 B–N5	P–K3
7 P–B4	B–K2
8 Q–B3	Q–B2

This accurate reply prevents B–B4.

9 O–O–O	QN–Q2
10 P–KN4	P–N4
11 BxN	PxB
12 P–B5	....

Ceding control of K5 in order to exert pressure on K6. Gligorich–Fischer, Zurich 1959 continued: *12* B–N2 B–N2; *13* KR–K1 O–O–O; *14* P–QR3 N–N3=.

An exciting draw in Padevsky–Evans, Havana Olympics 1966, resulted from *12* B–Q3 B–N2; *13* K–N1 N–B4; *14* P–B5 P–N5; *15* QN–K2 P–Q4; *16* BPxP QPxP; *17*

PxPch K–B1; *18* BxKP BxB; *19* QxB NxQ; *20* N–K6ch KxP; *21* NxQ R–R2; *22* R–Q4, etc.

12	N–K4
13 Q–R3	O–O

Fischer introduced this move against Gligorich at the Candidates' Tournament 1959. Black's game collapses after *13* ... B–Q2; *14* P–N5! PxNP (or *14* ... PxBP; *15* N–Q5); *15* PxP PxP; *16* NxKP.

14 P–N5	....

In the aforementioned game Gligorich proceeded with the more strategical *14* QN–K2 in order to increase the pressure against K6. After *14* ... K–R1; *15* N–B4 R–KN1; *16* R–N1 P–Q4; *17* PxKP QPxP; *18* N–Q5 Q–B4, Black's position hung by a hair.

14	P–N5?

An error which meets with a stunning refutation. Correct is *14* ... PxNP; *15* PxP PxP; *16* NxKP Q–Q2; *17* N–Q5 QxN; *18* QxQch BxQ; *19* NxBch K–B2; and Black has at least equal chances in the resulting endgame.

15 PxBP	BxP
16 R–N1ch	K–R1
17 Q–R6	Q–K2
18 N–B6!	....

Position after 17 . . . Q–K2

The shocker. When playing over this game for the first time, I remember thinking this was a misprint!

| 18 | .... | N×N |
| 19 | P–K5! | .... |

Now it is clear that White is fighting to clear the K4 square for his Knight.

| 19 | .... | B–N4ch |

Kholmov gives:

A. *19 . . .* N×P (worse is *19 . . .* P×KP; *20* N–K4 B–N4ch; *21* N×B P–B3; *22* N×RP!); *20* N–K4 N–Q2 (Black does best to take his chances with the inferior ending resulting from *20 . . .* N–N3; *21* N×B Q×N; *22* P×N Q–N2!; *23* Q×Qch K×Q; *24* P×BPch K×P; *25* R×P); *21* R×P P×P; *22* R×B R–KN1; *23* R×Rch K×R; *24* R×P/5 N–B1; *25* N–B6ch K–R1; *26* R–K5! B–K3; *27* R–N5 mates.

B. *19 . . .* B×P; *20* P–B6 B×BP; *21* B–Q3 B–N4ch; *22* R×B P–B4 (if *22 . . .* P–B3; *23* R–N3 P×N; *24* B×KRP wins); *23* QR–N1 R–R2; *24* N–K2 N–K4; *25* N–B4 and the

threat of N–R5 and R–N7 compels Black's resignation (if *25 . . .* R–QB2; *26* B×BP! P×B; *27* N–Q5 wins).

20	R×B	P–B3
21	P×QP	Q–KB2
22	R–N3	P×N
23	B–B4	P×Pch
24	K–N1	N–Q1

Position after 24 . . . N–Q1

| 25 | QR–N1 | .... |

Permitting Black to continue his resistance. More efficient is *25* P–Q7! B×P; *26* R×B, etc.

25	....	R–R2
26	P–Q7	R×P
27	P×P	N×P
28	B×N	R–Q8ch!
29	R×R	B×B
30	K×P	R–N1ch
31	K–R1	B×P

31 . . . B–B4 offers more fight, but White's material preponderance would still tell in the long run.

32	R/3–Q3	Q–K2
33	K×B	Q–K3ch
34	R–N3	Resigns

86

HASTINGS 1959–60
Sicilian Defense

WHITE: GLIGORICH   BLACK: BOBOTSOV

An important theoretical game which is important to an understanding of this variation. Today it looks like old hat, but Gligorich's Queen sacrifice was a trail blazer.

1 P–K4	P–QB4
2 N–KB3	P–Q3
3 P–Q4	P×P
4 N×P	N–KB3
5 N–QB3	P–QR3
6 B–N5	P–K3
7 P–B4	P–KR3
8 B–R4	B–K2
9 Q–B3	Q–B2

For *9* . . . P–KN4!? see Game 87. The text is more natural.

10 O–O–O	QN–Q2
11 B–Q3	. . . .

11 B–K2 may set Black more long-range problems. Bednarsky–Evans, Lugano Olympics 1968, continued: *11* . . . P–KN4 (if *11* . . . O–O; *12* P–KN4 is unpleasant to meet; and if *11* . . . P–QN4; *12* P–K5! B–N2; *13* P×N! B×Q; *14* B×B B×P; *15* B×B R–QB1; *16* B×P R–R2; *17* B–R5! R×B; *18* N×P Q–B5; *19* KR–K1! R×P—Klavins–Tal, Riga 1959; now *20* R–Q4! Q–B3; *21* B–B3! gives White a clear advantage); *12* P×P N–K4; *13* Q–K3 N–R2; *14* N–B3 P×P!? (*14* . . . N×N; *15* P×N P×P is probably necessary); *15* B–N3 (stronger is *15* N×P! N–N3; *16* P–

KN3) B–Q2; *15* Q–Q4 P–B3 with a solid position for Black.

11	P–QN4?

Black can obtain active play with *11* . . . P–KN4!; *12* P×P N–K4, etc.

12 P–K5!	B–N2
13 N×KP!	P×N
14 B–N6ch	K–B1

On *14* . . . K–Q1; *15* Q–R3! (or *15* P×N! B×Q; *16* P×Bch K–B1; *17* P×B K–N2; *18* KR–K1) P×P; *16* Q×P keeps up the pressure.

Position after 14 . . . K–B1

15 P×N!	. . . .

A Queen sacrifice to boot.

15	B×Q

Black's King is loose after *15* . . . B×P; *16* Q–R3.

16 P×Bch	K–N1
17 P×B	N–B3

18	BxN	PxB
19	P-K8(Q)ch	RxQ
20	BxR	P-Q4

A later game went 20 ... K-B1!;
21 B-R5 R-N1; 22 P-B5 P-N5!;
23 N-K4 R-N7; 24 N-Q2 Q-R4;
25 K-N1 RxN!; 26 RxR P-N6;
27 RPxP QxR; 28 PxP K-K2;
29 B-B7 P-B4; 30 R-N1 QxRP;
31 R-N7 Q-K4 and a draw was
agreed. This line may rescue Black.

21	R-Q4	....

With a Rook and two pieces for the
Queen, White can't miss. Sharper is
21 P-B5! Q-B5ch; 22 K-N1 QxP/4;
23 B-N6!

21	....	K-R2
22	B-R5	Q-B4
23	KR-Q1	R-QB1
24	R/1-Q2	P-B4
25	N-K2	K-N2
26	K-N1	K-B3
27	P-QR3	P-R4
28	N-N3	P-N5
29	P-QR4	Q-B3
30	P-N3	Q-B6

The only reason Black doesn't
resign is the awkward position of the
Bishop, which he hopes to keep

permanently out of play. It's only a
matter of time, however, before
White breaks through on the KN or
K file.

31	R/4-Q3	Q-B4
32	R-K2	Q-N8ch
33	K-N2	R-B6
34	R/3-Q2	P-Q5

A little better is 34 ... R-B1 to
prevent the Bishop escaping to K8.

35	R-N2	Q-K6
36	B-K8	P-Q6
37	PxP	Q-K8

Or 37 ... Q-Q5; 38 N-K2.

38	R-QB2	RxP
39	B-N5	R-B6

White forces mate after 39 ...
R-Q8; 40 N-R5ch K-B2; 41 R-
N7ch K-B1; 42 R-B8.

40	B-B4	RxRch
41	RxR	P-K4
42	PxPch	QxPch
43	K-R2	P-B5
44	N-K4ch	K-N3
45	R-N2ch	K-R4
46	N-B2	Q-K1
47	B-Q3	K-R5
48	R-N4ch	K-R4
49	B-N6ch,	Resigns

87
U.S.S.R. 1961
Sicilian Defense

WHITE: GASPARIANTZ   BLACK: EIDLIN

Here two unknowns enrich the
theory of the notorious Göteborg
Variation, which came into being one

day at the Interzonal in 1955, when
three Argentinians (Najdorf, Panno
and Pilnik) suffered terrible defeats

with their secret weapon at the hands of three Soviet stars (Keres, Geller and Spassky, respectively).

1	P–K4	P–QB4
2	N–KB3	P–Q3
3	P–Q4	PxP
4	NxP	N–KB3
5	N–QB3	P–QR3
6	B–N5	P–K3
7	P–B4	B–K2
8	Q–B3	P–R3
9	B–R4	P–KN4!?

A remarkable concept that typifies the modern approach to the openings. Black voluntarily smashes open his King side to obtain domination over his K4 square. It is even more remarkable that as the result of many key games with this sharp variation theory now regards it as drawish! 9 . . . Q–B2 is the prescription for maintaining tension nowadays.

10 PxP   KN–Q2

10 . . . PxP; 11 BxNP QN–Q2 does not yield enough for the Pawn.

11 NxP!?   . . . .

This is also the move those three Soviet players chose on that fateful day when confronted with Black's surprise. White might also try 11 Q–R5 (or 11 B–N3 N–K4; 12 Q–R5 BxP), N–K4 (not 11 . . . BxP?; 12 BxB QxB; 13 NxP! QxQ; 14 N–N7ch); 12 B–B2 BxP; 13 P–KR4 B–B3; 14 O–O–O with a double-edged game.

11	. . . .	PxN
12	Q–R5ch	K–B1
13	B–N5!	. . . .

Position after 13 B–N5

The purpose of this brilliant thrust is to clear the way for O–O, while the Bishop is also able to eliminate, on Q2 or QB3, a Knight which plays a vital part in many variations.

13 . . . .   KR–R2!

The original intention was 13 . . . N–K4 with which Panno defended against Geller. White whipped up a winning attack with 14 B–N3! BxP (14 . . . R–KR2! is necessary now); 15 O–Och K–K2; 16 BxN Q–N3ch; 17 K–R1 QPxB; 18 Q–B7ch, etc. After witnessing this slaughter (in the same round) Najdorf and Pilnik promptly switched to 13 . . . K–N2. But that fared no better after 14 O–O N–K4; 15 B–N3 N–N3; 16 PxPch RxP; 17 R–B7ch KxR; 18 QxR PxB; 19 R–B1ch, etc.

14 O–Och   . . . .

A good illustration of the creative evolution in opening theory. At the time this game was played it was well known that 14 Q–N6 gave White nothing after 14 . . . R–B2; 15 QxPch K–N1; 16 Q–N6ch R–N2; 17 QxPch K–R1; 18 BxN NxB; 19 O–O–O N–K4; 20 Q–Q5 B–N5;

21 QR–B1 (Gligorich–Fischer, Portoroz 1958), and now *21* . . . R–B1 (instead of *21* . . . BxPch; *22* BxB QxBch; *23* K–N1 Q–K2; *24* Q–Q2=) would give Black a plus.

14	. . . .	K–N1
15	P–N6	R–N2
16	QxP	. . . .

White might give his opponent an extra chance to go wrong by trying *16* R–B7 first. Then *16* . . . B–N4? (*16* . . . BxB!; *17* QxP transposes to the text) loses to *17* BxN NxB; *18* QR–KB1 N–K4; *19* BxB! PxB; *20* RxRch KxR; *21* Q–R7 mate.

16	. . . .	BxB
17	R–B7	. . . .

Although White is two pieces down, this position was no stranger to theory. The analysis which has been lavished on it shows that White gets at least a draw after *17* . . . RxR; *18* PxRch KxP; *19* Q–R7ch K–B1; *20* Q–R8ch K–B2; *21* Q–R7ch K–B1. But he can try for more with *22* P–K5 followed by R–B1ch and N–K4.

17	. . . .	Q–B3

If the aforementioned dangers can be avoided by giving up the Queen, this simplifies matters considerably for Black.

18	RxQ	BxQ
19	B–K2	N–K4

At last the key square is occupied.

20	B–R5	B–Q2

21	R–KB1	B–K2

With a Rook and two minor pieces for the Queen, Black is in good shape —particularly if he can pick up the KNP after . . . B–K1.

22	R–B7!	. . . .

Position after 22 R–B7

By applying the same maneuver again White just keeps his attack alive.

22	. . . .	NxR

The new sacrifice must be accepted. Not *22* . . . B–KB1; *23* RxBch KxR; *24* Q–R8ch R–N1; *25* P–N7ch wins.

23	PxNch	RxP
24	BxRch	KxB
25	Q–R5ch	Draw

After *25* . . . K–N2; *26* Q–N4ch K–B1; *27* Q–R5! Black must submit to perpetual check unless he wishes to lose by *27* . . . B–KB3?; *28* Q–B3 K–N2; *29* P–K5! followed by *30* QxP.

88

UNITED STATES CHAMPIONSHIP 1966
Sicilian Defense

WHITE: R. BYRNE BLACK: EVANS

This might well qualify as the most brilliant game by an American in modern times. *15* B-B6!? was the shot heard around the world.

1	P-K4	P-QB4
2	N-KB3	P-QR3
3	N-B3	P-Q3
4	P-Q4	PxP
5	NxP	N-KB3
6	B-N5	P-K3
7	P-B4	Q-N3
8	Q-Q2!?	....

The soundness of this sacrifice has eluded the best chess minds for over a decade. The pendulum favored first White, then Black, then White, then Black. . . . It is known affectionately as the "Poisoned Pawn Variation."

Black can force an equal endgame after *8* N-N3 Q-K6ch!; *9* Q-K2 QxQch; *10* BxQ QN-Q2; *11* B-B3 R-R2; *12* O-O-O P-N4; *13* N-R5 P-R3; *14* B-R4 R-B2, etc.

8	....	QxP
9	R-QN1	Q-R6
10	P-K5	....

Rehabilitating one of the discarded approaches. The "latest wisdom" in the line is *10* P-B5 N-B3; *11* NxN PxN; *12* PxP PxP; *13* P-K5! N-Q4 (Black barely escaped in Kavalek-Fischer, Sousse Interzonal 1967, after *13* . . . PxP; *14* BxN PxB;

15 N-K4 B-K2; *16* B-K2 P-KR4; *17* P-B4 P-KB4; *18* R-N3 Q-R5; *19* O-O!? PxN; *20* Q-B3 QxRP!; *21* B-Q1 R-B1; *22* BxPch K-Q1; *23* R-Q1ch B-Q2; *24* Q-K3 Q-R4!; *25* R-N7 B-B4; *26* R/1xBch K-B1; *27* R/Q-B7ch, Draw); *14* NxN BPxN; *15* B-K2 PxP; *16* O-O B-B4ch; *17* K-R1 R-B1; *18* P-B4 RxRch; *19* RxR B-N2 (Fischer-Geller, Monte Carlo 1967); and now *20* Q-B2 (or *20* B-Q1) gives a promising attack.

10	....	PxP
11	PxP	KN-Q2
12	B-QB4	B-N5

Fischer later introduced *12* . . . Q-R4! into master play.

13	R-N3	Q-R4
14	O-O	O-O
15	B-B6!?	PxB?

Loses by force. Correct is *15* . . . NxB; *16* PxN R-Q1; *17* RxB QxR; *18* Q-N5 P-KN3; *19* R-B4 Q-B1 (Zuckerman beat Byrne in the 1967 U.S. Championship with *19* . . . RxN; *20* Q-R6 Q-B1; *21* QxQch KxQ; *22* RxR N-B3); *20* R-R4 P-QN4; *21* B-Q3 P-N5; *22* BxNP! RPxB; *23* R-R6 RxN; *24* RxPch with a draw by perpetual check (Hartston-Mecking, Hastings 1966-67).

| 16 | Q-R6! | .... |

Black was hoping to muster up defenses after *16* PxP K–R1; *17* Q–R6 R–N1; but *18* B–Q3 N–B1; *19* N–B3 BxN; *20* RxB QxR; *21* P–KR4! renders Black helpless against the threat of N–N5, according to O'Kelly.

16	QxKP
17 N–B5!	PxN
18 N–K4!	....

An orgy of clearance sacrifices designed to free the third rank for the Rook.

Position after 18 N–K4

18	B–Q7

A valiant try. If *18* ... QxN (or *18* ... PxN; *19* R–KR3); *19* R–N3ch Q–N5; *20* RxQch PxR; *21* B–Q3 wins.

Also unsatisfactory is *18* ... R–K1; *19* R–KR3 N–B1; *20* NxPch QxN;

21 QxQ B–K3; *22* BxB PxB; *23* R–N3ch N–N3; *24* RxNch forcing mate shortly.

19 NxB	Q–Q5ch
20 K–R1	N–K4
21 R–N3ch	N–N5

21 ... N–N3 loses outright to *22* R–KR3. Also bad is *21* ... Q–N5; *22* QxP.

22 P–KR3	Q–K4
23 R–B4	Q–K8ch
24 N–B1	QxR
25 RxNch	QxR
26 PxQ	N–Q2
27 N–N3	K–R1
28 B–Q3	....

Even quicker is *28* NxP R–KN1; *29* BxP RxP; *30* B–K8 (threatening BxN). Black now prolongs the game, in desperation, until the time control.

28	R–KN1
29 BxP	R–N3
30 BxR	PxB
31 N–K4	P–QN4
32 P–N5	B–N2
33 NxP	N–B1
34 Q–R2	B–B1
35 Q–K5	N–K3
36 N–Q7ch	**Resigns**

The only thing he is left with here is the will to live.

89

VARNA OLYMPICS 1962
Sicilian Defense

WHITE: FISCHER   BLACK: NAJDORF

The originator of the Najdorf Variation encounters some surprising and effective tactics. After only twenty-four moves he is bound hand and foot, the victim of Fischer's supreme artistry.

1	P–K4	P–QB4
2	N–KB3	P–Q3
3	P–Q4	PxP
4	NxP	N–KB3
5	N–QB3	P–QR3
6	P–KR3	....

A recommendation of Weaver Adams—the first surprise. 6 B–QB4 used to be Fischer's pet recipe, and he still resorts to it from time to time with success.

6	....	P–QN4

White's last was specifically directed against the characteristic 6 ... P–K4 of the Najdorf Variation; after 7 KN–K2! B–K2; 8 P–KN4 O–O; 9 N–N3, White has a comfortable edge.

7	N–Q5!?	B–N2?

Black's troubles begin here. Correct is 7 ... NxP; 8 Q–B3 N–B4; 9 P–QN4 P–K3 (not 9 ... N–N2?; 10 Q–B3!); 10 PxN (10 N–B6ch QxN; 11 QxR QxN; 12 QxN QxR; 13 QxBch K–K2 is safe enough), 13 QxP R–R2=.

8	NxNch	NPxN
9	P–QB4!	PxP

More prudent is 9 ...BxP. By accepting the Pawn sacrifice Black subjects himself to tremendous pressure.

10	BxP	BxP
11	O–O	P–Q4
12	R–K1!	....

A very difficult move to find, but the only way to retain the initiative.

12	....	P–K4

Fischer gives 12 ... PxB; 13 RxB Q–Q4; 14 Q–B3 P–K3 as relatively best.

13	Q–R4ch!	N–Q2

If 13 ... Q–Q2; 14 B–QN5! PxB; 15 QxR B–Q3; 16 RxB! PxR; 17 QxKP followed by N–B5 with a bind.

Position after 13 ... N–Q2

14	RxB!	PxR

14 ... PxB leads to the same type of cramp, except that Black lacks any material compensation for it.

15	N–B5	B–B4
16	N–N7ch	K–K2
17	N–B5ch	K–K1

Now Black has lost the option of castling and his defensive task is hopeless.

18	B–K3!	BxB
19	PxB	Q–N3
20	R–Q1	....

Eschewing 20 BxPch K–Q1; 21 R–Q1 Q–N4. White just keeps piling up the pressure.

20	....	R–R2
21	R–Q6!	Q–Q1

Also futile is *21 ... Q×P* (or *21 ... Q–B2; 22 R×BP)*; *22 B×Pch!* K–Q1; *23 Q–R5ch K–B1* (if *23 ... R–B2; 24 B–K6* initiates another fatal pin); *24 N–K7ch K–N1; 25 N–B6ch K–R1; 26 N×R*, etc.

22 Q–N3   **Q–B2**

Or *22 ... R–B1; 23 N–N7ch K–K2; 24 Q–R3!* puts Black in a strait-jacket.

23 B×Pch   **K–Q1**

On *23 ... K–B1; 24 B–R5.*

24 B–K6   **Resigns**

The grand old master has no

Final position after 24 B–K6

appetite to continue. If *24 ... R–N2; 25 Q–R4 Q–B1; 26 Q–R5ch K–K1; 27 Q×RP K–Q1; 28 B×N R×B 29 R×Rch Q×R; 30 Q×Pch, K–B2; 31 Q×Pch K–N3; 32 Q×R.*

90
STOCKHOLM 1962
Sicilian Defense

WHITE: FISCHER   BLACK: BOLBOCHAN

Burdened with a bad Bishop against a good Knight, Black defends with extreme care but is gradually forced to retreat behind his lines. Fischer's invasion on the weakened squares is a model of accuracy, culminating in a keen combination.

1 P–K4	P–QB4
2 N–KB3	P–Q3
3 P–Q4	P×P
4 N×P	N–KB3
5 N–QB3	P–QR3
6 P–KR3	....

If now *6 ... P–K4; 7 KN–K2 B–K3; 8 P–KN4 P–Q4; 9 P×P N×QP; 10 B–N2.*

6	N–B3
7 P–KN4	N×N
8 Q×N	P–K4
9 Q–Q3	B–K2

More accurate is *9 ... B–K3!* so as to retreat the KN to Q2 without hemming in this Bishop.

10 P–N5	N–Q2
11 B–K3	N–B4?

11 ... B×P; 12 B×B Q×B; 13 Q×P Q–K2; 14 Q×Qch K×Q; 15 N–Q5ch K–B1; 16 O–O–O P–KN3 holds White to a minimal endgame edge.

12 Q–Q2	B–K3
13 O–O–O	O–O

| 14 | P–B3 | R–B1 |
| 15 | K–N1 | N–Q2 |

Regrouping. The Knight has no future on QB4, so Black tries to post it on QN3 where it can leap to B5.

16	P–KR4	P–N4
17	B–R3	BxB
18	RxB	N–N3
19	BxN!	QxB
20	N–Q5	Q–Q1
21	P–KB4	....

White has a strategically won game because of his domination of Q5 with the Knight. But not the hasty 21 NxBch? QxN; 22 QxP? KR–Q1 and Black wins.

Position after 21 P–KB4

In addition to his positional disadvantage, Black's King side is in a state of siege. It is instructive how White works with threats on both sides of the board in order to augment his superiority.

21	....	PxP
22	QxP	Q–Q2
23	Q–B5	QR–Q1
24	R–R3	Q–R2
25	R–QB3	....

Unconvincing is 25 N–B6ch (not 25 N–N4 P–Q4!; 26 N–B6 PxP!) BxN; 27 PxB P–N3; 28 Q–N5 K–R1.

Objectively best is 25 NxBch QxN; 26 RxRP KR–K1; 27 P–QR4! "But I was hoping to win in the middle game. Ironically, I wouldn't have been awarded the brilliancy prize had I chosen the best line here. They don't give medals for endgame technique" (Fischer).

25	....	P–N3
26	Q–N4	Q–Q2
27	Q–B3	Q–K3
28	R–B7	QR–K1

Black is being forced to the wall.

29	N–B4	Q–K4
30	R–Q5	Q–R1
31	P–R3	P–R3

Black has defended a difficult position rather well. On 31 ... P–B3 Fischer gives 32 Q–QN3! R–B2; 34 RxQP PxP; 35 PxP Q–K4; 36 R–KB6! R–KB1; 37 RxR RxR; 38 R–B8ch B–B1; 39 N–K6 wins.

32	PxP	QxP
33	P–R5	B–N4
34	PxP	PxP

On 34 ... BxN; 35 PxPch RxP; 36 RxR KxR; 37 R–R5! is the quietus.

| 35 | Q–QN3! | .... |

Less clear is 35 RxB!? QxR; 36 Q–N3ch P–Q4; 37 NxP K–R1!.

| 35 | .... | RxN |

What else? If 35 ... K–R1 (or 35 ... BxN; 36 R–R5ch wins the

Position after 34 . . . PxP

Queen); *36* NxPch QxN; *37* RxB R–B8ch (or *37* . . . QxR; *38* Q–R3ch mates); *38* K–R2 QxR; *39* Q–R3ch K–N1; *40* Q–R7ch K–B1; *41* Q–R8ch Q–N1; *42* Q–R6ch mates.

36	R–K5ch	K–B1
37	RxRch	Resigns

37 . . . KxR; *38* Q–K6ch K–B1; *39* Q–B8ch mates.

91

PORTOROZ 1958
Sicilian Defense

WHITE: FISCHER BLACK: LARSEN

Fischer slays the Dragon Variation after an ill-advised attempt on the part of his opponent to complicate. The result is an object lesson in how to mount an assault against the fianchettoed King.

1	P–K4	P–QB4
2	N–KB3	P–Q3
3	P–Q4	PxP
4	NxP	N–KB3
5	N–QB3	P–KN3
6	B–K3	B–N2
7	P–B3	O–O
8	Q–Q2	N–B3
9	B–QB4	NxN

Since this game, Black has tried many ways to neutralize the Yugoslav Attack. *9* . . . B–Q2 and Donald Byrne's *9* . . . P–QR4 lead to ultrasharp play; the fate of the

Dragon Vatiation rests upon the success of these two moves, if the text does not hold.

10	BxN	B–K3
11	B–N3	Q–R4
12	O–O–O	P–QN4

On *12* . . . BxB; *13* BPxB!, Black's counterattack is stymied.

13	K–N1	P–N5
14	N–Q5	BxN
15	BxB	. . . .

Probably stronger is the plan to obtain pressure along the King file and abandon the attack: *15* PxB Q–N4; *16* KR–K1 P–QR4; *17* Q–K2! (Tal–Larsen, Zurich 1959).

| 15 | . . . . | QR–B1? |

In a higher sense, the losing move. Correct is *15 ...* NxB!; *16* BxB (Fischer said he intended *16* PxN QxP; *17* QxP, keeping the game alive) N–B6ch!; *17* PxN (*17* BxN PxB; *18* QxBP QxQ; *19* PxQ KR–B1 renders White's Pawn useless) QR–N1!; *18* PxP QxNPch!; *19* QxQ RxQch; *20* B–N2 KR–N1 with equality.

16 B–N3! ....

Now this Bishop exerts a watchful eye on the King side.

16	**R–B2**
17 P–KR4	**Q–QN4**

If Black tries to slow down the attack with *17 ...* P–R4; Fischer gives *18* P–N4! PxP; *19* P–R5! PxRP; *20* PxP NxKP; *21* Q–K3 N–B3; *22* PxP P–K4; *23* P–R6 and wins.

18 P–R5! **KR–B1**

Again, Fischer gives *18 ...* PxP; *19* P–N4! PxP; *20* PxP! NxKP; *21* Q–R2 N–N4; *22* BxB KxB; *23* R–Q5 R–B4; *24* Q–R6ch K–N1; *25* RxNch RxR; *26* QxP mate.

19 PxP	**PxP**
20 P–N4	....

But not the impetuous *20* BxN? BxB; *21* Q–R6 P–K3! when Black not only defends everything, but threatens ... Q–K4 as well.

20	**P–R4**
21 P–N5	**N–R4**

21 ... N–K1 doesn't work either after *22* BxB NxB; *23* R–R6! P–K3; *24* Q–R2 N–R4; *25* BxP PxB; *26* RxPch N–N2; *27* R–R1, etc.

Position after 21 ... N–R4

22 RxN! ....

"I've made this sacrifice so often, I feel like applying for a patent" (Fischer).

22 .... **PxR**

Fischer gives *22 ...* BxB; *23* QxB PxR; *24* P–N6 Q–K4 (if *24 ...* P–K3; *25* QxQP); *25* PxPch K–R2; *26* Q–Q3! (intending P–KB4).

23 P–N6 **P–K4**

No better is *23 ...* P–K3; *24* PxPch KxP; *25* BxB KxB; *26* R–N1ch K–R2; *27* Q–N2 Q–K4; *28* Q–N6ch K–R1; *29* R–N5, etc.

24 PxPch	**K–B1**
25 B–K3	**P–Q4**

The best try. If *25 ...* P–QR5; *26* QxPch R–K2; *27* Q–Q8ch! RxQ; *28* RxRch R–K1; *29* B–B5ch is decisive.

26 PxP	**RxKBP**
27 P–Q6	**R–KB3**
28 B–N5	**Q–N2**
29 BxR	**BxB**
30 P–Q7	**R–Q1**
31 Q–Q6ch	....

31 Q–R6ch forces mate in three.

31 .... **Resigns**

92

UNITED STATES CHAMPIONSHIP 1967
Sicilian Defense

WHITE: EVANS   BLACK: ZUCKERMAN

Zuckerman is a player noted for his exhaustive book knowledge, and in New York circles he is often referred to as "Zuckerbook." He displays a rare piece of bad judgment in the opening by gobbling a tainted Pawn —the dose is lethal.

1	P–K4	P–QB4
2	N–KB3	P–Q3
3	P–Q4	P×P
4	N×P	N–KB3
5	N–QB3	P–KN3
6	B–K3	N–B3
7	P–B3	....

This setup is practically the only feared one against the Dragon; and it can be safely stated that if a reliable antidote were found the Dragon would enjoy a greater following. It has just begun to emerge again after a long period of desuetude.

7	....	B–N2
8	Q–Q2	O–O

The attempt to postpone (or avoid) castling with 8 ... B–Q2 and 9 ... R–QB1 has been found wanting, since Black's King is not secure in the center and he is minus the services of his KR.

| 9 | O–O–O | .... |

Zuckerman writes: "In my opinion Evans plays 9 O–O–O because he hopes that Black will reply 9 ... P–Q4, after which White can be a

pawn ahead, and everyone knows how Evans likes to have a pawn in his pocket. I don't think he believes 9 O–O–O is objectively superior. The main ideas behind 9 B–QB4 in this position are: (1) control of Q5 (preventing ... P–Q4); (2) attack on Black's King position (KB7); (3) safeguarding White's position on the Queen side after B–N3."

Actually, the answer is quite simple. I knew that Zuckerman would not invite this line unless he had a prepared variation up his sleeve. Since he was braced for 9 B–QB4, I decided to adopt an unfashionable move in order to make him play in my ball park. I also knew that he was familiar with a game that I had won from Padevsky at Havana 1964 in which I had flown in the face of theory by accepting the Pawn after 9 ... P–Q4; 10 N×N P×N; 11 P×P N×P; 12 N×N P×N; 13 Q×P Q–B2; 14 Q–QB5. Perhaps, therefore, he would be hoodwinked into an inferior reply, thinking that I was in possession of some pet recipe.

9	....	N×N
10	B×N	B–K3
11	K–N1	Q–B2

Not 11 ... Q–R4?; 12 N–Q5!

Again, Zuckerman writes: "It is

interesting to note that some annotators, because I lost the game against Evans, criticized this move, but all the alternatives they suggested were much weaker One of the main ideas behind *11 . . .* Q–B2 is the later transfer of the Queen to R4, after . . . KR–B1, without allowing N–Q5."

12	P–KR4	KR–B1
13	P–R5	N×P?

Position after 19 B–Q3

Opening the KR file proves fatal. Correct is *13 . . .* Q–R4!; *14* P×P RP×P; *15* P–R3 (*15* B×N B×B; *16* N–Q5 Q×Q; *17* N×Bch K–N2!=) QR–N1; *16* P–KN4 P–QN4; *17* N–Q5 (otherwise Black's attack comes first) Q×Q; *18* R×Q (not *18* N×Pch? K–B1) N×N; *19* P×N B×P!; *20* B×B B×P; *21* R–R3 B×P!; *22* R–N3 K×B; *23* R×B R–B4; *24* R–K4 R–N2; *25* P–N4 R–R4; *26* K–N2 Draw! (Evans–Zuckerman, U.S. Championship 1970).

14	B×B	K×B
15	P–KN4	N–B3
16	Q–R6ch	K–N1
17	P–K5!	....

This is the twist that Black overlooked.

17	....	P×P
18	P–N5	N–R4
19	B–Q3!	....

19 R×N P×R; *20* B–Q3 also works.

19	....	P–K5

There is no valid defense in the threat of R×N. If *19 . . .* P–B4; *20* R×N P×R; *21* Q×Bch K–R1; *22* Q×BP, etc.

20	R×N	P×R
21	N×P	....

Black can hold out longer after *21* B×P Q–K4; *22* B×Pch K–R1; *23* B–K4ch K–N1; *24* B×P KR–N1; *25* B×R Q×N; *26* R–Q8ch!

21	....	Q–KB5
22	N–B6ch	P×N
23	B×Pch	K–R1
24	B–B5ch	K–N1
25	Q–R7ch	K–B1
26	Q–R8ch	Resigns

Final position after 26 Q–R8ch

Etiquette dictates that a chessmaster not play on until mate—*26 . . .* K–K2; *27* P×P!

93

HASTINGS 1961-62
Sicilian Defense

WHITE: J. LITTLEWOOD   BLACK: BOTVINNIK

White launches a blitz attack against his renowned opponent which narrowly fails due to a very fine saving clause. As Botvinnik remarked at the time, it seemed that White had a 50–50 chance of success.

1 P–K4	P–QB4
2 N–KB3	P–Q3
3 P–Q4	PxP
4 NxP	N–KB3
5 N–QB3	P–KN3
6 B–K3	B–N2
7 P–B3	P–QR3
8 B–QB4	P–QN4
9 B–N3	B–N2
10 Q–Q2	QN–Q2

Black's Queen-side operations are designed to discourage White from castling on that wing, and he keeps his King in the center as long as possible until White declares himself. Reshevsky against Bisguier, 2nd Match Game 1957, tried the more pretentious *10* . . . P–KR4 and got the worst of it after *11* P–QR4 P–N5; *12* N–R2 P–R4; *13* P–B3.

11 O–O–O	N–B4
12 K–N1	NxB
13 BPxN	. . . .

Capturing away from the center generally is frowned upon, because the resulting Pawn configuration gives Black a won King-and-Pawn ending, if he can exchange all the pieces—a big *if*. White grants this concession in order to maintain his initiative. After *13* RPxN Q–B2 followed by . . . O–O–O, Black's opening problems are over, and he has the two Bishops as well. By contrast, after the text, Black dare not castle long, because of the open QB file.

13	O–O
14 B–R6	BxB
15 QxB	P–N5
16 P–K5!?	. . . .

This looks promising but meets with a stinging refutation. Objectively, best is *16* N–R4 P–K4; *17* N–B2 P–R4; *18* N–K3 with absolute control of Q5. White would then renounce his aggressive intentions and gang up on the Queen file by doubling Rooks.

16	N–Q2
17 P–KR4	. . . .

17 PxP P–K4!; *18* P–KR4 produces variations similar to the game.

17	PxN
18 P–R5	PxKP

Barden relates: "A dramatic moment. Here there was hubbub among the spectators, who had the vision of a new Saint George arising to slay the Continental dragons (Littlewood had defeated Gligorich

Position after 18 . . . PxKP

in the previous round). Even many
of the other masters were taken in,
and gathered round White's position,
which was viewed with a mixture of
amazement and envy. As Botvinnik
sat calmly at the board—and even
adjusted his tie—while Littlewood's
head remained buried in his hands,
doubts began to arise."

Most grandmasters are poker-faced,
but now and again one can observe
certain mannerisms which may be
interpreted as the external signs of an
inner reaction to an unexpected turn.
Fischer will rise, circle the playing
room, then rush back to his seat
while his opponent is still pondering
his next move. Petrosian will lean
back after a sacrifice and hum a
gentle tune. Gligorich will raise his
eyebrows a bit, while others toy with

a pencil, smile, massage their temples,
sway in their chairs, etc. Only
Botvinnik and Keres sit completely
unmoved, without a telltale batting
of the eye.

19	PxNP	N–B3
20	PxBP	. . . .

White is desperate now. He intended
20 N–B5, but saw the catch after
. . . P–B7ch! (the key to Black's
survival); 21 KxP Q–B1ch, followed
by . . . QxN.

Also inadequate is the plausible try
20 P–KN4 PxN; 21 P–N5 P–B7ch!
(again); 22 KxP Q–B2ch; 23 K–N1
BPxP; 24 PxN PxP, and White has
nothing to show for his piece.

20	. . . .	PxN
21	PxRPch	K–R1
22	RxP	. . . .

A better alternative was "Resigns."

22	. . . .	Q–R4
23	Q–K3	N–Q4
24	Q–Q2	NxPch
25	K–R1	QR–Q1
26	R–QB1	QxPch
27	QxQ	NxQ
28	RxR	RxR
	Resigns	

An antibrilliancy.

94

PIATIGORSKY CUP, CALIFORNIA 1966
Sicilian Defense

WHITE: LARSEN BLACK: PETROSIAN

Larsen's concluding Queen sacrifice is merely the frosting on the cake. What is remarkable is the way he ties the world champion up in knots —and makes it look simple.

1 P–K4	P–QB4
2 N–KB3	N–QB3
3 P–Q4	PxP
4 NxP	P–KN3
5 B–K3	B–N2

Allowing the dread Maroczy Bind, which could still be averted by 5 ... N–B3; 6 N–QB3 P–Q3, etc. But Petrosian has a predilection for cramped positions.

6 P–QB4	N–B3

This game is so convincing that one is left with the impression that Black does better with the thematic 6 ... N–R3; 7 N–QB3 O–O; followed by ... P–B4.

7 N–QB3	N–KN5
8 QxN	NxN
9 Q–Q1	N–K3

Theory gives White the nod after 9 ... P–K4; 10 N–N5! O–O; 11 Q–Q2 (but not 11 NxN PxN; 12 BxP Q–R4ch; 13 K–K2 R–K1).

10 Q–Q2	P–Q3
11 B–K2	B–Q2
12 O–O	O–O
13 QR–Q1!	....

An essential improvement which reduces Black to passivity. Now 14 P–B5 is threatened. Keres–Petrosian, Candidates' Tournament 1959, continued: 13 QR–B1 B–QB3; 14 P–B3 N–B4; 15 KR–Q1 P–QR4; 16 P–QN3, with only a slight spatial edge.

13	B–QB3
14 N–Q5	R–K1

"This move I do not understand. Why not 14 ... N–B4; 15 P–B3 P–QR4? I intended 16 KR–K1 followed by B–B1, but it would not be easy to attack the solid black position" (Larsen).

15 P–B4	N–B2
16 P–KB5	N–R3
17 B–N4	....

"A difficult decision—and probably wrong" (Larsen). Stronger is 17 P–QN4! N–N1; 18 P–N5.

Position after 17 B–N4

17	....	N–B4
18	P×P	RP×P

White maintains his advantage without any need for material sacrifice after *18* ... BP×P; *19* B×N P×B; *20* B–K6ch K–R1; *21* R–B7.

"Now I had the fixed idea of luring my opponent forward, giving him the possibility of attack in order, if the attack did not lead to success, to leave him no better off than when he began" (Petrosian).

19	Q–KB2	R–KB1
20	P–K5!	....

Rather than win the Queen, White sacrifices a Pawn! He refuses to break up his fulminant attack for the sake of a dubious material gain after *21* B×N P×B; *22* N–B6ch B×N; *23* R×Q QR×R. "This White can never win, and he might lose" (Larsen).

20	....	B×P
21	Q–R4	B×N
22	R×B	N–K3?

"The world champion overlooks my twenty-fifth move. He was probably a little depressed and dissatisfied with his position, and too quickly grasped what looked like a safe draw. ... In my opinion Black's best chance was *22* ... P–K3; *23* Q×Q KR×Q; *24* R×B P×R; *25* B×N. I did not like it very much, since it seemed to me that Black would get good counterplay, but now I believe that White would have winning chances —*e.g.*, *25* ... P–B4; *26* B–Q1 R–Q7; *27* B–N3! QR–Q1 (*27* ... R×QNP; *28* R–Q1); *28* R–K1 R×QNP; *29* B–R3 R/7–Q7; *30* B–B1 R/7–Q6; *31* B–N5" (Larsen).

23	R–B3	....

Threatening the murderous *24* R–R3. Black has only one chance—to play for a draw by repetition.

23	....	B–B3
24	Q–R6	B–N2

Hoping for *25* Q–R4 B–B3, etc. But now comes the stroke that shatters all illusions.

Position after 24 ... B–N2

25	Q×P!	N–B5

After *25* ... P×Q, White wins as in the game with *26* B×Nch. And on *25* ... N–B2; *26* Q×Bch! K×Q; *27* R–N5ch K–R1; *28* R–R3 mate.

26	R×N	P×Q
27	B–K6ch	R–B2

"*27* ... K–R2; *28* R–R4ch B–R3; *29* B×B P–KN4; *30* R×NP Q–N3ch is a very funny variation, since it shows that without the QBP the whole thing would have been incorrect! Of course there follows *31* P–B5! After *29* ... R–B4 in this variation, White plays *30* R×R P×R; *31* B–B7! P–K4; *32* R–R3, and the mating threat B–B8 decides" (Larsen).

28	R×R	K–R1

28 ... B–K4 staves off mate, but after *29* R–B5ch and *30* KR×B White wins easily with two Bishops versus Rook in the ending.

29 R–KN5   P–N4

"Black secures an exit for his queen, which has not done any work yet. Well, it is very late" (Larsen).

30 R–N3   Resigns

"My sense of self-criticism is probably not strong enough. I really do not blame myself for that mistake on move seventeen" (Larsen).

95
STUDENT TEAM CHAMPIONSHIP, CZECHOSLOVAKIA 1962
Sicilian Defense

WHITE: SPASSKY   BLACK: CIRICH

Good defense can be just as exciting as attack. Not convinced? Follow Spassky's thoughts in the days before he became world champion.

1 P–K4	P–QB4
2 N–KB3	N–KB3
3 P–K5	N–Q4
4 N–B3	P–K3!?

For 4 ... N×N see Game 96. White gets the edge after *4* ... N–B2; *5* P–Q4 P×P; *6* Q×P! N–B3; *7* Q–K4.

5 N×N   ....

The eccentric *5* N–K4 has also been tried. The text is the only attempt at a refutation.

5	P×N
6 P–Q4	N–B3

If *6* ... P–Q3; *7* B–N5ch! N–B3; *8* O–O B–K2; *9* P–B4 P×BP; *10* P–Q5 P–QR3; *11* B–R4 P–QN4; *12* P×N P×B; *13* P×P Q×P; *14* Q×P

with advantage. (Prins–Witkovsky, Munich Olympics 1958).

7 P×P	B×P
8 Q×P	Q–N3

The most aggressive choice in this risky variation. On *8* ... P–Q3; *9* P×P Q–N3; either *10* B–QB4 B×Pch; *11* K–K2, or *10* B–K3! B×B; *11* P×B Q×Pch; *12* B–K2 B–K3; *13* Q–KN5 is in White's favor.

9 B–QB4!	B×Pch
10 K–K2	O–O
11 R–B1	B–B4
12 N–N5	N×P!?

12 ... N–Q5ch; *13* K–Q1 N–K3; *14* P–B3 P–Q3; *15* P–QN4 B×P!; *16* P×B P×P is also complicated. (Bulyovchich–Minich, Yugoslav Championship 1962).

The idea behind this sacrifice is to swiftly mobilize his forces while White's King is stranded in the middle of the board. It nearly works.

Position after 12 . . . N×P

"This is a surprise, indeed! . . . Needless to say, I was far from a state of tranquillity at that moment. It isn't much of a pleasure coping with a special analysis, carefully thought out in a calm atmosphere at home. Even if this analysis has a slight inaccuracy, finding the latter during a vital game, where time for thinking over moves is limited, isn't easy at all. No wonder I pondered over my reply for exactly an hour before finally making up my mind" (Spassky).

13 Q×N   . . . .

"This was unquestionably the most crucial moment of the game. By accepting the sacrifice I, thereby, had to live up to this bold challenge. A continuation of *13 N×BP N×N; 14 R×N Q–K3ch; 15 Q×Q* (a sharp reply of *15 B–K3* also merited attention) gave me a somewhat better ending and a guarantee against all unpleasantness.

"I would feel more constrained if I were to play this game now. First of all, I would take into consideration the circumstance that I was playing in a team competition and on board

Number 1 at that, meaning that this contest would be of great psychological as well as sporting significance. Very often the 'duel' between the team leaders serves as a kind of barometer showing the combat spirit of the whole team. Naturally, in this case, one should take the least possible risk, or practically no risk at all.

"I would also take into account that the issue of who would receive the gold medals largely depended on the match between our teams. In the event of a victory, the Yugoslav students would be in a very strong position to capture the top laurels.

"It was possibly this sense of responsibility for the success of our team that would now force me (naturally, if I could not find a clear-cut plan of action after *13 Q×N*) to select a calm continuation: *13 N×BP* and, thereby, avoid a rather risky opening board debate with a well-prepared rival.

"But I must admit that at that time I was far from such reasoning. I was engrossed by the situation, and it even seemed to me that I was obliged to accept the challenge. I, of course, was aware of all the dangers this decision entailed. If 'calm' Cirich sacrifices a piece, it means that he has analyzed in detail all possible continuations. And yet intuition prompted me to think that my opponent's scheme was not correct. It was precisely intuition that guided my judgment and made me work intensively for a whole hour until I finally fathomed the position.

"I think that, even if I failed to

solve all the problems on the board to the end at that time, I still would not have made a reply of *13* N×BP with a transition to a somewhat better ending. A decision of this kind at that time would have been equal to my backing out of the fight, equal to the recognition of my helplessness in the face of my adversary's design.

"I accepted the Yugoslav player's challenge not so much because I had figured out all variants, but more because my intuition told me that I was right. This confidence, in the long run, helped me overcome an unexpected obstacle encountered in this game" (Spassky).

13 ....   P–Q4
14 Q×P!   ....

"Studying the variants arising after *14* B×P took up most of my time. It was clear to me that Black's reply to such a move would be *14* . . . B–N5ch. How should White play then?

"In the beginning, I regarded the possibility of moving my King back to K1: *15* K–K1 QR–K1; *16* B×Pch K–R1; *17* B×R (I rejected *17* Q×R in view of *17* . . . R×Qch; *18* B×R Q–B2 as, despite his material advantage, White finds it hard to prove that he has real chances of winning), Q–R4ch! convinced me that, in this event, the picture looks sad for White. Indeed, the side Queen check is fatal for him. If, for instance, *18* P–B3, the reply can be *18* . . . B–B7ch; whereas a decisive continuation to *18* Q–B3 can be *18* . . . R×Bch; *19* K–Q2 B–N5.

"Instead of making a retreat *15* K–K1, I began studying *15* R–B3, but I did not like the continuation *15* . . . Q–N4ch; *16* P–B4 QR–K1! In the event now of *17* N–K6, the continuation can be *17* . . . P×N; *18* B×Pch B×B; *19* R×Rch B×R; *20* Q×Q B×Pch, and Black wins.

"Giving up *15* R–B3, I concentrated my thoughts on variants springing up in case of *15* K–Q3. But here, too, after *15* . . . QR–K1; *16* B×Pch K–R1; *17* B×R R×R a completely unclear position would arise. And, lastly, I, in general, did not consider a reply of *15* K–Q2 at all, because I realized that it would also permit Black to build up quite unpleasant threats.

"Therefore, *14* B×P did not seem convincing to me, and I switched my attention over to *14* Q×P. Studying the variants connected with this move, I did not discover any particular danger for White, because, in the event of *14* . . . B–N5ch White had an excellent reply of *15* R–B3. Should Black now continue with *15* . . . B–N8, the next moves would be *16* K–B1 B×R; *17* Q×B, and White fends off the attack and retains his material advantage. A continuation of *15* . . . QR–Q1; *16* Q–K4 B×Rch; *17* P×B P–N3 would be a little better for Black, but this would probably give him only practical chances of salvation.

"It is truly remarkable the way a chess player's brain works during a game! I arrived at *14* Q×P, having rejected B×P. Why, then, did I study *14* B×P first? Was it because it looked like a more natural reply than *14* Q×P?" (Spassky).

| 14 | .... | R–K1ch |
| 15 | K–B3 | .... |

Stronger than *15* N–K4 B–K3; *16* Q×KB Q×Q; *17* N×Q B×Bch; *18* K–B2 B×R; *19* K×B QR–B1=.

| 15 | .... | Q–B3ch |
| 16 | K–N3 | .... |

It would be wrong to play *16* B–B4? in view of *16* . . . R–K6ch.

| 16 | .... | B–Q3ch |

Position after 16 . . . B–Q3ch

| 17 | R–B4! | .... |

"Evidently this reply was overlooked by my rival in the analysis he made at home. He probably reckoned only on *17* B–B4, after which *17* . . . R–K6ch would bring him a victory" (Spassky).

| 17 | .... | B–K3 |

"It is impossible to see how Black can keep up the dying flame of attack, because the danger to the KB2 spot is most unpleasant" (Spassky).

| 18 | N×B | R×N |
| 19 | Q×B! | .... |

The decisive blow.

| 19 | .... | Q–N3ch |
| 20 | R–N4 | R–K6ch |

After *20* . . . R×Q; *21* R×Q R×Rch; *22* K–B2, it becomes only a matter of time before the power of the two Bishops against a Rook will be felt.

21	B×R	Q×Qch
22	K–B2	R–K1
23	R–B4	R–K2
24	B–N3	Q–K4
25	R–K1	P–KN4
26	R–B3	K–N2
27	R–Q1	P–B3
28	K–N1	P–N5
29	B–Q4	Resigns

"We found out after the match that the variant with the piece sacrifice had been prepared by the Yugoslavs, especially for the contest with the Soviet players. The main expert was Minich, who finally persuaded mistrustful Cirich to employ this 'secret weapon.' But the surprise, as you can see, had both its merits and demerits" (Spassky).

96

34th U.S.S.R. CHAMPIONSHIP 1967

Sicilian Defense

WHITE: GURGENIDZE   BLACK: LEIN

Everything proceeds serenely until White's totally unexpected Knight sacrifice on move 11. Black must decline, but he never recovers from the disruption.

1	P–K4	P–QB4
2	N–KB3	N–KB3
3	P–K5	N–Q4
4	N–B3	NxN
5	QPxN	....

This capture away from the center violates principle but allows for rapid development. "Before the ending the gods have placed the middle game," wrote Dr. Tarrasch. After *5* NPxN P–Q4, Black's game is easier.

5	....	Q–B2

Black plans to mobilize his Queen side and perhaps castle there, but as the game goes he never gets a chance. Nimzovich opined that *5* ... P–Q4 is best, but then White retains his initiative with *6* PxPe.p. QxP (or *6* ... PxP; *7* B–QB4 B–K2; *8* B–B4 O–O; *9* Q–Q2!); *7* B–K3! N–B3; *8* B–Q3 P–K4; *9* N–N5 B–K2; *10* Q–R5 (Parma–Kozomara, Yugoslav Championship 1962).

Nimzovich once played *5* ... P–QN3? overlooking that White can win with *6* P–K6! P–B3 (or *6* ... BPxP; *7* N–K5); *7* N–K5!, and Black cannot withstand the double threat

of Q–B3 or Q–R5 (Votochek–Pachman, Prague 1944).

6	B–KB4	N–B3
7	B–B4	P–K3
8	O–O	P–QN3
9	R–K1	....

Overprotecting the KP in order to free the Knight.

9	....	P–B4

If Black continues his development with *9* ... B–N2 he must reckon with *10* N–N5, and if P–B4 (to deprive the Knight of K4); *11* PxPe.p.! QxB; *12* P–B7ch K–K2 (or *12* ... K–Q1; *13* NxPch); *13* BxP! wins.

The right course is *9* ... P–KR3 followed by ... B–N2 and ... O–O–O.

10	N–R4	P–N3?

The final error. Necessary is *10* ... N–K2, after which White would find it by no means easy to exploit his initiative. If *11* Q–Q6 N–Q4! equalizes.

11	NxBP!	....

Now the result of the game is practically decided.

11	....	N–R4

The only defense. After *11* ...B–QN2; *12* N–Q6ch BxN; *13* PxB, Black not only is a Pawn behind,

Position after 11 N×BP

but is tied up as well. There are two ways to accept the offer and both are bad:

A. *11* ... KP×N; *12* P–K6 P–Q3 (if *12* ... Q×B; *13* P×Pch K–Q1; *14* R–K8ch); *13* P–K7! B×P; *14* B×P Q–Q2; *15* Q–Q5 R–B1; *16* B×B N×B; *17* Q×R wins.

B. *11* ... NP×N; *12* Q–R5ch K–Q1; *13* QR–Q1 followed irremediably by *14* B×P, and Black's King will be caught in a crippling crossfire.

12 **B–Q5!**   ....

The prettiest and most effective way of continuing the attack. Also sufficient is *12* N–Q6ch (or N–K3) B×N; *13* P×B Q–B3; *14* B–KB1.

| *12* | .... | B–QN2 |

12 ... P×B loses to *13* N–Q6ch K–Q1; *14* Q×P with myriad threats.

| *13* | N–Q6ch | B×N |
| *14* | P×B | Q–B1 |

On any other Queen move comes *15* B×P. For instance, *14* ... Q–Q1; *15* B×P P×B; *16* R×Pch K–B2; *17* R–K7ch K–N1; *18* B–R6.

15 **B–R6!**   ....

Now Black's King is hemmed in the center, and victory is only a drop away.

15	....	R–KN1
16	Q–B3	B×B
17	Q×B	N–B3
18	QR–Q1	....

With the new and unpleasant threat of *19* R×Pch.

18	....	N–Q1
19	Q–N5	N–B3
20	Q–B6	P–KN4
21	R–K5	Resigns

Enough is enough. Of no help is *21* ... Q–Q1; *22* R×Pch.

97
LENINGRAD 1967
Sicilian Defense

WHITE: SUETIN   BLACK: TAIMANOV

A colossal struggle. Black staggers out of a beautiful combination bloody but unbowed, then falters in the quiet aftermath.

1	P–K4	P–QB4
2	N–KB3	P–QR3
3	P–B3	....

A legitimate attempt to profit from Black's last. White hopes to establish a Pawn mass in the center.

3	....	P–Q4
4	P×P	Q×P
5	P–Q4	N–KB3
6	B–K2	P–K3
7	O–O	B–K2
8	B–K3	P×P
9	P×P	O–O
10	N–B3	....

Finally White gains the tempo which Taimanov has been trying to deny him. But Black is already safely castled and can afford the slight loss of time.

10	....	Q–Q3
11	R–B1	QN–Q2
12	Q–Q2	N–N3

12 ... P–QN4 is more active, but Taimanov has another idea in mind.

13	B–KB4	Q–Q1
14	N–K5	KN–Q4
15	B–N3	B–Q2
16	P–B4	B–QN4!

When cramped, exchange pieces.

17	R–B3	B×B
18	Q×B	R–B1
19	R/1–KB1	B–N5

Too slow. 19 ... N×N; 20 P×N N–R5; 21 B–K1 P–QN4 produces the necessary counterplay. 19 ... P–B4, although it weakens the KP, also comes into consideration.

20	N–K4	N–K2
21	P–QR3	B–Q3
22	B–R4	P–B3

22 ... N/3–Q4 would prevent the following combination; but in that event the consequences of 23 P–B5 are ramified.

23	N×Pch!	R×N

Not 23 ... P×N; 24 R–N3ch N–N3

(24 ... K–R1; 25 Q–N4 N–B4; 26 Q–N8ch! R×Q; 27 N–B7 mate); 25 N×N P×N; 26 R×Pch K–B2; 27 Q–R5 with a firm mating web.

24	B×R	P×B
25	R–N3ch	K–B1
26	Q–N4	B×N

Not 26 ... P×N; 27 BP×Pch K–K1 (27 ... N–B4; 28 R×Nch! P×R; 29 Q–N8ch mates); 28 Q–R5ch K–Q2; 29 P×B K×P; 30 Q–K5ch K–Q2; 31 R–N7, etc.

27	BP×B	P–B4
28	R×Pch!	....

Position after 28 R×Pch

28	....	K–K1!

Forced. On 28 ... P×R (28 ... N×R?; 29 Q–N8ch K–K2; 30 Q×RPch wins); 29 Q–N7ch K–K1; 30 P–K6 Q–Q4 (on 30 ... R–B8ch, White simply strolls his King to Q3); 31 Q–R8ch N–N1; 32 R×Nch K–K2; 33 Q–N7ch K–Q3; 34 R×R N×R; 35 Q–Q7 mate.

29	R–B1	K–Q2
30	R–QN3	R–B3?

A pity that, after having survived the worst, Black does not offer the sturdiest resistance with 30 ... R–B5; after 31 R–B6 N–B4 he's still

alive (*32* KR×N P×R; *33* Q×Pch
K–B2; *34* Q–B7ch K–N1; *35* R×N
R–B8ch wins).

31 P–Q5!	N/3×P

31 . . . N/2×P; *32* Q–N7ch N–K2;
33 R–Q1ch N–Q4; *34* R×Pch leads
to a similar end.

32 R×Pch	K–B1
33 R–N3	Q–R4
34 P–R3	Q–Q7
35 K–R2	K–B2

Black is making a brave struggle to
consolidate, and it is not clear yet
that he must lose. *35* . . . N–K6 was
impossible because of *36* R–B8ch
K–B2; *37* Q–N7 N–B4; *38* R×N, etc.
Another try that fails is *35* . . . Q–
QB7; *36* R–B8ch K–B2; *37* R/8–
QN8 N–QN3; *38* R/8×N! R×R;
39 R–B3ch, etc. All things considered, *35* . . . N–KN3 is the best
practical chance.

36 R–B7	Q–QB7
37 R–QB3!	R×R

Position after 35 . . . K–B2

It's all over after *37* . . .N×R?;
38 R×Nch K–Q1; *39* Q–N7.

38 P×R	K–Q2
39 P–B4	P–KR4

If *39* . . . N–K6; *40* Q–Q4ch wins.

40 Q–R4	Q–N3
41 Q–B2	N–K6

On *41* . . . N–B2 the simplest win is
42 Q–B6.

42 R×Nch	K×R
43 Q×N	Q–B4
44 Q–Q4	P–R4
45 P–B5	Resigns

98
6th MATCH GAME 1968
Sicilian Defense

WHITE: SPASSKY BLACK: GELLER

Spassky's lopsided score of 3½–½
with the "closed" system in this
match did much to revive its popularity. Black is defeated with apparent
ease when his Queen-side counterplay
proves ineffectual.

1 P–K4	P–QB4

2 N–QB3	. . . .

Tchigorin employed this variation
with great success at the turn of the
century, and it was later adopted by
Mieses and Smyslov. White's plan
is to control his Q5 and hinder
. . . P–Q4, which means that it will be

difficult for either player to open the center. Thus, the variation is known as "closed," because the struggle is confined to the wings and generally flares up in the middle game.

2 ....   P–Q3

It is sharper for Black to keep an eye on his Q5 with an immediate *2* ... N–QB3 followed by *3* ... P–KN3, etc. If Black continues with ... P–K3 and ... KN–K2 he may be able to advance this QP to Q4 in one move.

3	P–KN3	N–QB3
4	B–N2	P–KN3
5	P–Q3	B–N2
6	P–B4	....

The most elastic continuation, reserving B3 or R3 for the Knight. The older moves were *6* KN–K2 and *6* B–K3.

6 ....   N–B3

For *6* ... P–K4 see the next game. A more viable system is *6* ... P–K3 followed by ... KN–K2 and an eventual ... P–B4. Only after this crushing defeat did Geller switch to that plan in the last game of this match.

7	N–B3	O–O
8	O–O	R–N1
9	P–KR3	....

The opening is over and the two sides develop strategies characteristic of such formations. Black has sufficient control of the center and prepares to advance his Pawns on the Queen side, where he has more space; White strives to develop activity on the other wing, where his prospects are better.

In their second match game Spassky tried *9* N–KR4 N–Q5; *10* P–B5 P–QN4; *11* B–N5 P–N5; and now he played the somewhat strange *12* N–N1, after which Black's chances were better.

Position after 9 P–KR3

| 9 | .... | P–QN4 |
| 10 | P–R3 | .... |

A novel treatment. White, in order to exchange a potential weakness and open the QR file, invites the opening of lines where his opponent is pressing.

10	....	P–QR4
11	B–K3	P–N5
12	P×P	RP×P
13	N–K2	B–N2

The Bishop remains inactive for the rest of the game and does not help in defending the King. Better is *13* ... N–K1; *14* R–N1 N–B2; *15* P–B5 N–N4 (Reshevsky–Korchnoi, Match 1968).

14 P–N3!   ....

Until now play has followed the fourth match game, in which Spassky tried *14* Q–Q2. The point of the text is that the Pawn will not be under fire when Black's Rook arrives at QR7; it also hinders . . . P–B5.

14	. . . .	R–R1
15	R–B1	R–R7
16	P–N4	Q–R1

Once again, as in the fourth game, Geller brings his Queen to this flank in search of counterplay.

17	Q–K1	Q–R3
18	Q–B2	. . . .

Not *18* Q–R4? NxKP! Now Black might try *18* . . . N–Q2! with equal chances.

18	. . . .	N–R2
19	P–B5	N–N4
20	PxP	RPxP?

After *20* . . . BPxP; *21* N–B4 B–B1; *22* N–N5 White's positional advantage, in view of the hole at Black's K3, would be obvious; however, *22* . . . N–B2 would stem the attack which Spassky gets now.

21	N–N5	N–R6
22	Q–R4	R–B1
23	RxN!	PxR
24	Q–R7ch	K–B1

The fever seems to have subsided, and it appears that there will be a lull. But the next blow dispels Black's illusions of safety.

25	NxP!	RxP

Position after 24 . . . K–B1

Black already lacks the power to offer meaningful resistance. If *25* . . . KxN (or *25* . . . R–B2; *26* N–R6); *26* B–R6 R–KN1; *27* N–B4 P–Q4; *28* PxP P–B4; *29* N–K6 wins.

26	B–R6	RxRch
27	NxR	KxN

No better is *27* . . . BxB; *28* NxB K–K1; *29* QxPch K–Q2; *30* Q–B7ch K–B3; *31* P–K5ch, etc.

28	QxBch	K–K1
29	P–N5!	P–B4

A last gasp. Mate is unavoidable after *29* . . . PxP; *30* BxP.

30	QxPch	K–Q2
31	Q–B7ch	K–B3
32	PxPch	Resigns

On *32* . . . K–N3; *33* QxBch QxQ; *34* BxQ KxB; *35* P–B6, and the Pawns cannot be stopped.

BUCHAREST 1968
Sicilian Defense

WHITE: BILEK   BLACK: GHEORGHIU

Seldom is castling too early so drastically punished. White's energetic combination gives some measure of the potential of his hitherto unfashionable system.

1	P–K4	P–QB4
2	N–QB3	P–Q3
3	P–KN3	N–QB3
4	B–N2	P–KN3
5	P–Q3	B–N2
6	P–B4	P–K4

The text is recommended in Gligorich's book on the Sicilian, but he does not consider White's reply.

7	N–R3	KN–K2
8	O–O	O–O

The right plan is *8* ... PxP! as in Bilek–Evans, Lugano Olympics 1968, which continued: *9* NxP O–O; *10* N/4–Q5 NxN; *11* NxN B–K3; *12* N–B4 B–Q2; *13* P–B3 P–QN4, with equal chances, although Black's Queen-side counterplay carried the day. (I was not familiar with this game at the time, but instinct told me castling was premature.)

9	P–B5!	PxP

Necessary is *9* ... P–B3 either here or on the next move.

10	PxP	BxP?
11	RxB!	NxR
12	B–K4	KN–Q5

12 ... KN–K2 is refuted by *13*

216

Position after 10 ... BxP

BxPch KxB; *14* Q–R5ch K–N1; *15* KN–N5. The hardest resistance, however, is offered by *12* ... NxP!; *13* PxN P–B4.

13	Q–R5	R–K1

Or *13* ... P–B4; *14* B–Q5ch K–R1; *15* N–KN5 P–KR3; *16* Q–N6! PxN; *17* Q–R5ch mates.

14	QxRPch	K–B1
15	B–N5	Q–Q2
16	N–Q5	R–K3
17	R–KB1	NxP
18	B–N6!	....

The finishing touch. Black's King cannot escape from its tight wedge. *18* ... RxB; *19* QxR makes it hopeless for Black.

18	....	N/7–Q5
19	B–R6	Resigns

19 ... RxB; *20* QxR BxB; *21* QxBch mates next.

WORLD CORRESPONDENCE CHAMPIONSHIP 1968

Two Knights Defense

WHITE: ESTRIN BLACK: BERLINER

While the opening duel is of great importance to theory, the endgame is no less worthwhile. World Correspondence Champion Berliner's handling of the entire game is impeccable, and his notes are unusually instructive.

1	P–K4	P–K4
2	N–KB3	N–QB3
3	B–B4	N–B3
4	N–N5	. . . .

Position after 4 N–N5

Condemned by Dr. Tarrasch as "a duffer's move," this sortie is nevertheless a logical way to exert pressure against KB7. It has withstood numerous attempts at refutation, and probably will survive this setback as well (see note to White's 8th).

"When I found out that International Master J. Estrin of the Soviet Union was among the finalists of the World Individual Correspondence Chess Championship, one thought that immediately came to mind was that he plays the Two Knights Defense from the White side. This was of special interest to me since I used to play this opening a long time ago, but stopped playing it shortly after a catastrophic loss against Larry Friedman in 1946, in a game which cost me the U.S. Junior Championship. Although I made some opening mistakes in that game, I became convinced that the whole *4 N–N5* variation was unsound. However, this conviction was not borne out by anything one could find in opening books or by any other analysis at hand. However, the conviction was strong enough that even though I did not know what color I was ultimately to get *vs.* Estrin, I determined to begin some research on this pesky problem.

"When the tournament pairings were announced about two weeks before the start of play, I was delighed to learn that I had Black in the game in question. My work then began in earnest. The result of this effort is shown in the game and notes below. Since Black never has worse than a draw after White's fourth move, this line logically refutes the whole *4 N–N5* variation unless some improvement for White over the notes here published is sound. In addition to making this important theoretical contribution, I gained a valuable point in the tournament" (Berliner).

4 ....   **P–Q4**
5 PxP   **P–N4**

Ulvestad's Variation. The usual *5 ... N–QR4* (on *5 ... NxP; 6 P–Q4!* is best); *6 B–N5ch P–B3: 7 PxP PxP* favors White.

6 B–B1   **....**

6 BxP QxP; 7 BxNch QxB; 8 O–O B–N2 is thought to give Black equal chances.

6 ....   **N–Q5**

Transposing to Fritz's Variation (*5 ... N–Q5* immediately). Unsound is *6 ... NxP; 7 BxP B–N2; 8 P–Q4*, etc.

7 P–QB3   **NxP**
8 N–K4   **....**

Theory gives this as best, but a reassessment seems to be in order. Very exciting but dubious is *8 NxBP!? KxN; 9 PxN PxP; 10 Q–B3ch N–B3!; 11 QxR B–QB4; 12 BxP R–K1ch* with a stinging attack.

Right is *8 PxN! QxN; 9 BxPch K–Q1; 10 Q–B3! P–K5!; 11 QxKP* (not *11 QxBP B–Q3) B–Q3; 12 O–O B–N2; 13 P–Q3?* (necessary is *13 R–K1! P–QB3; 14 B–B1*, a critical line which may serve to rehabilitate White's fourth move), as in Fischer–Unknown, simultaneous exhibition, Montreal 1964. Now Black could have pulled off a neat win with *13 ... BxPch!; 14 KxB N–B5!; 15 BxN Q–R5ch; 16 K–N1 BxQ*, etc.

8 ....   **Q–R5!**

"This move is condemned in every opening book despite its natural appearance and its function in helping to keep White off balance. The recommended move is *8 ... N–K3*, which leads to equal positions. This in itself is enough to censure the whole variation for White. The game Berliner–Friedman, 1946, went: *8 ... N–K3; 9 BxPch B–Q2; 10 Q–R4? N/4–B5; 11 BxBch QxB; 12 QxQch KxQ; 13 P–KN3?? N–Q6ch; 14 K–K2 NxBch; 15 RxN P–KB4*, and the Knight is lost!

"After *8 ... Q–R5* the question is whether or not Black can successfully storm White's undeveloped position. If the attack fails, Black will be lost" (Berliner).

9 N–N3   **B–KN5**
10 P–B3   **P–K5!**

"This is the new move that turns the tables on existing theory. Book is *10 ... N–B4; 11 BxPch K–Q1; 12 O–O! B–B4ch; 13 P–Q4!* and White wins" (Berliner).

Position after 10 ... P–K5

The element of surprise is much less effective in postal chess than it is over the board, so it is important that an innovation be sound. Therefore, when novelties are employed successfully the opening books must take note.

11 PxN   ....

11 PxB is still met by Black's next.

11 ....   B–Q3
12 BxPch   ....

Not 12 PxB? BxNch; 13 PxB QxPch; 14 K–K2 N–B5 mate.

12 ....   K–Q1
13 O–O!   ....

"On *13* K–B2 P–KB4 yields an overwhelming attack, and *13* PxB BxNch; *14* PxB QxRch; *15* B–B1 N–N5!; *16* N–B3 R–K1 followed by . . . Q–N8 hardly merits serious consideration by White" (Berliner).

13 ....   PxP
14 RxP!   R–QN1!
15 B–K2?   ....

"After this natural move White is lost by force. *15* B–B6 N–N5 is not attractive either. Best is *15* B–B1! R–K1; *16* N–B3 P–QB3!; *17* P–Q3! NxN!; *18* PxN R–N4, with an attack good for at least a draw— e.g., *19* B–K2! R–KR4!; *20* NxR QxPch; *21* K–B2 Q–R5ch, etc. The next fourteen moves are forced for both sides" (Berliner).

15 ....   BxR
16 BxB   QxQPch
17 K–R1   BxN!
18 PxB   R–N3
19 P–Q3   N–K6
20 BxN   QxB
21 B–N4!   P–KR4!

Black must be careful not to get sidetracked with *21* . . . R–R3ch; *22* B–R3. Now White must prevent the opening of the KR file.

22 B–R3   P–N4
23 N–Q2   P–N5
24 N–B4   QxNP
25 NxR   PxB
26 Q–B3   PxPch
27 QxP   QxQch
28 KxQ   BPxN!

Black violates principle by capturing *away* from the center. But after *28* . . . RPxN?; *29* P–R4–5 forces a draw. Now the Queen-side Pawns cannot be liquidated.

29 R–KB1   K–K2
30 R–K1ch   ....

"Now Black must assess how to win this position. The Black Rook and KRP appear ideally placed, but if White can successfully attack Black's Queen-side Pawns with his Rook, Black will be unable to win. On close examination one discovers that Black must win this endgame on the Queen side, where he can concentrate all his forces while using his King-side Pawns as decoys" (Berliner).

30 ....   K–Q3!
31 R–KB1   R–QB1!

"One of the best moves I have ever made. The point is that instead of tying down the Rook to defend the weak King-side Pawns, Black gives up one of them in order to reach a passed-Pawn situation in which Black has the outside KRP versus the worthless White center Pawn. The rest of the game will be played on the Queen side, while the White King is

unable to join the fight there"
(Berliner).

32 R×P   R–B2!

"One of the points: of course, the
King-and-Pawn ending will be lost
for White" (Berliner).

33 R–B2   K–K4!

Position after 33 . . . K–K4

34 P–R4?   ....

"This makes things easy by voluntarily weakening his Queen-side
Pawns in the hope of exchanging one
of them. The very difficult variations
I had to calculate when making my
31st move were: *34* K–N3! K–Q5;
35 K–R4 K×P; *36* K×P R–B7! and
now:

"I: *37* R–B3ch K–Q7!
    A. *38* P–N4 R–B6!; *39* R–
       B2ch K–K8!; *40* R–R2 R–
       QR6!; *41* K–N5 R–R5; *42*
       R–QN2 K–Q8 and wins.

    B. *38* P–N3! K–B8!; *39* P–R4
       R–QN7!!; *40* P–R5 (else
       Black plays . . . P–R4) P–
       N4; *41* P–R6 P–N5; *42* K–
       N4 K–B7; *43* R–B7 R×P;
       44 R×P R–QR6; *45* R–QN7

P–N6; *46* P–R7 P–N7 and
wins.

    C. *38* R–QR3 P–R4; *39* R–
       QN3 R–B4ch; *40* K–N4
       P–N4; *41* K–B4 K–B7; *42*
       K–K4 K–N8; *43* K–Q4
       R–R4; *44* R–QR3 P–R5!;
       45 K–B3 R–R5! and wins.

"II: *37* R–B7 R–B4ch!; *38* K–N4
R–QR4; *39* R–B3ch! K–Q7!!;
40 P–R3 K–B7; *41* R–B2ch K–
N6; *42* K–B4 R–QN4!; *43* K–
K4 K–R7!; *44* R–B7 P–R3!; *45*
R–QR7 R–QR4!; *46* R–QN7
P–N4 and wins.

"These variations could hardly be
more exquisite in a composed study.
Lines IB and II especially are worthy
of close study" (Berliner).

It is unfortunate that one of these
lines did not crop up in the actual
game; but it is not likely that Black
would have been able to calculate so
deeply had this been a tournament
with the clock ticking. The accuracy
of his analysis resembles the kind of
work that goes into dissecting ad-
journed positions in general. (For a
detailed discussion of this subject
see chapter on "Midnight Oil" in my
Chess Catechism.) This kind of
perfection is possible in postal chess,
but the element of direct human
tension is lacking.

34 ....   K–Q5
35 P–R5   K×P
36 R–B3ch   K–B7!
37 P–N4   ....

37 P×P P×P; *38* R–B6 R–QN2 is an
easy win.

37	....	P–N4!
38	P–R6	R–B5
39	R–B7	R×P
40	R–QN7	....

No better is *40* R×P R–QR5.

40	....	R–N5ch
41	K–B3	P–N5
42	R×RP	P–N6
	Resigns	

The QNP cannot be stopped after *43* R–B7ch K–N8; *44* R–B5 R–QR5.

The sacrifice of a Pawn to produce a winning position of Rook and two Pawns versus Rook and two Pawns on the same side facing each other is an extraordinary concept (initiated with *31* ... R–QB1). Every move of this contest merits further study.

101
YUGOSLAVIA 1968
Two Knights Defense

WHITE: KARAKLAICH   BLACK: TRAIKOVICH

White is caught flat-footed by a neat opening innovation. Although he manages to survive to the endgame, he cannot recover from the initial shock

1	P–K4	P–K4
2	N–KB3	N–QB3
3	B–B4	N–B3
4	P–Q4	....

Theory still has arrived at no verdict after *4* N–N5 P–Q4. The text is more natural, because the first player strives to profit from the early opening of lines.

4	....	P×P
5	P–K5	P–Q4
6	B–QN5	N–K5
7	N×P	B–QB4

A definite improvement over *7* ... B–Q2; *8* B×N P×B; *9* O–O B–K2; *10* P–KB3 N–B4; *11* P–KB4 N–K5, where Black can indeed hold his own, but with fewer active chances than the text.

8	B–K3	....

White must avoid the trap *8* N×N? B×Pch; *9* K–B1 Q–R5!; *10* N–Q4ch P–B3; *11* N–KB3 N–N6ch; *12* K×B N–K5ch!; *13* K–K3 Q–B7ch; *14* K–Q3 B–B4.

8	....	O–O!

This continuation improves on *7* ... B–Q2.

9	N×N!?	....

More prudent is *9* B×N P×B; *10* O–O B–R3; *11* R–K1.

Other tries for an advantage after *9* B×N P×B fail—*e.g.*, *10* P–B3 B×N!; *11* Q×B (not *11* B×B Q–R5ch; *12* P–KN3 N×P; *13* B–B2 Q–N5ch) P–QB4; *12* Q–R4 (or *12* Q–Q3 Q–R5ch) P–Q5, with active counterplay.

9	....	P×N
10	B×B	N×B

11 B×P　　　　B–R3!

This fine sacrifice contains a remarkable hidden point.

Position after 11 . . . B–R3

12 Q×P?　　　. . . .

No better is *12* N–B3 P–Q5!; *13* N–N5 B×N; *14* B×B R–N1 regaining the Pawn with advantage.

The crucial variation is *12* B×R Q–N4!; *13* B×P (*13* Q×P transposes into the game) Q×Pch; *14* K–Q2 Q×Bch; *15* K–B1 Q×NP; *16* N–B3, where White remains an exchange ahead and his King reaches safety after P–N3.

12 . . . .　　　　Q–N4!
13 B×R　　　　. . . .

Forced. If *13* N–B3? QR–Q1; *14* Q×N Q–Q7 mate.

13 . . . .　　　　Q–B8ch
14 Q–Q1　　　　Q×NP
15 P–KB4　　　　Q×R

A blemish. Even stronger is *15* . . . R×B!; *16* N–Q2 R–Q1.

16 B–Q5　　　　Q–N7
17 K–B2　　　　N–K3!
18 B×N　　　　. . . .

Not *18* K–N3 R–Q1. After the text White consolidates, but Black regains his Pawn and remains with an overwhelming position.

18 . . . .　　　　P×B
19 K–N3　　　　. . . .

Equally bad is *19* P–N3 Q×KP; *20* R–K1 Q–B4ch.

19 . . . .　　　　Q×RP
20 Q–Q2　　　　B–N2
21 N–B3　　　　Q–B5
22 R–QN1　　　　B–R1
23 N–K2　　　　. . . .

23 R–QR1 runs into R×P!; *24* Q×R Q×Nch and . . . Q×R next.

23 . . . .　　　　Q–K5
24 R–KN1　　　　P–N4!

This causes White's carefully contrived structure to collapse.

25 P–R4　　　　P×BPch
26 N×P　　　　Q×KP
27 R–KB1　　　　P–QR4
28 R–B2　　　　. . . .

White is all tied up and a Pawn down as well. Not *28* R–K1 Q–N2ch; *29* K–R2 R×N!; *30* Q×R Q×P mate.

28 . . . .　　　　P–R5
29 R–K2　　　　B–K5!
30 Q–K3　　　　Q–N2ch
31 K–R2　　　　Q–N5
32 N×P　　　　. . . .

This almost gets White out of trouble. *32* P–N3 loses to . . . P–K4.

32 . . . .　　　　Q×N
33 Q×B　　　　Q×Q
34 R×Q　　　　R–R1

White has fought hard to reestablish material equality, only to land in a hopeless Rook-and-Pawn ending. The finale is curious.

Position after 34 ... R–R1

35	R–K1	P–R6
36	R–QR1	P–R7

37	K–N3	K–B2
38	K–B4	K–K3
39	P–B4	....

If White tries to deny Black's King access to Q4 with *39* K–K4, then *39* ... R–R5ch; *40* K–Q3 K–B4 followed by ... K–N5 proves decisive.

39	....	K–Q3
40	K–K4	K–B4
41	K–Q3	K–N5
42	K–B2	R–KN1
	Resigns	

If *43* R–KN1, RxPch forces a new Queen.

ALPHABETICAL LIST OF
CONTESTANTS *(numbers refer to games)*

ADDISON
  Sigurjonsson 36
AVERBACH
  Estrin 50
BAKULIN
  Bronstein 5
BEDNARSKY
  Saidy 32
BENKO
  Fischer 44, 71
  Horowitz 55
  Zuckerman 45
BERGER
  Evans 4
BERLINER
  Estrin 100
BILEK
  Gheorghiu 99
BISGUIER
  D. Byrne 53
  Evans 39
BLACKSTONE
  Evans 80
BOBOTSOV
  Gligorich 86
  Tal 31
BOGDANOVICH
  Suetin 77
BOLBOCHAN
  Fischer 90
  Tal 67
BOTVINNIK
  Littlewood 93
  Portisch 10
BRONSTEIN
  Bakulin 5
  Foguelman 47
  Kholmov 85
  Spassky 24
  Tal 25
BYRNE, D.
  Bisguier 53
BYRNE, R.
  Evans 88

Fischer 23
Kozomara 34
CELLE
  Fischer 12
CIRICH
  Spassky 95
DELY
  Fischer 70
DODA
  Vladimirov 30
DONNER
  Ivkov 58
  Portisch 38
  Tal 14
DUBORIK
  Sorokin 43
EIDLIN
  Gaspariantz 87
ESTRIN
  Averbach 50
  Berliner 100
EVANS
  Berger 4
  Bisguier 39
  Blackstone 80
  Byrne, R. 88
  Koehler 74
  Zuckerman 92
FISCHER
  Benko 44, 71
  Bolbochan 90
  Byrne, R. 23
  Celle 12
  Dely 70
  Geller 69
  Geller, U. 18
  Gligorich 27
  Larsen 91
  Letelier 26
  Miagmarsuren 17
  Najdorf 89
  Nikolich 33
  Reshevsky 48
  Stein 56

Tal 15
FOGUELMAN
  Bronstein 47
FUSTER
  Tal 6
GASPARIANTZ
  Eidlin 87
GELLER
  Fischer 69
  Keres 49
  Smyslov 21
  Spassky 98
GELLER, U.
  Fischer 18
GHEORGHIU
  Bilek 99
  Uhlmann 16
GLIGORICH
  Bobotsov 86
  Fischer 27
  Matulovich 3
  Tal 57, 84
GUFELD
  Kavalek 60
GURGENIDZE
  Tal 2
  Lein 96
HECHT
  Tal 54
HENNINGS
  Moehring 68
HOROWITZ
  Benko 55
IVKOV
  Donner 58
  Portisch 13
JOHANSSON
  Pomar 37
KARAKLAICH
  Traikovich 101
KAVALEK
  Gufeld 60
  Matulovich 29
KERES

Geller *49*
Tal *59*
KHOLMOV
  Bronstein *85*
KLAVINS
  Lutikov *73*
KOEHLER
  Evans *74*
KONOVALOV
  Mordkovich *40*
KOZOMARA
  Byrne, R. *34*
LARSEN
  Fischer *91*
  Petrosian *94*
  Matanovich *52*
  Tal *1, 63*
LEIN
  Gurgenidze *96*
LETELIER
  Fischer *26*
LIBERSON
  Smyslov *11*
LITTLEWOOD
  Botvinnik *93*
LUTIKOV
  Klavins *73*
  Tscheshkovsky *41*
MATANOVICH
  Larsen *52*
  Padevsky *42*
MATULOVICH
  Gligorich *3*
  Kavalek *29*
MIAGMARSUREN
  Fischer *17*
MEDINA
  Pomar *66*
MOEHRING
  Hennings *68*
MOHRLOK
  Tal *62*
MORDKOHVIC
  Konovalov *40*
NAJDORF
  Fischer *89*
NEZHMETDINOV
  Tal *79*

NIEVERGELT
  Tal *61*
NIKOLICH
  Fischer *33*
  Velimirovich *64*
O'KELLY
  Penrose *72*
OLAFSSON
  Tal *75*
PACHMAN
  Uhlmann *20*
PADEVSKY
  Matanovich *42*
PARMA
  Szabo *83*
PENROSE
  O'Kelly *72*
PEREZ
  Trappl *7*
PETROSIAN
  Larsen *94*
  Polugaievsky *35*
  Tal *81*
POLUGAIEVSKY
  Petrosian *35*
  Tal *82*
POMAR
  Johansson *37*
  Medina *66*
  Szabo *28*
PORTISCH
  Botvinnik *10*
  Donner *38*
  Ivkov *13*
  Stein *76*
  Tal *8*
REISSMAN
  Rossolimo *19*
RESHEVSKY
  Fischer *48*
  Seidman *22*
ROSSOLIMO
  Reissman *19*
SAIDY
  Bednarsky *32*
SEIDMAN
  Reshevsky *22*
SIGURJONSSON

Addison *36*
  Szabo *51*
SMEJKAL
  Smyslov *46*
SMYSLOV
  Geller *21*
  Liberson *11*
  Smejkal *46*
  Tal *9*
SOFREVSKY
  Velimirovich *65*
SOROKIN
  Duborik *43*
SPASSKY
  Bronstein *24*
  Cirich *95*
  Geller *98*
  Suetin *78*
STEIN
  Fischer *56*
  Portisch *76*
SUETIN
  Bogdanovich *77*
  Spassky *78*
  Taimanov *97*
SZABO
  Parma *83*
  Pomar *28*
  Sigurjonsson *51*
TAIMANOV
  Suetin *97*
TAL
  Bobotsov *31*
  Bolbochan *67*
  Bronstein *25*
  Donner *14*
  Fischer *15*
  Fuster *6*
  Gligorich *57, 84*
  Gurgenidze *2*
  Hecht *54*
  Keres *59*
  Larsen *1, 63*
  Mohrlok *62*
  Nievergelt *61*
  Nezhmetdinov *79*
  Olafsson *75*
  Petrosian *81*

Polugaievsky 82
Portisch 8
Smyslov 9
TRAIKOVICH
Karaklaich 101
TRAPPL
Perez 7

TSCHESHKOVSKY
Lutikov 41
UHLMANN
Gheorghiu 16
Pachman 20
VELIMIROVICH
Nikolich 64

Sofrevsky 65
VLADIMIROV
Doda 30
ZUCKERMAN
Benko 45
Evans 92